Purch. Fri. Dec. 7/2001 at Dollar Bills in
@ $1.00 Hmd.

BIG GOVERNMENT

BIG GOVERNMENT

A NOVEL BY EV EHRLICH

WARNER BOOKS

A Time Warner Company

Copyright © 1998 by Everett M. Ehrlich
All rights reserved.

Warner Books, Inc., 1271 Avenue of the Americas, New York, NY 10020
Visit our Web site at http://warnerbooks.com

 A Time Warner Company

Printed in the United States of America
First Printing: September 1998
10 9 8 7 6 5 4 3 2 1

Library of Congress Cataloging-in-Publication Data

Ehrlich, Everett M.
    Big government / Ev Ehrlich.
      p.   cm.
    ISBN 0-446-52385-2
      I. Presidents—United States—Election—fiction. 2.
    United States—Politics and government—Fiction. I. Title.
    PS3555.H718B5 1999
    813'.54—dc21   98-13275
                                      CIP

For Tony Phipps and Dave Weinfurter
They Were an Under Secretary . . . So I Didn't Have to Be!

VI

Acknowledgments *goes to pg VIII.*

If you want to know if your wife loves you, tell her that you cannot tend to a squalling infant because you are working on your book. I did not invoke this defense too often and there were times when my muse was told to take a hike. But without Nancy's unceasing encouragement and nurturing, this endeavor, like any other, would have failed. My thanks to her are endless.

Mark Steitz and Alan Stone provided confidence and clarity to this project and knew at every moment which was appropriate. And they taught me something about myself in the process. I am grateful to both of them for their exceptional friendship.

When Amity Shlaes introduced me to David Chalfant at IMG Literary, I was a fellow with a book in a box. Today, thanks to him, I am a fellow with a book in your hands. And, as the song says, he's lovely to look at and delightful to know. Through David, I met a series of people for whom I have great gratitude and affection: Susan Lohman at IMG Literary, whose charm is equaled only by her competence; Howard Mittelmark, my "coach," who taught me respect for my own voice as well as skepticism about neologisms; and Rick Horgan at Warner Books, whose cunning eye read a flabby early draft and saw the statuesque beauty within. My heartfelt thanks to all of them.

Last, I want to mention—and thank—my three wonderful children—Nick, Carl, and Alice—simply because they're wonderful. Hi kids!

"End of Acknowledgments"

BIG GOVERNMENT

Prologue) goes to pg. 7

The February night was cold and dark. Icy winds skimmed over the homeless encamped in Lafayette Park, and on through the fence surrounding the White House. The Marine guards at the White House sentry gate huddled at their stations. The nation's elite, the brightest and the best, sat by their hearths in Washington's most exclusive neighborhoods, far from the ghetto that sprawled across Rock Creek toward the deep, violet sky.

Missing from their firesides, however, was the select group invited to the White House that night. "Tonight's dinner is not an official White House function," President Wade F. Hoak's press secretary told the White House press corps. "It is a private dinner and we would appreciate it if you treated it as such." But the press pool could not help but be intrigued by the number of limousines driving up to the West Gate of the Executive Mansion. They contained President Hoak's most important friends, fund-raisers, and advisors: in sum, the nation's business leaders. President Hoak insisted that they come that night, and if he insisted, they could only accept, remanding mergers, divestitures, overthrows of foreign governments, and other excellent pursuits to another day.

And not just because it was the president, but because it was

President Hoak. People loved President Hoak. He was strapping and good-looking. He had large shoulders and a massive chest that kept them apart. He had a wide smile full of naturally engineered teeth and a full mane of gray and brown hair. And in the presence of these assets people had the feeling of being somehow smaller, as if they were under a shade tree or within a walled city.

He was neither liberal nor conservative, left nor right. He was the center; he defined the center as does a fulcrum. He favored laying bare the facts, helping those who helped themselves, maintaining safety in our streets and neighborhoods, helping those who could not help themselves, and keeping America strong. He opposed special treatment for the few, helping those who would not help themselves, compromising our national security, helping those who had not helped themselves, and turning a deaf ear to the needs of the people. How could anybody argue with a stance so well reasoned? Despite his native Texan twang, he could bridge almost every regional and ethnic gap. He knew that a knish was a perogy, a calzone, and an empanada, that a tamale was a crepe, that chitterlings were derma, and that all of them gave you indigestion. His captivating smile, his immense presence, and his completely average and uninformed view of the world made him the biggest kid in the American schoolyard. "Finally," the voters said when they pulled the Hoak levers just three years before, "a president who will fight our battles for us."

President Hoak's inner circle was ushered into the East Room for cocktails, where they exchanged speculation and innuendo masked as pleasantries.

"You've been a Hoak man for a long time, Leo," the managing director of the investment bank said to the chairman of the integrated steel producer. "What are we doing here?"

"Honestly, Harry, it beats me," said the chairman as the media conglomerate mogul nodded along, "but the president's reelection's only a year away, and it's time to—"

Their conversation was suddenly drowned out by a shrill fanfare and "Hail to the Chief." Resplendent in their creased white pants, the White House Guard entered. All this! thought the chairman of Datacompusoft, and he only takes in two hundred Gs.

President Wade F. Hoak and Vice President Herbert J. Honeycutt appeared at the door of the East Room. The executives burst into spontaneous applause out of as much respect for their offices as they could muster, and began to file out past the president and the vice president, each shaking the First and Second Hands as they walked to the State Dining Room, where dinner was served.

Two hours and several courses later, President Hoak rose and looked out over the gathering. He cleared his throat and stoked his cigar.

"Thanks very much for coming," the president said. "I appreciate your being here, and that you've all kept this meeting low-key. Sometimes I think that the only way to keep a secret around here is to tell Herb Honeycutt about it because nobody listens to him anyway." There was a ripple of laughter as Vice President Honeycutt cheerily waved his hand. President Hoak grinned and continued.

"Well, it's been a little over three years since I took the oath of office, even if it seems like yesterday. So I thought that this would be a good time for us to get together to discuss my plans.

"You know," he drawled, "this isn't a bad job. I've enjoyed lots of the places that I've had the chance to go. I've been pleased to meet all of those world leaders—even the Russians and the Arab types, though you can't trust them as much as you want to. And living in the White House is a pretty good deal. They've got movies here and a bowling alley and a swimming pool. It's not Graceland, but it's home."

He stoked his cigar again. "The rest of it, though, has been pretty close to hell." His guests laughed at this as they always laughed when President Hoak talked this way. It was part of his charm, his public persona. As a noncandidate, his steadfast desire not to be a candidate had propelled him to the nomination. As a candidate, his take-it-or-leave-it attitude led to his landslide election. As president, his indifference to his office was the key to his unbridled authority. His service as chief executive was the Official National Favor. "Sometimes I find this job," he continued, "well . . . depressing. I just can't help feeling the decisions I make are going to determine whether some poor kid—maybe a Mexican kid, I don't know," he shrugged indifferently, "is going to have dinner, or a job or a car or something. I know it's been proven scientifically that if you get a job or a car or something, it's because of how hard you've worked, but it would be a pretty sobering thought if it turned out they were wrong. Sure, you all tell me not to worry about it, and Euraline," he said, referring to his second and current wife, "tells me there's nothing I can do about it anyway. But I just can't help it sometimes.

"And another thing is all those nuclear weapons," he said. "Now I know that to most of you, it's a product that meets a need in the marketplace just like any other. But if you decide you're never going to use them, you guarantee the other side is going to walk all over you, even if we don't know who the other side is anymore. But if there is another side, and if you do use them, the other side is going to use theirs, too, and before you know it, the world is going to look like the barn floor at milking time. I don't want to sound like some folksinging college professor, but it's a frightening business.

"And when it's not depressing or frightening, being president is just annoying. I'm tired of meeting Boy Scouts and Girl Scouts and Olympic heroes and people with diseases. I live in a fishbowl and I'm surrounded by Secret Service agents. I have to wear a bulletproof vest that makes me sweat like a pig. I have to fly everywhere and you know how I hate that. I've forgotten how to balance my checkbook, and how to light a barbecue. I'm sixty-two years old and, frankly, I don't need it. Particularly since Euraline won't be sixty-two for twenty more years yet. Sure, making history is interesting work, but the fact is, we can't all be Nixons. And after three years, I can safely say that I'm not."

He contemplated his cigar smoke. "Before the last election, you fellows came to me with a problem. You said there was going to be a Democratic president and a Democratic Congress and pretty soon the country was going to be run by lesbians and people on Prozac. You-all came to me and said, 'Wade, you've got to run.' Well, you got what you wanted. The party's intact, we've won the White House, and you even let me have Herb here to help me run the show.

"So this is the way I see it. We had a deal. You wanted me to keep the country out of the hands of a bunch of liberal whale-huggers and I did it. Well, it's three years later and the country's in fine shape. But I don't like being president, and Euraline doesn't like being first lady. Hell, Euraline doesn't like being any kind of lady. So from where I sit, I can only see one solution."

He sucked in a chestful of air and paused.

"I quit."

Silence filled the room. President Hoak's guests were stunned. Some of them began to chuckle, convinced this was the latest instance of President Hoak's unique approach to leadership.

"Don't laugh," President Hoak insisted. "You've all known from square one how I felt about this job. Look at the bright side. I've served three full years, so Herb here is eligible to finish my term and serve two terms all on his own. He'll have nine years to do whatever it is that you-all want him to do." He paused and swept his eyes over the tables of his assembled guests. "Trust me on this, boys. I'm out."

The small trickle of nervous laughter yielded to the subtle sounds of coffee cups, cordial glasses, and silverware being set down on plates. It wasn't a joke. The realization swept through the room faster than inside information. He was—the word crept into everyone's mind at the same time—*serious.*

"There's only one remaining point," President Hoak continued. "I came to Washington with a minimum of capital, if you get my drift. And what I've got today might have been enough for me and the ex, but it's not enough for Euraline. So I'm going to need a bankroll. I'm not going to be a TV commentator and I don't want to join any boards of directors. I'm not smart enough to write a book. Heck, for that matter, I'm not smart enough to read a goddamned book. So I'm going to need some money. I figure there are a hundred of you here, and you're all from big companies, so if each of you could raise $500,000 for me, that would give me $50 million. I could make do on that."

He rubbed his palms together, happy to be past the hard part. "So that's the story. We've been real friendly so far, you and me, and there's no reason we can't be friendly some more. The folks out there love me, you know—hell, everybody loves me, don't they? And right now they love you, too, 'cause we're all buddies," he said with a dangerous grin. "You guys see what I mean? There's only one good way to settle this thing. So what do you say?"

America's corporate leaders are regularly called upon to make immediate decisions. It's lonely at the top, where the buck comes to rest and the bullet must be bit. But questions plagued them. Could a president simply get up and quit? Could the office of Jefferson and Lincoln be vacated for a life of endless summer vacation? Could the president be paid off for his efforts? Would the payoff be tax deductible?

President Hoak was right: America loved him and, therefore, his friends. What's more, if he was intent on quitting, he would probably find his money somehow. If it didn't come from them, there would be hell to pay later. But could he be allowed to walk away with $50 million in full view of the public?

They had bought presidents before, but they had never sold one.

Warren Weddington, chairman of the largest financial institution in the country, rose from his seat. His peers looked up at him, their breaths held tightly. He moistened his lips, prepared

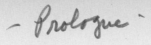
for the bullet's bitter taste, drew his shoulders back, and looked up at President Hoak.

"No problem, Wade," he said. "We appreciate everything you've done for us."

"Spoken like a gentleman, Warren," President Hoak said, the smile never leaving his face. "We can work out the details in the morning." He reached for his glass and raised it as he spoke. "To President Honeycutt."

They rose as one. "To President Honeycutt."

End of Prologue

Chapter One ⟩ *grees to pg 18*

"And it is my pleasure to introduce to you," said the pastor of the Walcott Falls Lutheran Church, "our neighbor, our friend, and our representative in Washington, D.C., Congressman Ezra T. Wheezle." A round of applause wafted through the autumn air as Congressman Ezra T. Wheezle (D.-Pa., 4 C.D.) rose and walked to the podium. A banner stretched across the top of the band shell behind him:

WELCOME!
WALCOTT FALLS INTERFAITH LEAGUE PICNIC
WALCOTT FALLS STATE PARK

Congressman Wheezle gave the audience a practiced appreciative smile for as long as seemed appropriate, and then began to speak. Having nothing substantive to say about any of the issues of the day—the Falkland Islands, budget-busting tax cuts, the unforeseeable decline of disco music—and speaking to an audience with no collective interest save the fact that their churches held their picnics on the same day, Congressman Wheezle chose to speak about freedom and government. In particular, he decided to speak about the freedoms that allowed people such as them to come to picnics such as this and listen to representatives such as him. It would be grave if they forgot the value of these freedoms, he warned, although there was no evidence that they intended to. As for government itself, Congressman Wheezle emphasized his support for it—not *big* government, the bad kind, but *good* government, the kind that he personally favored. It was the kind of government that cared about the average person and built projects like the Walcott Valley Water Supply System that provided that average person with cheap power, drinkable water, and parks such as this one. "This is the kind of government that I am proud of," he said. "It was my personal privilege to have championed the congressional decision to build the Walcott System and this park," he said, reinterpreting the transaction in which he had bartered his support for an African coup d'état in exchange for the appropriation for his local project. "And it reminds me that government *can* work if we want it to."

"There's a girl drowning in the river!" an excited voice shouted from the back of the crowd by the riverbank.

Congressman Wheezle muttered to himself. He never failed to be surprised by where and when hecklers showed up. "If you'll excuse me, my friend," he said, leaning possessively into the microphone, "I'd like to—"

"There's a girl drowning in the river!" the voice repeated.

"Excuse me, Congressman," said the pastor, "but I think a girl is drowning in the river." Congressman Wheezle looked up from his notes, craned his neck to see, and bit his lip pensively. If the girl drowned, it would put a pall over the entire affair, with which he unfortunately would be associated. And if she drowned, how exactly should he respond? He snarled and wondered whether better staff work might have anticipated this contingency. But, then again, the incident could warrant congressional hearings on the safety of federal water projects. He could move the hearings to Walcott Falls. His attitude began to improve.

Congressman Wheezle pondered as all eyes turned to the river.

A small girl had fallen in and the current swept her out to the middle. Suddenly, a young man jumped in and stroked frantically to catch up to her. In a moment he was near enough to grab the girl's dress and gathered her in his arms. Rolling in the white water, he tried to bounce against the rocks and, by luck and a series of caroms, came up against a lodged tree trunk, pinned above the rushing water.

Some men in the crowd formed a chain, and a man with a rope around his waist finally reached them and passed them into the arms of the waiting crowd. The girl was quickly given to her anxious parents. Her rescuer, actually just a boy himself, was barely out of the water when he was whisked up to the stage, his hair plastered over his forehead in strands, to stand next to Congressman Wheezle. He looked to be about twelve. He had an intelligent and pleasant face, and wore an understandably bewildered expression.

"What's your name, lad?" Congressman Wheezle asked.

"It's Lenny Keeler, sir," the boy, water slowly forming a pool around his feet, replied politely.

"Well, you're a very brave young man, Lenny. You've done a very brave thing."

"Thank you, sir," the boy said.

"Stay right here with me," Congressman Wheezle whispered to the boy and put a fatherly hand on his shoulder. "I'm sure that we all feel the way I do right now," he said, turning back to the audience. "And what I feel is pride, intense pride, that a young person in our community has the stuff of which heroes are made. This young man has just given us a perfect example of what our country stands for, each of us working to help the other. Ladies and gentlemen, won't you join me in a round of applause for a wonderful young man from our own city, Lenny Keeler." There was a wave of applause and Lenny's dripping hands were suddenly clasped by beaming clergymen of every denomination, none of whom offered the boy what he wanted most in all the world, a towel.

Fifteen years later, Lenny Keeler sat at his desk in Congressman Wheezle's office. The girl had moved away five years after Lenny saved her, when he was a high school senior. Her father had worked at the railroad switching yard, but the railroad, acquired and reorganized by the federal government, was reacquired by the company that originally disorganized it so as to necessitate its subsequent reorganization, and the switching yard was shut down. Lenny, on the other hand, graduated from college with an interest in politics and the public good, and knew who to call.

Lenny was Congressman Wheezle's legislative assistant, which meant he was in charge of matters of substance, a notably unrewarding job given Congressman Wheezle's decided lack of interest in substantive matters. He worked closely with Congressman Wheezle and Jeff Monge, Congressman Wheezle's office director, an overreaching young carnivore of thirty who handled all matters of backroom politics (in which Congressman Wheezle had a decidedly strong interest). Jeff Monge agreed with everything that Congressman Wheezle said and disagreed with everything somebody else said. As a consequence, his opinions always corresponded with those of Congressman Wheezle, who gave him high marks for political judgment. Among his duties as office director, Jeff took note whenever the three bells rang to indicate that a congressional vote was taking place. He would then ask Lenny what the vote was about and how Congressman Wheezle should vote, information he would share with Congressman Wheezle, who would exit the private door of his office, take the elevator to the basement, take the underground tram to the Capitol, take the Capitol elevator to the House floor, ask Speaker Rollo Plank (D.-Oh., 10 C.D.) if he was voting the right way, vote, backslap for a few moments with his colleagues, and return to his office by the same route.

Congressman Ezra T. Wheezle (D.-Pa., 4 C.D.) was a small man with sparse gray hair waxed over a balding dome, well past sixty but animated by a certain nervous energy, who smoked too much and wore expensive suits and starched shirts to shore up a

rotting frame. He was the second most senior Democratic congressman on the Committee on National Economic Affairs. It
was a situation that led naturally to wanting to be the most senior Democratic congressman on the Committee on National
Economic Affairs, and, therefore, committee chairman. Becoming a chairman was a goal that called for almost endless waiting
and Congressman Ezra T. Wheezle took up the task with relish.
He chose the Committee on National Economic Affairs not for
intellectual challenge or parochial interest, but because its existing chairman, Congressman Senior Younger, Jr. (D.-Id., I C.D.),
was seventy-eight years old when Congressman Wheezle first arrived in the Congress, and had been in the Congress for forty-
two years, more years than Congressman Wheezle had been
alive. His departure, therefore, appeared imminent.

It was a strategy that would have worked had it not been for
the fact that, thirty-six years later, Congressman Senior Younger,
Jr., was 114 years old and had been in the Congress for seventy-
eight years, still more years than Congressman Wheezle had been
alive. Other congressmen veered from membership on his committee, having come to see his age as fool's gold not worth the
mining. Congressman Wheezle waited it out nonetheless, convinced that somehow a 114-year-old man was bound to screw up.

Congressman Wheezle's plan, however, had a second flaw. He
was about to be voted out of office. Changing economic winds
were eroding the base of foundries, hearths, and loading docks
that made up his district, and a trend toward the right had
emerged in an electorate disgruntled by hermaphroditic teenage
musicians, steadily shrinking paychecks, and Americans taken
hostage. Congressman Wheezle had seen the polls and knew
that a viable opponent could end his career with voters who were
coming to like their laissez-faire straight up.

Lenny worried about that, too, partly out of self-interest and
partly out of what remained of his conviction that Congressman
Ezra T. Wheezle was a better agent for good in the world than
whoever might take his place. It was a sentiment to which he

clung despite ever accumulating evidence to the contrary. Congressman Wheezle's reelection, he knew, was going to be a problem. And it was the reason Lenny was summoned one afternoon to Congressman Wheezle's office.

Lenny entered to find Congressman Wheezle at his desk with Jeff in front of him. A young blond man sat on the sofa next to a heavyset man in a blue pinstripe suit. The first was Steve Lowry, The Speaker's point man, a political troubleshooter dispatched whenever the affairs of the party were in disarray. Congressman Wheezle nodded Lenny toward a chair, and Steve Lowry began to speak. "Ezra, I've brought Buddy Youngblood along from Message Concepts in New York, one of the leading political consulting firms. The Congressional Campaign Committee has signed up Buddy to help out on the campaigns of selected senior members, and you're very high on our list."

"Is Ezra in trouble?" interrupted Lenny.

"No," Steve Lowry said, "but we regard the fundamentals in Ezra's district as a problem." He spoke so quickly and forcefully that it took Lenny a moment to understand that his answer was yes. "Ezra's demographic base has been changing. Walcott Falls isn't a mine, mill, and foundry town anymore. It's about computers, services, industries of the future.

"We can appeal to that base. Don Green, in fact, is a voice for them," he noted, referring to their party's presumptive candidate in the upcoming election against President Hoak, although everyone present knew Hoak was going to be tough for anybody to beat.

"Nonetheless," Lowry continued, "we can't afford to run a mill town candidate in a high-tech election. And we have to consider Congressman Wheezle's age. Sixty-four isn't old, but it dovetails poorly with the demographics issue, and puts us at a disadvantage with Congressman Wheezle's opponent, who *really* isn't old. So we need a strategy that makes Ezra's age and experience a plus. That's why we've asked Buddy to come in today."

Buddy Youngblood moved to the edge of the sofa as Lowry

retreated into it. He was the best media man The Speaker knew, a chubby, double-chinned man of fifty with graying, frizzled hair. He had a moist jowly face that he dabbed with a small pudgy hand. He had rocketed his way through advertising, starting with paper towels and laundry soap, moving through vaginal preparations, soft drinks, and automobiles, until the only thing left unsold was people and, rising to the challenge, he became a campaign consultant. "Thank you, Steve," he began. "My firm, Message Concepts, has been asked to outline Congressman Wheezle's reelection campaign." With that he rose to his feet and began walking about the room.

"With all due respect, Congressman Wheezle is old, slovenly, knee-jerk, and sexually unappealing. But that view of the situation doesn't tell us what to do about it. That's where Message Concepts fits in. So if you don't mind," Buddy continued, oblivious to whether anybody minded, "let me talk a bit about Message Concepts and how we see our work.

"Why do you use the media?" His eyes swept the room. "You use the media to distinguish your product from its substitutes. The closer the product to its substitutes the greater the need to draw a distinction. The more things are the same, the more you have to prove they're different, whether it's a product, service, concept, message, deity, or sentiment. Many are called, few are chosen. Three car companies, two soda companies, one elected candidate. The only real question is how to differentiate what you're selling from what everybody else is selling."

He had their rapt attention. "Let me tell you something, gentlemen. Advertising directors, media consultants, and campaign managers have wasted billions of dollars and thousands of hours of their valuable time trying to figure out a product's distinguishing characteristic. Even more time and money have been squandered inventing meaningless differences, and then actually building them into the product itself, in the hope that a trivial distinction would trigger waves of decisiveness in the minds of the public.

"At Message Concepts, we find that approach futile at best and pitiful at worst. Product design is the last refuge of the unimaginative. There's no need to change the product. All you need to change is what you claim the product does. The public has enough on its mind already without you adding to it. It doesn't need advertising that instructs it to want new things, it needs to be told how to get what it already wants. It doesn't want new ideas, it wants the ideas it already has figured out. If you can figure out what the public wants, there's no need to give it to them: telling them that you have it is just as good."

Having outlined this basic proposition, Buddy pushed forward. "Now let's consider Ezra. He's old when everybody else is young. He's liberal when everybody else is conservative. He's low-tech when everybody else is high-tech. His opponent is young, handsome, dissembling, and a latent crypto-fascist. He's obviously going to do well on television. His advantages are so compelling that he would walk away with this election if he weren't making the mistake of running on the basis of who he is rather than who the voters want. We are going to beat him because we've figured out what the public really wants, and we'll convince them we've got it, even if we don't."

Lenny looked about the room to see if anybody else was as confused as he was. Congressman Wheezle sat impassively in his chair. Jeff sat with one eye on Congressman Wheezle, waiting to see what Congressman Wheezle's, and thus his own, response would be. "The important question then becomes," Buddy Youngblood continued, "what kind of a candidate does the public want? I can answer that question with three words: *dependability, familiarity,* and *convenience.*"

Lenny looked up, incredulous. "Are you saying that people judge candidates the way they judge fast food?"

"Precisely!" Buddy Youngblood said, delighted that somebody had expressed his point with such economy. "That's exactly what I'm saying! A candidate has to look dependable, seem familiar, and be convenient. Say all you want about war and peace, pros-

perity and tolerance; voters still pick candidates the way they select a convenience store. Is it dependable? Is it familiar? Is it convenient? That is exactly how our system works. People elect
representatives so that they don't have to get involved; the same
way we have frozen foods so they don't have to cook, and calcu-
lators so they don't have to add. Civilization is a history of sub-
stituting *things* for *effort*. The American colonists didn't fight for
the right to make their own laws. They fought for the right to
pick somebody to do it for them. They fought for the political
right to be consumers." Buddy Youngblood paused, moved by his
own vision.

"That's how we intend to build Congressman Wheezle's campaign," he continued, "on these three traditional American values: dependability, familiarity, and convenience. And this is the
cornerstone of that campaign, the idea that expresses it best."
Buddy Youngblood unzipped a large leather folio and extracted
a campaign poster. It was a black-and-white photo of Congressman Wheezle looking congressional. Underneath, in large red
letters, it said:

WHEEZLE!
HE'S A CONGRESSMAN . . .
SO YOU DON'T HAVE TO BE!

Buddy Youngblood gleamed. "This," he said, "says it all."
Lenny stared at the poster. Steve Lowry looked at his watch.
Jeff looked at Congressman Wheezle. Congressman Wheezle
sat mesmerized with his feet up on his desk, his hands folded in
his lap, and a cigarette dangling from his lips. There was a long
silence. "You know," he said slowly, "you may really have something there, Buddy." He lowered his feet to the floor and sat forward in his chair, all eyes upon him. "Isn't that exactly what we're
trying to say?"
"I think you're right, Congressman," Jeff chimed in. "It has a
really good feel to it."

"I'm glad you feel that way, Ezra," Buddy said. "In fact, I want everyone on your staff to feel that way, because we see them as a major asset in the campaign. You see," he said, addressing the room at large, "the fact that Congressman Wheezle is a congressman with a large staff becomes a compelling advantage when you ask people to vote on the basis of who looks more like a congressman. A large staff is so . . . congressional. People may legitimately wonder if Congressman Wheezle's opponent will ever have any staff at all. They have no assurance that a new guy is even going to get a desk and a telephone. But Congressman Wheezle has all those things, and that's a big advantage for us.

"Ezra," he said, turning back to Congressman Wheezle, "you're going to have the most advanced campaign that any democracy has ever seen. Once we get in gear, you could go to sleep on Labor Day and wake up reelected in November," he said with satisfaction.

Congressman Wheezle looked up and smiled. "That's the ticket," he said, sitting back in his chair. "Maybe I will." He lifted his feet onto his desk and leaned back in his chair until its wheels skidded out from under him, sending him to the floor with a crash.

End of chpt.1

Chapter Two goes to pg. 28

For Dr. Burton Horton, being chairman of the Department of Geophysics at the South Florida Institute of Technology was an exercise in personnel management. First, he had to convince the assistant professors to teach extra courses and work for minimal pay in the hope of receiving tenure. That part was easy, since most assistant professors arrived at the South Florida Institute of Technology hoping to receive tenure and were willing to do virtually anything to get it. Second, he had to tell the assistant professors who had taught extra courses and worked for minimal pay that they were not going to receive tenure, given the university's extreme financial duress and its freeze on new tenured positions, and to point them toward career opportunities outside education (which would eliminate any future contact with them). Third, he had to convince those assistant professors who successfully appealed their tenure reviews and were promoted to associate professor that they should forgo immediate raises and provide extensive university service in the hope of becoming full professors. Of course, the associate professors readily acceded to this request. Finally, he had to inform those associate professors who had been promoted to full professors that they would not be given large raises or easy teaching assignments. The full professors did not like this, but accepted it when they realized that they probably would be unable to bring their tenure and rank to another institution. Dr. Horton dreaded having these conversations, since telling people that they could not have what they wanted seemed to put them off. But transacting his chairmanly responsibilities was a price worth paying for his chairmanship.

Dr. Horton was about to work the second stage of this sequence on an assistant professor named Dickie Vanderhaltz. Dickie Vanderhaltz was a tall young man with an impressive carriage and unmistakably American good looks—blond hair crisply parted on the left, clear blue eyes, a strong chin and nose, and thin lips that formed a rugged expression. He was thirty-two years old, older than most of the other assistant professors in the Geophysics Department, having spent nine years in graduate school pursuing his Ph.D. He had failed his Ph.D. exams twice, formulated several dissertation experiments involving volcanic heat transfer that provided no results of scientific value, and lost his fellowship money after failing to produce his dissertation on time. He finally wrote one after spending two years in the Icelandic hinterlands taking ground temperature readings during a period of volcanic activity, including the grim day he lost his only companion, a stray dog named Vulcan, to a lava flow.

He obtained his position at the South Florida Institute of Technology by inducing his dissertation chairman to provide Dr. Burton Horton with a recommendation based on pity rather than merit. Once at S.F.I.T., he discovered that there was little interest in the geophysics of volcanic heat in a state dominated by swamps and flatlands. He persevered nonetheless, attending stultifying conferences, presenting uninteresting scientific findings, and writing for geophysical journals inept articles that were not accepted.

Dickie did not merit tenure nor had he the guile to get it. Dr. Horton was therefore doubly frustrated that Dickie's general ineptness would also make it difficult to recommend a career opportunity outside academia. It would have to be a clean kill.

Outside the window it was springtime in Florida. Mosquitoes the size of dragonflies and dragonflies the size of sparrows bounced against the windowpane. Dr. Horton diverted himself with the morning's mail. It contained a variety of announcements concerning new books in geophysics. Most of these he threw away. As chairman, he had no need to collect books and no desire to read them. There was a memo from the dean of science requesting course schedules for the coming semester by the fifteenth of the month. It was now the eighteenth of the month, so he threw that away, too. There was a memo from the academic vice president, reminding him that tenure-recommendation decisions for assistant professors were due at the end of the week. He exhaled deeply and looked at his watch. Dickie Vanderhaltz would be in to see him in fifteen minutes.

The return address on the last envelope in the stack read: Metkovich, Earth Sciences, M.I.T. Metkovich was the chairman at M.I.T. and he enjoyed talking about M.I.T.'s various geological programs. He didn't enjoy talking about the work being done at less prestigious institutions, like Dr. Horton's.

He opened the envelope. Metkovich wrote that he had received a sizable grant from the National Association for Physical Science allowing him to select several young graduate students or faculty members in the physical sciences for Public Policy Fellowships. The recipients would receive a stipend to serve on a congressional committee or in the office of a congressman or senator. Nominations, Metkovich wrote, should be sent to him immediately, along with letters of recommendation.

Dr. Horton burned as he read the letter. He had proposed such a program several years before but was told that funding was not available. That plagiarizing bastard. Dr. Horton was contemplating how much he loathed Metkovich when his concentration was interrupted by Dickie Vanderhaltz, who appeared at the door.

"Come in, Dickie," Dr. Horton said, and extended his hand toward a chair in front of his desk.

"You asked to see me, Dr. Horton?" Dickie said, seating himself.

"Yes, Dickie. It's time for us to talk about your relationship to our department and this institution," he said by way of introduction. "You've been with us for—"

"This is about my tenure review, isn't it?" he interrupted.

"Well, yes, Dickie, it is," responded Dr. Horton. "I've given the matter a considerable amount of thought—"

"I'm not going to get it, am I?" Dickie asked.

"No, you're not," Dr. Horton agreed. This was going to be easier than he thought.

"I knew I wasn't, Dr. Horton. I knew it all along." He immediately went about defending himself from dismissal using the same tactic he'd used to get his Ph.D. and the recommendation for his first job at S.F.I.T.—unabashed self-immolation in the hopes of mercy. "It was a mistake to have come here, sir. There's no interest in volcanic heat experiments in Florida, and if there were, there are probably plenty of people who could do them better than me. I fully understand your position, sir, I really do."

His self-denigration took Dr. Horton aback. "Don't be too hard on yourself, Dickie. The university is under extreme financial duress and has put a temporary freeze on new tenured positions," he found himself reciting again, "so it's impossible—"

Dickie's eyes began to mist. "I'm sorry. It's just that nothing seems to work out for me." He wiped his nose with his forearm in a sweeping gesture. "What am I going to do?" He looked up, hoping that Dr. Horton might tell him, having no idea of his own.

Dr. Horton looked down at his desk to avoid Dickie's forlorn gaze and his eyes fell upon the letter from Metkovich.

"Well now, Dickie, perhaps I can offer a suggestion. I've been asked to nominate a candidate for a fellowship offered by the National Association for Physical Science. The fellowship allows young scientists to go to Washington, D.C., to learn about the policy-making process. Would you be interested in that kind of situation?" Dr. Horton's enthusiasm for the idea grew as he spoke. Why not make him Metkovich's problem as opposed to his own? The thought of Dickie in Washington, D.C., made perfect sense. It was far away, and he could imagine no better place for somebody who wasn't good at anything. "Frankly, Dickie, I think you could go far with this," Dr. Horton said, cryptically. He retrieved a package of tissues from his desk and pushed them over to Dickie. "Has the thought of going into government ever occurred to you?"

"No, it hasn't, sir," Dickie said as he dried his eyes.

"I'll tell you what," Dr. Horton said enthusiastically. "Put your vita and a publications sample together and let me call Metkovich about it."

"Metkovich? *The* Metkovich at M.I.T.?" Dickie asked, in awe of the great man's reputation. "Why, yes," Dickie said, warming to the idea. "I'd appreciate it if you did." A smile flashed across his face. Washington, a new place! He had no friends in Washington, but he had no friends at S.F.I.T. either, and at least in Washington he could tell himself he lacked friends because he'd never been there before.

"I really appreciate this opportunity, Dr. Horton," Dickie said earnestly as he rose. "I'll get my materials together as soon as possible." He pumped Dr. Horton's hand in gratitude and left the office. Dr. Horton smiled to himself. He would never hear from Dickie Vanderhaltz again.

Lenny sat at his desk and stared down at the work still awaiting his attention. An empty pizza box balanced atop his wastepaper basket. It was about eight in the evening and everyone else had gone home for the day.

The television droned on in a corner of the room. The Congress was not in session that evening, so C-SPAN was covering a live Col. Cody Clark event. Col. Cody Clark, the evangelical investment advisor, was now on the screen, saving his flock's soul and solvency. "*There's a woman sitting in her living room in Topeka,*

Kansas," he said. "I'm getting a reading from her right now. She is in great pain, and she has had several operations. She hasn't been able to move her right arm for several years, but she will now. This same woman, who can now move her arm for the first time in years, is holding a major portion of her late husband's estate in utility common stocks. But she must sell those common stocks and switch to higher-yield preferreds because of her low taxable income. Yes, Jesus wants us to be spiritually well and financially well, Hallelujah! So let this woman, we pray, Lord, realize high returns and great stability and preservation of capital, Amen."

Lenny looked about his desk for the remote control but couldn't find it. *"Ladies and gentlemen,"* Col. Cody Clark persisted, *"let me ask you a question tonight. Let me ask you: why is the free enterprise system like the Kingdom of Heaven? Friends, do you know why? Because those are the only two places you can invest with the expectation of earning a fair return. Because that is what God guarantees us,"* he said. *"Nothing more, and nothing less, than a fair return."*

Lenny opened the folder in front of him. On top was a letter to Congressman Wheezle from the Executive Committee of the Committee for Government by the People. The Committee for Government by the People was a public interest group that supported good government in general and themselves in particular. They stood for everything President Hoak stood for but never supported any of President Hoak's proposals, all of which struck them as tawdry sellouts of the principles they so vehemently supported. They criticized most government activities and supported all initiatives to reform them until those initiatives became law, at which time they opposed them. Their unequivocal opposition to all administrations, coupled with their unqualified support for each administration's objectives, cemented the sanctity of their reputations. Toward this end they would raise enough money to buy newspaper advertisements announcing these positions, making sure that enough was left over to pay their salaries, rent their offices, and to write ponderous policy memoranda to influential individuals such as Congressman Wheezle.

The Committee for Government by the People in this par-

ticular instance was writing in opposition to a bill that had been
directed to the Committee on National Economic Affairs, the
equipment-that-doesn't-work tax credit. Enclosed was a copy of
the bill itself. Lenny quickly turned through the various Findings and Whereases and tried to find the place where somebody
got something. Every bill had a place where somebody got something and no bill was truly understood until Whom and What
were clear. He was only vaguely aware of Col. Cody Clark in the
background. *"Yes, the Lord watches all of us, and in return for our deeds,
our investments in holy grace, we are provided with a reward, a spiritual return. The righteous will truly witness God's bottom line. And in return for
your prayers, I will recommend for you Patterson-Wylie, a medium-size machine tool company out of Muncie, Indiana, that specializes in microelectroni-
cally assisted lathing machines and is now selling at a price-to-earnings ratio
of only 6.5 due to strictly transient financial restructuring problems. Act now
and be rewarded."*

Lenny turned his full attention to the monitor, though, when
it began to emit music of dramatic moment and Col. Cody
Clark was replaced with a graphic heralding a special report.
"Good evening, ladies and gentlemen," a news anchor said from
a desk before a blue drape. "And welcome to a special broadcast
from the White House." The camera moved in for a tighter
shot. "Tonight, we are told, President Wade F. Hoak will make
a historic announcement. In a departure from usual procedure,
he has not provided us with an advance copy of his speech, so
we're just as curious as you are to find out what he's going to say."
The news anchor's head tilted slightly as he listened to the voice
in his headset. "I understand that he's ready now . . . very good
. . . ladies and gentlemen, the President of the United States,
Wade F. Hoak."

President Hoak suddenly appeared on the screen, sitting at
his Oval Office desk, smiling his magnificent and widely loved
smile. "Good evening, my fellow Americans," he began. "I want
to thank you for taking the time to be with me tonight. This is
a special night for both of us, for me and you. I'm probably

going to surprise most of you with what I have to say tonight. But I want you to remember that nothing I ever do is going to hurt you. You can count on that."

Lenny looked down at the folder on his desk and let his attention slip for a second. President Hoak said something about something being just the point. "I've always felt that if you wanted to be president, you had to take the responsibility seriously," he continued. "You had to want to do it. You had to want to get out of bed in the morning and run the country. And when I took office three years ago, that's how I felt. If there was one word to characterize the Hoak administration, it was *determined*. We were determined to bring prosperity back to our great nation. And the prosperity we now enjoy is the result of the sound economic policies that my advisors and I have put into place. And let me tell you something, folks," he said. "My advisors are smart guys, really smart guys. But if their advice hadn't worked, I'd have fired every last one of them. I can promise you that."

President Hoak paused and adopted a reflective tone. "Now, you all know why I came here to Washington, D.C.," he said, allowing his audience to forget that he had been a senator for years. "It was because I was determined to fix up the mess that the other party handed us, to clean house. And you all know that I didn't chase this job. But when I was asked, when you, the people, came to me and said, 'Wade Hoak, it's time for you to be president,' I told myself: set yourself some goals, get some determination, and you can be just as good a president as the next guy.

"And I'm mighty proud of everything we've accomplished. We were determined to fight crime, and we're fighting it. We were determined to save the environment, and we're saving it. We were determined to get the cheaters and the loafers off the welfare rolls, and now they're gone. You remember the woman I told you about during my campaign, who was getting welfare benefits and drove around in a brand-new Lincoln Continental? Well, I'm proud to say we were able to get the car back and take her off the welfare rolls, and that woman lives in poverty again today!" He beamed.

"But I'm not here tonight to talk about my accomplishments. What I'm trying to say is that when I took this job, I was determined to accomplish my goals. Well, I've accomplished them. So now what? I could stick around in the Oval Office and be president some more. I could cut some ribbons and sign some treaties and entertain myself, I suppose, but would that be fair to you? I don't think so. It would be like paying someone for eight hours' work when they could get all the work done in four. You've had your fill of do-nothing presidents, and I don't intend to become one. So I'm going to do the one honorable thing that there is to do. I'm going to resign."

Lenny looked up at the television set in the hope that it would have the decency to offer an instant replay to confirm what he thought it had just reported to him.

"I know what you're thinking," President Hoak said with a wry smile. "You're thinking, 'Presidents don't quit.' But why not? Haven't you ever quit your job before? Haven't you ever felt that the job you had was wrong for you, wasn't paying you enough, or was just plain done? Well, my job's done.

"There might be some of you who think I'm just doing this to collect my pension. You know how it is for ex-presidents. They write their memoirs and sit in their big presidential libraries that you, the taxpayers, pay for, and they have Secret Service agents waiting on them hand and foot. Well, I can promise you there'll be none of that for me. I don't want one blessed dime of your money. Why should all you hardworking Americans pay for me when I make a pretty good living as it is? I'm never going to be a burden to you. I promise you that, and you know I keep my promises.

"Vice President Honeycutt will take the oath of office tomorrow at noon. He's going to be a great president, folks, believe me. And after he takes the oath of office and they give him the football—that's the special device that allows the president to begin a nuclear war no matter where he may be—I'll be on my way. It's been nice knowing you, folks. God bless all of you, and God bless America."

And with that, President Hoak was gone.

"Let me turn to you first, Tom Baines," said the news anchor to the commentator. "What's the real message that President Hoak was trying to convey tonight?"

Lenny looked down at the file on the equipment-that-doesn't-work tax credit and closed it. He sat there agape for a moment as the miracle of Constitutional succession acted itself out on the television before him. Then it occurred to him that suddenly, maybe, possibly, Congressman Ezra T. Wheezle (D.-Pa., 4 C.D.) had a chance.

Chapter Three ⟩ goes to pg.

Dickie Vanderhaltz strode briskly down the fifth floor of the Dirksen Senate Office Building, wondering what great adventures lay behind each of its silent oaken doors. This was more than his first day at work, he thought. It was his first day in history.

He stopped and presented himself to the door numbered 654. *Committee on Science and Engineering*. He fumbled for his letter from Metkovich and compared its contents to the information on the door. He drew a breath, ran his hands over his hair, and squared his corduroy sport coat under his down vest. He shook each leg to fight off the numbness that unfamiliar hard leather shoes had sent climbing up both shins.

He opened the door and entered. A receptionist smiled up at him from underneath a poster advertising Florida vacations.

"Can I help you?" she asked.

"Yes, uh, I'm Dickie Vanderhaltz."

"Yes?" she prompted.

He did not understand why she did not recognize his name. "I'm Dickie Vanderhaltz," he repeated seriously. She looked at him quizzically. "I'm here on a fellowship from the National Association for Physical Science."

"Oh, of course," she said. "Mr. Brock told me you'd be arriving today. Won't you take a seat while I see if he's available?"

"Certainly," said Dickie. He sat and looked about. Opposite him was a door with a sign above it: HEARING ROOM. His imagination swirled with visions of witnesses speaking for the commonweal, gavels punctuating the nation's progress, laws constructed by panels of solons. He inserted himself into the picture. Perhaps that was him, sitting behind the senators, maintaining a vigilant expression. Perhaps that was him, passing a note to a senator, perhaps to Senator Luther A. Moss himself: *"This witness is lying. Ask him if his design for an impervious geological repository for strategic minerals would survive the intrusion of a hot magma formation moving through a sedimentary fault trap on the repository's perimeter."* Perhaps that was him, sitting back smugly, as the witness broke down into a pitiful stammer, confessing that his plan to build a geological repository to store strategic minerals was little more than a hastily crafted fraud, that he might as well have proposed leaving the nation's stores of tungsten, chromium, and vanadium under the front porch for a few summers. *"These hearings are adjourned!"* bellowed the imaginary Senator Moss as his gavel guillotined the witness's perfidy.

His reverie was broken as a matronly woman of fifty approached him. "Dickie Vanderhaltz?"

He nodded.

"I'm Elsie, Hugh Brock's secretary," she extended her hand, confident in her authority.

"Who is he?"

"Mr. Brock is the staff director. He runs this committee."

"I think I'm here to see Senator Luther A. Moss," he said apologetically.

The woman acted as if she hadn't heard him. "Would you come with me?" she said and turned and opened the door before Dickie could open it for her. He followed her past a confusing sequence of corridors, bookshelves, Xerox machines, and secretarial stations to another door. She opened it and poked her head in. "Dickie Vanderhaltz is here," she said, and then turned back to him. "Go right in."

Dickie entered and saw a man of forty with an unforgiving expression rise from his desk. The American flag and the flag of the State of Florida flanked the window behind him. "I'm Hugh Brock," the man said. "Welcome. Won't you sit down?" Dickie sat himself in front of the desk.

Hugh sat down rigidly, as if his reflexes were about to be tested. For Hugh, life was a series of tests. He was the product of a military academy as a youth and had spent several years in the service on board a submarine. "His temperament would be unaffected by prolonged confinement," his psychological record reported coyly, and so off he went for three submarine crossings of the Arctic Ocean. After his requisite years of service he hastened to Washington, where Senator Moss gave him a job on the committee. By the end of the year he looked down on the world as staff director.

He smiled at Dickie. "We're always very pleased to have a physical science fellow on staff. Were you a colleague of Dr. Metkovich?"

"No, I'm from the South Florida Institute of Technology."

"Of course. Florida. Our chairman's home state. Well," he said, reasserting control of the conversation, "let's talk about the things that we do here. Have you ever been involved in government before?"

"No," said Dickie apologetically.

"Did you vote for President Honeycutt?" Hugh asked.

"Nobody voted for President Honeycutt."

"I meant for President Hoak," Hugh said.

"Oh. Well, I didn't vote in that election." He saw Hugh's eyebrows rise. "But I certainly would have voted for President Hoak, though, if I had voted."

"Good, good," Hugh said. "I'm glad to hear it." He looked at his watch and decided that he had undergone enough formality. "Now, you're going to have to learn the routine here. But, first, remember this," Hugh offered, throwing back his head and addressing the soundproofing dots on the paneled ceiling above him. "Politics is at once both very simple and very complex. The first principle is always the same: keep your old friends and make some new ones."

Dickie had a hard time following what Hugh said, but he agreed. If politics meant having friends, he was all for it.

"We always work on that first principle of politics: we keep our old friends and make some new ones, groups of like-minded people whose interests parallel our own. You'll be doing lots of new things with the committee," Hugh assured Dickie, "but keep the first principle in mind and you'll be fine. Your work, of course, will be designed to take advantage of your background as a scientist and your specialty in . . . what was it again?"

"Geophysics," Dickie responded.

"Of course," Hugh said. "I can't recall, offhand, a project that we have in that area right now," his voice trailed off as he ransacked his memory, "but oil and gas are always important and they're geological, aren't they?" Dickie nodded in agreement. "Good, then. Let's get the show on the road, shall we?" he said as he picked up the phone. "Would you ask Miriam to come in here, please?" he said. He hung up. "I'm going to ask Miriam Moskowitz to join us," he said, having just done so. "Miriam's a valuable member of my staff. If you have any questions, Miriam will take good care of you."

Dickie was pleased that somebody would take care of him and wondered if Miriam Moskowitz would be the first friend he would get and keep. In a moment, she entered. She was taller than Dickie expected, about thirty years old. She wore a gray flannel suit, white blouse, and black shoes. She was attractive, almost pretty, with dark hair that curled to the bottom of her neck, and dark brown eyes that studied Dickie as intently as he was studying her.

"Dickie is a geophysicist with us under a fellowship from the National Association for Physical Science," Hugh told Miriam.

"I'd like you to take him around the office. There's that desk next to yours in the back room behind the galley. Why don't we put Dickie there?"

Miriam nodded in agreement as she cursed under her breath. She had planned to have the properties office remove that desk and then rearrange the remaining furniture to annex that space into her own. She clenched her teeth and looked at Dickie, the interloper. "Sure," she said with a forced smile.

"Very good. Dickie, welcome aboard," Hugh rose and shook Dickie's hand. He tried to retract it but Dickie gave it a few extra pumps to signal his commitment. Dickie walked backward a few steps and said, "See you later" to Hugh, who did not look up as Miriam followed him out.

"Did you work with Metkovich at M.I.T.?" she asked as they began to walk.

"No," he said. "With Burton Horton at S.F.I.T."

"Where?" she asked, passing a row of dividers and leading him into the galley where most of the senior committee staff worked.

"South Florida Institute—" Dickie was saying when he looked up and saw Miriam already beckoning him from the other end of the galley.

She opened the door into a second room. It was cluttered with old furniture, bookshelves, file cabinets, and stacks of reports, papers, and newspapers. Two desks faced the window on the left. Miriam walked over to the far one and gestured toward the other. "This one's yours," she said. Nearby were a set of bookshelves, and a chair. He sat down at his desk and looked out the window. The view was of another wing of the building, an endless white wall with a matrix of windows like his own. Across the top of the window was a ribbon of blue sky. A dying plant had been left on the sill.

He dropped his knapsack on the desk and took off his down vest. His hands ran over the flat of his new desk. "What do I do now?"

Miriam had already put some papers in front of her in a studied effort to look busy. "I'll give you some background materials on the things the committee's doing this session. Did you ever hear of the equipment-that-doesn't-work tax credit?"

"What's the equipment-that-doesn't-work tax credit?" Dickie asked.

"It's a bill that gives companies a tax credit if they give equipment that doesn't work to colleges and universities."

Dickie considered for a moment. "We're against that, aren't we?"

"Oh, no," Miriam answered. "We're against tax loopholes. Tax loopholes force the many to pay taxes for the few. But the equipment-that-doesn't-work tax credit isn't a loophole. It's a legitimate incentive that supports colleges and universities. We're all for legitimate incentives. And our support for colleges and universities is unqualified."

"But don't we need the tax money to balance the budget? Aren't we for keeping the federal budget in balance?"

"What's that have to do with it? We're definitely for keeping the federal budget in balance. The budget deficit is the most pernicious economic force in our country today, even if we don't have one. After all, the budget deficit is linked to the trade deficit and the savings deficit."

"It is?"

"Of course it is. All deficits are related."

"They are?"

"Until somebody suggests otherwise, it's unambiguous."

"Then what are we going to do to keep the budget balanced?"

"Senator Moss is for strong action."

"Is Senator Moss for cutting spending?"

"Without a doubt, except for science and technology."

"Then what programs would he cut?"

"None in particular."

"But how can Senator Moss be for cutting spending without cutting any particular program?"

"Easy. Everybody else is. Why shouldn't he?"

"But if you're for cutting spending you have to cut something!"

Miriam looked at Dickie and shrugged. She studied the vest and knapsack lying at Dickie's desk. Instead of an easy chair and a tree in a tasteful planter, she was going to share her office with a down vest, a knapsack, and a geophysicist. He was an imposition in every sense of the word, an affront to her framed Monet print and bountiful hanging plants, a denial of her efforts to expand not only her office space, but her career with the committee. For Miriam, the point of sitting in the back room was to sit in the front room. And now she was presented with a back-room challenger. She knew how these things went—biology professors came to Washington on one of these science fellowships and became deputy staff directors; physics professors became defense issues experts before taking jobs as lobbyists.

She resolved then and there that Dickie would not beat her into the front room. It was only a matter of time before one of the people out there went somewhere else; everybody went somewhere, sooner or later. But what if Hugh were impressed by the new man, with his advanced degree in—what was it?—geophysics? After all, he had been a professor at the South Florida Institute of whatever it was, hadn't he? He had to have something upstairs, even if it wasn't immediately apparent what that might be.

She would have to be careful, she thought. She could never give the appearance of trying to sabotage him. But she had invested three years preparing for the day when a new job would open up for her. She certainly wasn't going to let a science fellow stand in her way. She looked his way and felt the slightest twinge of pity for what was going to happen to him.

It was nine o'clock: the morning light came in through Dickie's window at the Science and Engineering Committee. Miriam was busily returning her phone messages. She had divided her stack of messages into two piles. The first pile contained messages from the people to whom she wanted to talk. She put this pile aside for later. The second pile were calls that she did not want to return. She returned these calls immediately, before the callers arrived at their desks. If they then called her back during the morning, she would return their returned calls during lunch, when they would be out again. She repeated this procedure until they stopped calling. You could learn plenty just watching her, Dickie thought.

Dickie had only been with the committee for a week and a half, but his desk and work area were already as cluttered as everybody else's. Before him sat stacks of *Congressional Records*, hearings transcripts, and appropriations records. Next to him lay technical and scientific journals. On top of the journals sat lists of witnesses for committee hearings. Atop these lists sat memos from Hugh asking him to prepare questions that Senator Moss could ask if he were awake and interested. Atop these memos were drafts of statements for Senator Moss, giving his views on the state of America's readiness in the area of particle acceleration; on providing more funds for upgrading and maintaining the nation's particle accelerators at those educational institutions with particle accelerators but without the means to upgrade and maintain them; on building new particle accelerators at those educational institutions that did not have particle accelerators but were capable of upgrading and maintaining them; and on dedicating new graduate fellowships to address the imbalance between the projected widespread availability of particle accelerators and the unavailability of students interested in doing particle accelerator research.

"Umm, excuse me, Miriam," Dickie said as he leaned over toward the next desk, "but could I ask you a question?"

Miriam's smile clicked like a switchblade. "Sure, Dickie, what's the problem?"

"Well, I've got all these things to do. I just don't know where to begin."

"I see the problem, Dickie," she said sympathetically as she swam toward the smell of blood. "Let me ask you this: what are you here to do?"

Well, that was a good question. He had come to Washington, he told himself, to gain valuable insights that would allow him, a geophysicist, to fathom the workings of public policy. Actually, he had come because he had been fired at S.F.I.T. and dumped in Metkovich's lap, but he had managed to forget his life at S.F.I.T. in the intoxicating rush of his new Senate career. As his memory reprogrammed itself, he became a geophysicist Minuteman who left the comforts of blackboard and faculty lounge to answer his nation's call—a scientist-patriot, a spokesman for the colleagues he had forgotten he never had. "Well, I guess I'm here to be the resident scientist."

She liked that. It sounded irrelevant. "Then that's exactly what you ought to be doing, Dickie."

Her logic was unshakable. How could he serve as a scientific resource if he was unaware of the latest work by his fellow scientists? He sat forward in his chair and carefully stacked the hearings transcripts, witness lists, Congressional Record insert drafts, executive agency submissions—everything that required immediate attention—and set them aside. He took the stack of scientific journals and opened the first one. "I'm sorry to ask questions like that, Miriam, but I'm just so new around here."

He had just begun to read when his phone rang. "Vanderhaltz here." He nodded a few times. "Got it." He hung up and grabbed his notebook. "Hugh needs me," he said proudly, and strode out of the room.

Hugh was sitting in his office with two men. The taller one introduced himself to Dickie as Chance and the other as Collins. "Mr. Chance and Mr. Collins are from the A.E.I.O.U.," Hugh said. Dickie nodded, although he did not know what the A.E.I.O.U. was. "Dickie," Hugh told the visitors, "is a professor of geophysics at the South Florida Institute of Technology. He's with us on a fellowship from the National Association for Physical Science, a program run by Leonard Metkovich."

Chance and Collins were impressed.

"He's quite a man, isn't he?" said Chance.

"He certainly is," said Dickie, forgetting to mention that he had never met him.

"Tell me, Dr. Vanderhaltz. Have you ever worked on groundwater issues and power plant siting?" Chance asked.

"No," Dickie said. "My work has been in volcanic geocalimetry." He smiled awkwardly.

"I see," said Chance, secretly embarrassed that he did not know what volcanic geocalimetry was.

Hugh was pleased that preliminaries had gone so well. "Let's get down to business, shall we?"

"Sure," Collins began, extracting some stapled papers from his briefcase. "First, Dr. Vanderhaltz, are you familiar with the A.E.I.O.U.?"

Dickie suppressed the instinct to panic. "Well, no, actually."

"Of course," said Collins, who imagined that a prestigious scientist like Dickie had little time for following the activities of a group like the A.E.I.O.U. "Dr. Vanderhaltz, the A.E.I.O.U. is the Association of Electric Investor-Owned Utilities. We represent the companies that provide electricity to American industry and consumers. Our nation faces a wave of disastrous utility financial failures that will pose a crippling burden for our ongoing economic expansion. Our industry has been savaged by a system that allows anyone to hold up power plant construction by telling a judge with no engineering or business training whatsoever a sad story about somebody's theoretical lymphoma. One day a utility is going to go bankrupt, and then we'll see the consequences. A utility that goes broke will never build another power plant again, I can assure you."

Dickie nodded, although he could not help but think that it might be a good thing if a utility that went broke did not build a power plant ever again, since building power plants was how it got to be broke in the first place. But Dickie held his tongue because the only thing he knew about power plants was how they worked, how they could be represented in thermodynamic terms with either a Rankine or a Brayton cycle diagram in temperature-enthalpy space, and how such power plants had a maximum Cournot efficiency that could be approached in practice by using feedwater heaters and recirculators inside the coolant loop. But that was how power plants actually worked, and how things actually worked, he was learning, was not very important.

Chance now took the floor. "We've been working on a proposal to address the issue of electric utility financial failures. But if we tried to help utilities on the brink of failure, people are bound to say, 'Oh, that's fine for utilities, but it's unfair to everybody else.' Well, we agree. In fact, it would be particularly unfair to utilities that have avoided financial crises, denying them assistance simply because of their good fortune. If you only bail out the failures, you penalize the successful ones, don't you?"

There was no arguing with that, Dickie thought.

"So we've designed a proposal that helps the entire investor-owned electric utility sector without the need for expensive federal bailouts. Our idea is to institute daylight saving time on a year-long basis with bonus saving time between June 30 and Labor Day, which would advance the clock another hour. We believe this, what we call 'universal saving time,' would increase electricity demand substantially, since households and businesses would have to air-condition their premises later each day in the summer, and would use more heating and lighting during winter mornings.

"Electricity is a bridge between man's needs and the limitations of his environment. Anything that enlarges the gulf between man's needs and his environment's ability to satisfy them increases the demand for electricity, which is the key to averting a wave of disastrous utility financial failures."

There was a round of solemn nodding. "I have these fact sheets," Collins added, "that deal with the nature of the utility financial crisis and some possible benefits of universal daylight saving time and we've put together a draft for a bill."

There was yet more nodding. Chance leaned forward in his seat. "Well, Dickie, that's our proposal in a nutshell. As a scientist, what do you think?"

Dickie rubbed his palms together and looked down at the floor, lost in thought. He noticed that the longer he held his pose the more interested Chance and Collins became. Finally, he looked up and offered his considered scientific opinion.

"I think it will have no geological significance whatsoever."

Hugh looked at Dickie with confusion. "What?" he demanded.

"Exactly that," he said, reveling in his role as science advisor and advocate. "Moving the clock forward an hour will have absolutely no geological significance, because the logic of geology does not require a fixed measurement index, only a fixed metric," he discoursed. "After all, there are only x hours in the day."

"That's not what they're asking, Dickie," hissed Hugh. "What do you think of the idea?"

"Oh, as an idea? I think it's very good. I'm all for the extra hour of light in the afternoon, myself," he said placatingly, assessing Collins and Chance as two friends he could make and then keep. "And, of course, it offers the opportunity to save several investor-owned utilities from financial failure," he said, beginning to get the point.

Collins and Chance nodded along with Dickie's recitation of the correct answer, pleased that a scientist of Dickie's stature recognized the merit of their plan. "Dickie," Hugh said, "I want you to take charge of this proposal. The A.E.I.O.U. is a good friend of ours and it has a very good idea. Why don't you get a feel for it? You might want to write some notes up for discussions and public consumption. Lay some groundwork. What kinds of arguments should we put forward? What forums should we select? Perhaps we should write some kind of report or article."

Dickie nodded and wrote down Hugh's instructions carefully,

hoping later to understand what they meant, and making a note to remind him that the plural of *forum* was *fora*.

"Report back to me once you've got something," Hugh concluded. Dickie nodded. He would ask Miriam's advice before he did anything. "You understand," Hugh said, turning back to the two men, "that we're new to this issue. But we'll get started, and see what we can come up with." Hugh nodded once, ending the meeting.

There was a round of polite handshaking, an exercise Dickie never failed to enjoy. "Thanks so much for coming over," said Hugh, as he led Chance and Collins out the door, dismissing Dickie a moment later.

Hugh sat down at his desk and reviewed the state of play. The A.E.I.O.U. had plenty of money and a good national organization, the kind of people that Senator Moss needed at this point in his career. Hugh was less than enthusiastic about the prospect of year-long daylight saving time, of course, and suspected that Senator Moss felt the same way. But he was enthusiastic about the A.E.I.O.U.'s money and assigning Dickie to their proposal would stall them for a while. He was mulling the possibilities when his phone rang.

"Art Mack called while you were in your meeting," Elsie began. "He wants to get a copy of the hearing schedule for next month." Art Mack ran Senator Moss's personal staff. He could screw himself, Hugh thought. Personal staff was always trying to tag along after the senator.

"Bring me some coffee," he said and then dialed Senator Moss's office number. "This is Hugh," he barked. "Is the senator available?" He waited a moment and the senator came on the line.

"Hello, Hugh?"

"Yes, Senator. How are you today?"

"Very well, Hugh. How are things?"

"Going nicely, Senator. I had the visit from the A.E.I.O.U.

that you told me about. Remember you had dinner with Conrad Scott from Florida Heat Steam and Light?"

"Right. He said his organization had a new idea about electric utility finances, something like that. How did it go?"

"Frankly, Senator, there could be problems. Their idea is to put the entire country on daylight saving time all year long. And an extra hour's advance all summer. They figure they'll sell more juice. They want you to submit a bill to that effect."

"Jesus, Hugh. I can't do that. Can you imagine how the hotels in Miami would react if it didn't get dark until ten at night? Or the dog tracks?"

"I can see that, Senator. But if I remember correctly, you've already taken Conrad Scott's check."

"Damned, yes," Senator Moss said. "And I've been promised more. Do you think we ought to give it back? It was a pretty good piece of change, wasn't it?"

"Five hundred thousand dollars, Senator."

"But isn't there a legal limit on how much we can take from them?"

"Yes. There's a $5,000 limit on contributions from any one source. But Conrad Scott arranged for a hundred utilities to give us $5,000 each."

"Isn't that illegal?"

"No, it's absolutely legal. And we can always give the money back if we're caught."

"I suppose so," Senator Moss thought aloud. "Then what do you think we should do?"

"Well," Hugh began, preparing to reveal his plan, "we've just added a new person on committee staff, some kind of science fellow. He can hold their hands for a while and, if need be, we can let him write a report about the advantages and disadvantages of their proposal. Hell, he's got nothing else to do. And we can let the A.E.I.O.U. go wave that around for their money. Besides, all they want is a foot in the door. If they can get a better

bailout plan out of somebody else, they'll drop universal day-light saving time."

"Good thinking, Hugh. But can this science guy handle it?"

"No," laughed Hugh, "and that's why he's perfect for it. If he screws up, I can fire him and express our sincere regrets, that sort of thing. Frankly, it could buy us a year. As long as it looks like we're doing something, I don't see any problem."

"I suppose you're right, Hugh. Good work," Senator Moss said, and hung up the phone.

Damn right, Hugh thought, as he leaned back in his chair. After all, who else could turn an overeager geophysicist into a $500,000 campaign contribution?

End of chpt. 3.

Chapter Four) *goes to pg.*

Dickie emerged from Hugh's office with his head spinning. He had been in the halls of Congress for only a week and a half, and he was in charge of a major piece of legislation. His meandering days as a geophysicist were over. He was now a man with a mission.

"So what did Hugh want, Dickie?" asked Miriam, burning curiosity masked by her most casual tone.

"He wanted me to meet the A.E.I.O.U."

"The utility guys?"

"Yeah. They have a proposal to put the country on daylight saving time all year long."

Miriam's eyebrows shot up in surprise. "Daylight saving time? Why do they want daylight saving time?"

"Because daylight saving time would increase the demand for electricity and stop utilities from going broke. Electricity is a bridge between man's needs and his environment's ability to satisfy them. Anything that enlarges the gulf between—"

Miriam interrupted him. "You mean the A.E.I.O.U. wants to get the country on daylight saving time to sell more electricity?"

"Is that surprising?" he asked.

"It's not surprising, it's outlandish. Nobody wants to bail out electric utilities. Can you imagine the public outcry if people found out the utilities were using the clock to manipulate electricity demand? This one's a nonstarter, Dickie."

Dickie would have sooner been hit with a club. "But that can't be," he pleaded.

"Dickie, every so often somebody suggests having more daylight saving time. And then there's a hearing and up pops a mother of eight children, all of whom walk to school alongside an interstate highway with eighteen-wheel trucks speeding by at seven-thirty in the morning, when it would be as black as night if there were daylight saving time, and so on. And then out come the drive-in theater owners and the farmers and the Orthodox Jews."

"You mean somebody's thought of this before?"

"I'm sorry to tell you this, Dickie, but there was a government before you got here." She got up and walked over to the file cabinets.

"If it doesn't have a chance, then why are we having meetings about it?"

"Because the A.E.I.O.U. wants to say it has a chance, so they can write exciting newsletters for their member organizations that describe how hard they're working for a bailout program. Memberships love newsletters, Dickie. The fact that it hasn't a chance hardly makes a difference."

"But what about Senator Moss?"

She was prepared to give him a simple answer when the possibilities of the situation and the urge to toy with him overcame her. "Dickie, Senator Moss has been around here for eight years," she began, "and unless Franklin D. Roosevelt and Martin Luther King return to earth and run on a national ticket that favors capital punishment and school prayer, there's probably nothing that can take Senator Moss out. That's not bad in and of itself, but Senator Moss is only fifty-two. He's got enough time left to do something else."

"But what else could he do?"

"Well, he could do one of three things. First, he can stay a senator and retire in the Senate. If he has it in him to wage two more campaigns, and they wouldn't be strenuous, he could have this job until he's sixty-eight. Then he could retire. Or, he could do the second thing—move up in the Senate leadership. Senator Moss's party is going to control the Senate for a few decades, so why not? Senator Moss could get a better committee. He even could run for majority leader or whip. And there's the third option—going for it."

Dickie was confused. "Going for what?"

"Running for president," she explained.

"Does Senator Moss want to be president?"

"Yes, Dickie. But the odds of getting to be president are low, since there's only one president at a time and everybody wants to be him."

"President Hoak didn't want to be president."

"But President Honeycutt wants to be president, and that's what counts. If he beats Don Green, then he could be president for eight more years," she said, referring to the likely Democratic nominee.

"So does Senator Moss have a chance?"

"It depends," she said coyly, finally baiting the trap, "on whether he can make himself more of a national figure. He's got to make some national friends, friends with organizations and connections coast to coast. And he has to be thought of as a national figure in the public mind. He needs to stand for something, an idea. He needs to mean something. And to do that, he needs a political action committee."

"To do what?"

"To give out money. He's got to have a political action committee with a campaign fund. That way, he can promote other people's candidacies. So if you needed campaign money, you'd come to Moss."

"Is that legal?"

"Think about who'd have to make it illegal, Dickie."

He stroked his chin in an attempt to hide his incredulity. "Do you think the A.E.I.O.U. is giving Senator Moss money?"

"Dickie, you're making it sound like bribes. They're trying to build a relationship. Moss is the chairman of a committee that can get them something. But that gets us to the important question, Dickie. What are you going to do for them?"

Dickie's heart accelerated—a quick quiz! "Well, the first rule is make friends and keep them, so that's what I'd do. I'd try to figure out who could be a friend, and then I'd keep them. I'd build a coalition, that's it, build a coalition!" he said excitedly. "Isn't that right?" He hadn't had as much fun since identifying minerals in freshman laboratory.

Miriam could not figure out where he had learned the "first rule," but was too fascinated not to hear the rest. "Go on."

"Well," beamed Dickie, "I'd also want to make it national. That's the important part. You'd have to make this into a national issue."

"But how?" she spurred him on. "It's about unpopular electric utilities that are going broke while the average household cheers them on. And their proposal amounts to using more electricity on cold winter mornings. You can't create a national movement over that."

Got me again, he thought. "That's right. You've got to make it bigger than electric utilities. You've got to tie it in to everything that's popular nowadays—exercise, old-fashioned values, the environment, good schools, no drugs. You have to tie it all together!"

"Tie it all together?"

"Why not? Isn't that the point? That must have been what Hugh was talking about when he said to develop some arguments and write some notes for public consumption. That's exactly what he meant!"

His earnest smile never wavered as he outlined his plan. She listened to him as he thought out loud, mapping a position paper about universal daylight saving time that would be the basis for a national campaign. It was the most inane, half-cocked stunt she'd ever heard. If she didn't stop him then and there, she thought, it would be too late. "Well, it would be something if you pulled it off," she said with a whimsical smile.

"You bet it would," he said with relish. He stared out his window, as if in a trance. She could not figure out what he would possibly say to make universal daylight saving time a national issue. But who cared? The course of the conversation allowed her to deny encouraging Dickie to do whatever he might end up doing. She had taken the Pilatean wash.

President Herbert Honeycutt sat at his desk in the Oval Office with his two trusted advisors. President Honeycutt had been the conscientious governor of a Midwestern state with little in the way of national aspirations, and even less in the way of charisma or vision, when Wade Hoak received his party's nomination for president. Wade Hoak's own trusted advisors advised him to pick a vice presidential candidate who would add luster, who would attract a different demographic segment, and who would be able to project the vision of the Hoak candidacy to the American people. "Nonsense," said prospective President Hoak. "I'm going to win this thing in a walk," and he proceeded to pick the one individual with legitimate credentials who would stay out of his way. *The Mouse That Roared*, said *Time* magazine below their cover picture of Governor, soon-to-be Vice President, Honeycutt that week, and they would have hit the nail on the head had Governor Honeycutt ever done any roaring. Instead, he did what Wade Hoak told him to do, and now found himself sitting in the Oval Office for his efforts.

On the desk before President Honeycutt lay a phone list prepared by President Honeycutt's two trusted advisors, who were urging him to move through it. "Herb, you've got to make these calls," the first advisor said.

"He's right, Mr. President," the second advisor said. "You've got to broaden your base, reach out to new constituents, be president of all the people," he said enthusiastically, trying to deal with President Honeycutt in the cheery, upbeat tone to which he appeared most responsive.

"Aw," President Honeycutt whined, "who's next on the list?"

"Colonel Cody Clark," the second advisor said.

"Him! Aw, come on," President Honeycutt complained. "With

that loopy evangelical financial business? Why do I have to call him?"

"Because he's got an audience of ten million people, Mr. President," the second advisor said with some amount of exasperation. "Because he's capable of raising millions of dollars and you've got an election less than a year away!"

"Okay, okay," President Honeycutt conceded. "Go ahead and ring him up."

Half a continent away, Col. Cody Clark sat in a hotel room. His shoes were being shined and an aide sat in an easy chair nearby when the phone rang. "Get that," he said flatly.

"Hello," said Col. Cody Clark's aide as he picked up the phone.

"This is President Honeycutt calling for Colonel Clark," President Honeycutt's first advisor said officiously to Col. Cody Clark's aide.

"It's President Honeycutt," Col. Cody Clark's aide said, the phone stuffed against his palm. "Do you want to talk to him?"

"About what?" Col. Cody Clark asked.

The aide shrugged and spoke into the phone again. "Colonel Clark is here, and can be summoned to the phone," he said, nodding knowingly to Col. Cody Clark.

"Then could I ask you to summon Colonel Clark to the phone," President Honeycutt's aide insisted, "so that I can tell President Honeycutt that he's on the line?"

"I can't very well summon Colonel Clark to the phone if President Honeycutt isn't available to speak to him, can I?" Col. Cody Clark's aide noted, grinning knowingly at Col. Cody Clark.

"I can assure you that President Honeycutt will be available for Colonel Cody Clark once Colonel Cody Clark comes to the phone."

"Is President Honeycutt there?"

"Of course President Honeycutt is here. He's calling for Colonel Cody Clark."

"But if he's not on the phone he's not there, is he?"

"Of course he's here," President Honeycutt's advisor puffed. "He's in his office."

"Then put him on the line, would you?"

"President Honeycutt would like to speak to Colonel Cody Clark," the advisor deflected.

"Well, Colonel Cody Clark is available to take President Honeycutt's call," said Col. Cody Clark's aide.

"But this isn't Colonel Cody Clark, is it?" President Honeycutt's advisor noted. "Is Colonel Cody Clark there?"

"If he were there, would President Honeycutt be ready to speak to him?"

"Most certainly," said President Honeycutt's advisor.

"Well, he's here," Col. Cody Clark's aide chirped.

"Very well, then. I'll get him." He turned to President Honeycutt. "They're getting him," he said to President Honeycutt.

"I hate it when people do this," President Honeycutt said, shaking his head regretfully. "It's so petty. It used to happen all the time when I was vice president."

"I agree entirely," his advisor said. "Moreover, the man's merely a television personality while you're the—" He was interrupted by Col. Cody Clark's aide's voice.

"Colonel Cody Clark is ready to speak to President Honeycutt," he said.

"Fine," President Honeycutt's advisor said. "Put him on."

"If President Honeycutt is interested in speaking to Colonel Clark, he might wish to call back at a later time," Col. Cody Clark's aide said, playing his trump card.

President Honeycutt's trusted advisor rolled his eyes and palmed the mouthpiece. "It's for you," he said, extending the phone to President Honeycutt. Exasperated, President Honeycutt snatched it from him and began to speak. "Colonel Clark, my old friend! How are you doing?"

"I'll be pleased to get Colonel Clark for you, Mr. President," said the aide, who passed the phone to his boss.

Col. Cody Clark regarded the trophy for a moment, then put it to his lips. "Why Mr. President, it's a heavenly dividend to hear your voice!"

*   *   *

Senator Moss was out of town during what was euphemistically called the District Work Period, a term with no intuitive meaning unless Senator Moss's district had been redrawn to include Bermuda. Hugh was on a field trip to California, but Miriam, like Cinderella, was left to grouse her way through a stack of newspaper articles on the equipment-that-doesn't-work tax credit. Hugh was very high on the equipment-that-doesn't-work tax credit, the idea being that corporations could donate equipment that didn't work to state universities and community colleges and write off the value against their taxes. Miriam recalled the meeting at the Treasury Department at which the proposal for the equipment-that-doesn't-work tax credit was unveiled. The assistant secretary of the treasury announced that he, with the help of the deputy assistant secretary, had put together a bold new proposal that would allow the nation's state universities and community colleges to obtain valuable research equipment at no cost whatsoever, while providing the nation's private sector with compelling new incentives to modernize their research and development facility's capital stock. He went on with the assistance of impressive flow charts and diagrams. He explained that the equipment-that-doesn't-work tax credit would allow firms to buy a piece of scientific equipment, receive an investment tax credit equal to 10 percent of its purchase price, qualify it for the tax credit of 25 percent of the purchase price allowed for all research and development expenditures over and above the average level of those expenditures over the previous three years, write off 100 percent of its value over a period of three years by depreciating it, and then deduct its original purchase price from its tax bill when it donated it to a college or university.

Miriam nodded sagaciously. She had absolutely no idea of what he was talking about. Everybody in the room appeared to be very impressed by the assistant secretary's presentation, his flow charts, his diagrams, and his careful analysis, including Miriam, who did not understand any of it, when the assistant director of the Office of Management and Budget sat forward in his chair. "Now wait a minute," he began. "A firm goes out and buys a piece of equipment that costs, let's say for the sake of argument, one dollar, and it turns out not to work. Then what happens? First, they get ten cents back immediately through the investment tax credit. Then they get twenty-five cents back immediately through the Section 44F tax credit for incremental research and development expenditures. Then they get ninety-five cents back over the next three years through the section 174 expensing election for R&D, but since it's a deduction and not a credit, that's only worth about forty-four cents immediately. So they've already made seventy-nine cents on their dollar." Miriam was completely lost, so she nodded in agreement, as if doing the calculations herself. "Then, in three years," the assistant director continued, "they donate the equipment that cost them a dollar to a university and deduct the dollar from their taxes. But a dollar three years from now is worth about seventy-five cents today. So that's ten plus twenty-five plus forty-four plus seventy-five; that's a dollar fifty-four in tax benefits for every dollar that a firm spends on a machine." The assistant secretary and his deputy grinned proudly as he spoke.

"Well, frankly, I think this is a pretty good way to give away money," said the assistant director of the Office of Management and Budget. "If we went along with your proposal, a firm could buy a piece of equipment, let it sit in an unopened box for three years, claim it didn't work, donate it to a university or community college, and make fifty-four cents profit for every dollar it spent. That's a profit of 54 percent for doing absolutely nothing!"

Miriam thought that this argument could have merit. But the assistant secretary obviously became very agitated. "Granted," he granted, "but it all goes back to the kind of government we want to have and the kind of president we want President Hoak to be. Do we want to be a government that holds the hands of our state universities and community colleges, that makes decisions for them, that tells them what they can and can't have? Or do we want a government that lets the private sector take the risks it thinks appropriate in pursuit of the rewards it considers attractive, and that preserves our freedoms by supporting the economic system that allows those freedoms to exist? Oh, sure, we might save a few pennies by buying equipment for our state universities and community colleges and cutting the private sector out of the loop. I know that Don Green thinks so," he said with a sneer. "But when do we decide that raising taxes now only inhibits growth and economic progress and leads to a smaller tax base later? When," he asked with finality, "do we decide that it's counterproductive to keep squeezing the turnip?"

The assistant director of the Office of Management and Budget seemed prepared to escalate the argument when the White House staffer leaned forward in his chair. "I think that we've just touched on an important point. President Hoak is not about to undertake initiatives that undercut the foundation of our country's progress. Let's do it," he said, rising from his chair to conclude the meeting.

Sitting in her office, Miriam, of course, realized that the equipment-that-doesn't-work tax credit was a dog, but if Hugh wanted it and Senator Moss wanted it, and if Miriam helped them get it, then all to the good. The next three years promised two senatorial elections. Senator Moss could end up being chairman of the Banking Committee. The senator would certainly make Hugh staff director, and anybody that Hugh liked was going to get a first-class ticket.

Miriam imagined herself at the Banking Committee. Banking lobbyists surrounded her in search of bailouts, squandering huge sums on lunches explaining their positions on archaic regulations whose minutiae were the stuff of which fortunes were made. She would write such regulations, creating meaningless yet career-making ambiguities and problems of construction that were easily resolved in grammar but not in law, devising regulations so impenetrable to those who would divine congressional intent that a multitude of banks would spring forth and offer her employments beyond her wildest imaginations, an office in glittering downtown Manhattan, and an outlandish salary to boot. "Ms.

Moskowitz," they would say to her in her moment of triumph, "we've come to you because we need somebody in our strategic planning department who has a good handle on the implications of the Banking Code and Financial Practices Act. We've been watching your staffwork over the past few years, and frankly, we're pretty damned impressed." That's right, she thought, gazing into her daydream. And it's going to cost you.

Having found this motivation, she was ready to work. She had established her concentration when Dickie came bursting through the door and bounded to his desk. He shrugged off his knapsack and dropped it on the floor.

"Miriam, I think I've got it."

"Good morning, Dickie," she said.

"I'm fine, thanks," he responded. "You were absolutely right, Miriam," he continued, as he sat at his desk and pulled the knapsack up into his lap. "I really have to thank you. I wrote it all up."

She stared at him with detachment. He produced a folder from his knapsack and extended it toward her. "What is this?"

"The piece on universal daylight saving time. Remember? You suggested I write a piece about the significance of the issue, the underlying content. Something that would broaden the base. It was a great idea!"

"It was?" She looked down for a second and suddenly it all came to her. Dickie had gone out and, completely uncritically, had done exactly what he had said he would do. He had written an essay on why having daylight saving time all year long was going to have some meaningful impact beyond its obvious inconvenience. She looked at him. He was smiling broadly and self-contentedly, offering her this manifestation of her facetious advice. She reached out and took the folder from his hands.

"What's it about, Dickie?"

"It's about . . ." he paused for effect, " . . . daylight! And about why daylight's so important. To all of us." He smiled so broadly he almost glowed. "I really want you to read it, Miriam, if you don't mind."

"Sure, Dickie," she said. The folder had a handful of pages of typewritten text in it, single-spaced with little sense of margin and numerous cross-outs. She looked up at him. He was leaning forward in his chair, as if he expected her to begin reading it right then and there. She patted the folder in her lap. "Well, it looks great, Dickie, but I've got a couple of things to do right now . . . "

"Sure, sure, I understand," he said quickly. "I've got a few errands to run, too, so I'd better get along myself. I'm going over to the fast food restaurant group, what's their name again?" He reached for a small notebook in his back pocket and began flipping through it. "The National Association of Fast Food Restaurants. And then there's the National Athletic Goods Association, I've got to see them, too."

"Why are you seeing hamburger and running shoe people, Dickie?" she asked, in the hope of a ludicrous answer.

"Like the first rule says, Miriam, they're our friends," he said, never disappointing. "If there's an extra hour of daylight, people are going to be outside, and they're going to want to eat. There's a very good chance that they're going to spend that hour at a fast food restaurant. I mean, that's the only way they can enjoy the extra hour of daylight outdoors and still have dinner, isn't it? What if we were talking about a sales increase of 15 or 20 percent? Not only would that help the bottom line for fast food franchise operators, but it would probably increase the actual number of fast food licensees, wouldn't it? And if it increased the actual number of fast food franchise operators, then it would actually increase the membership of the National Association of Fast Food Restaurants. And isn't that the point, more dues-paying members?" Dickie looked up with satisfaction, replaying his words to himself. It all seemed to make sense.

"I guess so," said Miriam, following his surprising, if angled, logic.

"And they'll play tennis, or go jogging," Dickie enthused. "And they're going to go to malls. I should have thought of this before," he said self-reproachingly. "There must be a trade association for malls somewhere. Wait until they hear about this. Daylight until six during the Christmas season!" He hunted the worn nub of a pencil out of his pocket and wrote a message to himself. "I really appreciate your help."

"No problem, Dickie," she said, sliding the folder into the center drawer of her desk.

Dickie got up, ran his hands through his hair, and picked up his knapsack. Miriam regarded him silently. "Well, I'm off," he said as he bounded out of the office. "I'll see you later, and thanks."

"Don't mention it, Dickie," she said as he left. She looked down at her newspaper articles for a moment, then bolted upright to see if he was really gone. She snatched the folder out of her drawer and opened it to the first page:

Daylight and Mankind
By Senator Luther A. Moss

Her eyes widened as she began to read.

When I talk to the American people, I hear a sentiment I often find shared by my own constituents, the good people of Florida. Something has gone wrong, I hear them saying. They point to drugs, to our kids hanging out outside their schools with their heads full of dope and hip-hop music instead of thoughts. They point to sex and our modern desire to use our bodies to emulate animals instead of gods. They point to economic malaise, and the humbling of our industries, once the world's mightiest, in international markets. They point to the breakdown of the family, to the rising divorce rate, to circumstances that make us wonder what our children will think life is really all about.

There are many explanations for these disturbing trends. Some of the experts tell us that we must expect these developments as our standard of living rises and we become a materially better-off civilization, as we have under the Hoak-Honeycutt administration. Some say that it is a sign of the stress that comes from the pressures of modern life, and that sex, drugs, and amorality are escape valves we turn to when our modern world corners us, and without which we would go mad.

But these explanations won't do.

Let's start by going back to the basics. Who is this animal called man? Where does he come from? Early man lived according to a rigid natural cycle. By day, man was at his fullest evolutionary glory. He mastered agriculture and the arts of cultivation. He organized family groups and primitive communities. But at night, this evolutionary progress broke down. Out of the protective shield of daylight, man withdrew to his cave dwellings. Here he was at the mercy of his fellow animals and their more accurate sense of smell and night vision. And so, by day, early man searched for food. By night, he was food.

This is an important observation——that man is a daylight animal, an animal whose progress in the biosphere depends on daylight activity. But as our civilization has evolved, so have the dangers and the temptations posed by our lives at night. The night now offers us a broad range of "entertainments." It offers us films that we are afraid to let our children see. It offers us the cult of alcohol and the opportunity to descend into the netherworld of random sexual coupling. It offers us the life of "disco," of marijuana and cocaine, of music that is rhythm only, where anything is available for a price. And at home, it offers us television, the blinking idiotgod, with its montage of jiggling breasts and buttocks and its wanton celebration of drunken violence. Remember the word for all of this activity——it is called "nightlife."

Our lives are becoming ever more night-oriented. The Roman artisan, the medieval serf, and the worker of the early Industrial Revolution rose before dawn and returned to their abodes at nightfall. But people today rise well after the sunrise and spend their days waiting for the night and the deceptive excitement that it brings. Our children go through their paces in school, oblivious to the opportunities that school provides and the dreams it will one day allow them to fulfill, waiting instead for nightfall, with its promises of drugs, petting, and empty-headedness. Is it any wonder that our school systems fall apart, and that our children don't learn anything? Adults see work as a debilitating obligation that stands between themselves and their nighttime social lives. Is it any wonder that our economy is worn and sapped, when the average worker has his head in a singles bar and not on his vocation?

Would that we could legislate when our families, our parents and our children, our workers and our students, rose and slept. But we cannot set a national bedtime. How, then, can we direct our society back to the natural order of things, back to the fundamentals of daylight and daytime activity?

My own answer is this. If we cannot move the times that people rise and work, study, and live together as families, then we should change something else—the clock. Accordingly, I intend to submit to my colleagues in the Senate a bill entitled "The Universal Daylight Saving Time Act." That bill requires that all states and localities adopt the provisions of daylight saving time for the entire year, beginning next January 1 at 2:00 A.M., Eastern Standard Time. In addition, it would establish a new category of "bonus saving time," an additional hour's advance of the clock, between June 30 and Labor Day. It also provides special grants and loans to individual states and localities to help them defray the expenses involved in this transition.

By moving the clock ahead, we would provide our families with extra hours of daylight in the evening all year long. It would be an extra hour that families could use to their best advantage. It would be an hour conducive to exercise and appreciation of nature, an hour in which we would enjoy a reduced fear of crime. And it would be an hour when our families could be together. In a word, the Universal Daylight Saving Time Act would bring us closer to nature and the natural way for man to live. I ask for your support for my legislation and for the goal of unifying man and the natural world he has abandoned.

Miriam closed the folder and looked up, so overwhelmed that she wondered whether she could trust her senses. The article was overblown and grandiose. It was extreme and vindictive. It was ridiculous. It made no sense. It was too good to be true. Miriam could hardly contain her glee. Let them stick some dried-up scientist next to me, she thought. This would ruin him.

60.1

Chapter Five ⟩ *goes to pg.*

The following morning Lenny reached into his in-box. He began to scan the first item for issue keywords when he realized that what he was reading was not constituent mail but a memorandum from Jeff. It concluded:

> *Following our meeting with Buddy Youngblood, we've decided to update our positions on selected issues. The first of these is the equipment-that-doesn't-work tax credit. As part of our efforts to appear in tune with the development of the high-tech economy, we feel that it would be worthwhile to support this proposal. Lenny, please take appropriate actions. Congressman Wheezle and I would like to see documents supporting our new position as quickly as is possible.*

Lenny read the memo a second time and walked into Jeff's office. "Did you write this?"

"Depends," Jeff said, not looking up from his terminal. "What is it?"

"This memo about the equipment-that-doesn't-work tax credit."

"Sure," Jeff nodded, tapping a series of keys. "I wrote it. What about it?" Jeff said, plunking his ENTER key a final time and turning in his chair.

"Why are we turning around on this?"

"It's just like it says." Jeff shrugged. "We're going to support the tax credit, try to look a little more modern."

"Has Ezra talked about this with Congressman Younger?" Lenny asked.

"Why should we tell him anything?" Jeff snorted a laugh.

"Because he's the chairman of our committee, that's why," Lenny explained. "You can't just back out of a position and move into conflict with the chairman without talking to him about it. Or at least warning him."

"He's 114 years old," Jeff said. "He won't be chairman forever."

"But he's chairman now," Lenny snapped before he composed himself. "Look, have we traded this vote for something? Some of the computer industry people are working hard to get this thing through committee. If we're going to change our position and make it easier for them, then let's at least get them to support us on something we want."

"Look," Jeff spat. "We're not getting anything, we're not making any deals, we're simply changing our position, and frankly, I'm getting a little steamed about having to explain to you what I've already explained in the memo. Now is there some other reason why I should be listening to this?"

"There's something going on here, Jeff."

"Yes, well, Buddy and Steve Lowry and I are busy trying to get Ezra reelected, Lenny. So in that sense, you're absolutely right."

There was no sense arguing with him, Lenny thought, at least not then. He turned without saying a word and went back to his desk and started scanning the constituent mail that the two interns had opened that morning. The two interns were fraternity brothers from Walcott Falls who were getting academic credit toward their degrees in political science for arriving at Congressman Wheezle's office every morning slightly hungover, opening all of the incoming mail, sorting it, answering the phones, delivering parcels, running errands, and going out each night to the bars on Pennsylvania Avenue and getting lopsided enough to come in the following morning slightly hungover and begin the process again.

Constituent mail took many forms. Some of it occurred in bulk mailings, done on high-speed computer printers that could hit all 435 congresspeople in a few minutes. Some of it was written by real constituents who were so moved by an issue that they took pen in hand to exercise their basic right to waste a stamp. Then there were the astrological charts, the women claiming to be Congressman Wheezle's wife, the people who claimed that Congressman Wheezle owed them money. There would occasionally be a missive from, say, King Leopold of Pennsylvania, who would hereby order the United States government to cease and desist in their efforts to force him to give up his claims to . . . well, whatever. And then there were the death threats, but the rising number of these over the years had left the F.B.I. in the position of not wanting to read them unless they truly gave you chills.

The two interns would sort through this tangle, segregating the requests for constituent service, and sorting them out by agency . . . who wanted Social Security, who wanted veterans, who wanted jails, who wanted housing, Medicare, Medicaid, and so on. They would highlight the request with a pen, toss it on the right pile, and send the pile over to the agency's liaison office.

Lenny put the memo on the equipment-that-doesn't-work tax credit in his desk and started to flip through the constituent mail. He was not halfway through the stack of service requests when he came upon a meticulous handwriting that captured his attention. "Dear Congressman Wheezle," the letter began.

I have now not received my Social Security check for four months in a row, and I have no money. I cannot receive Medicare or Medicaid since those agencies will not provide assistance to anybody without Social Security identification. I am writing to you for help now because I have been a proud American for these many years, have always worked, and have never broken the law. God bless America and God bless you, Congressman Wheezle, for having tried your best to help me.

It occurred to Lenny that instead of visiting his wrath upon Jeff, he could take it out on the Social Security Administration and give himself a breather. He folded the letter into his pocket and took the underground tram to the Senate side of the Capitol, and found the Social Security Liaison Office. It was staffed by four or five people obviously selected for their courtesy, understanding, and ability to be the subjects of abuse without reacting in any discernible manner. They dutifully clucked their tongues as Lenny told them about the letter writer's situation. They wrote down his name and Social Security number more times than Lenny had, on legal pads and forms and in the blank spaces of interoffice correspondence. They assured Lenny that the man's troubles were over until Lenny believed them, and he headed back toward Congressman Wheezle's office with a feeling of relief.

A sign in the hallway announced that the tram would be closed that afternoon for repairs. Lenny looked at his watch. He had only a few minutes to reach the other side of the Capitol and catch the last underground car back to the House Office Building. He picked up his pace as he moved through the catacombs of the Capitol basement. He was doing fine until he made a wrong turn and headed into an unfamiliar corridor at a near run. In an instant a flash of chrome came out of a doorway on his right and he heard metal crashing to the floor as he fell. When he lifted his head from the floor, Lenny saw the back of a toppled wheelchair with an old man's head at one end and his feet at the other, both motionless, and a cane lying nearby.

"Are you all right?" Lenny shouted as he scrambled to his feet. He swung around to the front of the wheelchair, expecting to find the man expiring. Instead, he saw an old man lying on the floor looking as composed and lucid as a judge presiding from the bench. "Congressman Younger!" Lenny exclaimed.

"Yes," Congressman Senior Younger, Jr. (D.-Id., I C.D.), said. "What of it?"

Lenny recoiled. He had toppled Senior Younger, Jr., himself. "Mr. Chairman, Congressman Younger, I'm so sorry," he stuttered. "I had no idea. Please accept—"

"Accepted," Senior Younger, Jr., said sharply.

"Are you all right, sir? Did you hurt yourself?"

"No, I'm not all right, I'm lying on the floor. And I haven't hurt myself, *you* hurt me," Senior Younger, Jr., snapped. "Would you please hand me my cane?"

Lenny gave him the cane.

"Good," Senior Younger, Jr., said. He raised his arm from the floor and whipped the cane across Lenny's shin with a sharp snap. Lenny winced and hopped up in pain. "Don't just stand there hopping," the old man jeered. "Help me the hell up."

Lenny wanted to hop away holding his throbbing leg, but instead eased the old man into his wheelchair and righted the two in unison.

"That's much better," Congressman Younger said. "Now, who are you?"

"My name is Lenny Keeler, sir."

"And do you work here?"

Lenny was still focused on providing Senior Younger, Jr., with an ample apology. "I'm sorry that I toppled you, sir. I was careless and wasn't watching where I was going. Are you well enough to continue on your own?"

The old man whipped his cane across Lenny's shin a second time. "The hell with that, son," he said. "Now tell me, where do you work?"

"In Congressman Wheezle's office," he said.

"Ezra! Wonderful!" exclaimed the old man. "A very good friend! What a nice young fellow he was when he first got here. Nineteen sixty-four, it was. He was a Landslide Lyndon baby

Fourth C.D., Pennsylvania. Took it for the party for the first time since the war and held it. Isn't that right?"

"Yes it is, Congressman."

"Of course it is. And now he's the second ranking Democrat on my National Economic Affairs Committee, isn't he? In fact, I'm all that stands between Ezra Wheezle and the chairmanship of a major committee, aren't I?"

"I suppose that's true, Congressman Younger."

"Yes it is." He leered up into Lenny's face and winked. "Think he's waiting for me to die? You don't have to answer that, because we all know the truth," he said, nodding solemnly. "The truth is that I'm never going to die." He fell back in his wheelchair in a burst of laughter, wiping his nose with back of his hand as he snorted. He was old and gaunt, and his laughing exposed purple, spotted gums. "Well, you seem like a nice fellow. I suppose I might even be sorry I hit you with my cane," he said cautiously.

"It did smart a bit," Lenny agreed.

Congressman Younger pulled his wrist back and cracked his cane over Lenny's shin yet another time. "You mean you accept my apology, don't you?"

"Of course, Congressman," Lenny agreed quickly.

"Good. Now, were you going anywhere in particular when you toppled my chair and spilled me to the ground?"

"I was trying to get a ride to the Rayburn Building before they shut the tram down for the afternoon."

"Well, so was I, but it's probably too late now."

"I'm sorry, Congressman."

"Yes, well, I suppose that you'll have to push me."

Lenny couldn't argue. "Yes, I suppose I will."

"Very well then, I accept your generous offer. Now hurry up." Senior Younger, Jr., sank deeper into his wheelchair. "Tell me," he commanded as they started, "how long have you worked for Congressman Wheezle?"

"Less than a year, sir."

"Well, what do you think of working in the Congress?"

"Well, I'm not sure that I've been here long enough to have an opinion."

"Yes, well, I have an opinion," Senior Younger, Jr., said. He stuck his tongue between his lips and raspberried.

"Excuse me, Congressman?"

Senior Younger, Jr., raspberried again. "That's what I think of the Congress. I'll tell you something else, young fellow. Do you realize how old I am?"

"No sir. How old are you?"

"I'm 114. I'm probably the oldest Democrat there is, and that's saying something. I've been a congressman for almost eighty years." He sighed and shifted in the chair. "Things have changed," Congressman Younger reminisced. "My father, Senior Younger, Sr., was in the Congress for thirty years himself. He was the first congressman ever from the State of Idaho, incorporated into the union in 1890. He arrived here ten years before McKinley was shot by an Antichrist."

"Anarchist."

"Antichrist, anarchist. Enemies of the republic. My father died in 1920. On his deathbed, he said to me, 'Senior, my son, I'm going to do you the biggest favor a man can do for his son. I'm going to leave you my seat in the House of Representatives.' Then he died. Left me his seat, too, just like he said. It was there in his will."

"In his will? Is that legal?"

"If Senior Younger, Sr., said it was legal, it was legal. A congressman had authority back in those days." He sighed anew. "Being a congressman meant something then. Not like now."

"Doesn't being a congressman mean anything anymore?"

"It's like being a harlot, son. You dress up and meet a lot of people, but they don't respect you."

"Don't you like being a congressman?"

"I hate being a congressman."

"Then why don't you retire?"

"Retire from Congress? Do you think I'm crazy?"

"I didn't say you were crazy."

"No, you didn't. But if I retired, everybody would. They'd say I was senile. If you're 114 years old and you say what's on your mind, they call you senile. But if you're 114 years old, say what's on your mind, and you're a congressman, they call you the Honorable Mr. Younger, Jr."

"But you can't want to be a congressman forever."

"Young man, every congressman wants to be a congressman forever, once he's lost his Senate race. Of course I want to be in Congress forever. That's why I keep running. Why would I give up wanting to be a congressman forever just as I was about to get it?"

"But you said you hate being a congressman."

"Of course I do. But if I wasn't a congressman I'd have to go live in a home. Besides, being a congressman is the only thing I know how to do. I was five years old when my father, Senior Younger, Sr., was first elected. In high school I was his office boy. In college I answered his correspondence. When I was in law school I handled his legislation. When I graduated from law school I ran his office. And when he died, I took his seat. Barely survived the Harding landslide. And from 1921 to this day I've represented the good people of the First Congressional District of Idaho. And I never took a dishonest dollar."

"At least you were honest."

"I wasn't honest, I was stupid. That's the story of life. First you're stupid, then you're senile."

"But you're not senile."

Congressman Younger turned and cracked his cane across Lenny's shin. "Are you calling me stupid?"

"I didn't say you were stupid," Lenny pleaded.

"Sure, you didn't. But if I weren't a congressman, everybody else would. They'd say I was broke, too. Broke, stupid, and senile. No," he shook his head sadly, "if you're old, broke, stupid, and senile, there are only two places for you. In a home or in the

Congress. And I don't want to live in a home, so I'd better stay here."

"But why do your constituents keep reelecting you?"

He shrugged. "Probably because after nearly eighty years I've done something that each of them approves of."

"But after eighty years you've probably done something that each of them disapproves of."

"But I only did it because I had the courage of my convictions. If you do things that people disapprove of and you're 114, you're cantankerous. If you do things people disapprove of and you're 114 and a congressman, then you have the courage of your convictions. I'm a Grand Old Man now. I don't stand for anything anymore, period."

"But what about your politics?"

"I gave that up long ago," Congressman Younger said.

"I thought you were a centrist."

"Never!" Senior Younger, Jr., spat.

"A liberal?"

"Not even I'm that old," Senior Younger, Jr., snickered.

"A neoliberal?"

"I can't tie my shoes without help. I can't be a neoanything."

"A conservative?"

"Never! Not as long as there's a rancher left to be protected from a railroad."

"What?"

"Nothing. Just something I used to say in the old days." Senior Younger, Jr., sighed.

"Then what are you?"

"I'm a radical populist!" Congressman Younger said with a flourish.

"But there are no radical populists anymore!"

"The hell there aren't. I'm one."

"But nobody thinks of you as a radical populist."

"That's because I've kept it a damn good secret. The electorate would never tolerate it. Either you're a radical populi who says what he thinks and gets beaten by a right-wing political action committee, or you're a radical populist who thinks what he pleases, keeps his mouth shut, and gets reelected."

"What good is that?"

"Plenty good. If I said what I thought, I'd lose my election and they'd put me in a home. Believe me, the only thing that's sadder than a radical populist in Congress is a radical populist who used to be a congressman and now lives in a home. Besides, somebody's got to stand up to the big monopolies and the banks and the bosses and the fat cats and tell them, 'No more!'" he said, shaking his fist before him.

"What are you talking about?"

"Who knows?" Congressman Younger shrugged. "Do you think it'll go over? In front of a crowd, I mean."

"I really couldn't say."

Congressman Younger sighed. "I don't think so, either," he confessed. "I could be in big trouble next time around, you know. They got some television commentator with name recognition to run against me. Hell, he's got face recognition. I've got to run against him as something. Why not a radical populist?"

"I'm the wrong one to ask. Congressman Wheezle had a meeting with his campaign people last week and it was all over my head."

"What does Ezra have you do?"

"Well, I just started working on the equipment-that-doesn't-work tax credit."

Senior Younger, Jr., turned in his chair and raised his cane. "You lousy little—! What the hell is wrong with you?"

"Nothing's wrong with me, sir!" Lenny exclaimed, leaping back from the wheelchair to get out of range.

"Then why did your boss just change positions on it?"

"Congressman Wheezle and his campaign consultant decided he needed to look more modern. They figured that supporting the equipment-that-doesn't-work tax credit would help."

"Modern? Why doesn't he just shave his head and be done

with it?" Senior Younger, Jr., sneered. "Do you have any idea what a bad idea the equipment-that-doesn't-work tax credit is?"

"It's a terrible idea."

Senior Younger, Jr., nodded to himself. "Yes, it's a terrible idea. And the problem is that people like Ezra don't really like it but they can't afford not to support it. If I only had some decent staff around me, I could do something about it."

"But you have plenty of staff."

"Nonsense. I've no staff at all. Who in their right mind would work for me? I'm 114 years old, and everyone thinks I'm going to die soon, so there's no reason for anybody with any talent to associate themselves with me. No future in it."

"I see."

"Do you know anything about the equipment-that-doesn't-work tax credit?"

"I guess so," Lenny said. "I've got a file on it in my desk with all the arguments we're going to use to support it."

Senior Younger, Jr., turned in his seat. "Stop pushing me for a second," he ordered. "I want you to give me a copy of that file."

"But I have an obligation to Congressman Wheezle," Lenny protested.

"You can do whatever Congressman Wheezle needs you to do just as well, can't you? Besides, you have an obligation to do the right thing, don't you?" Lenny agreed, this being the first time anybody in Washington had mentioned doing the right thing. "Bring it by my office tomorrow afternoon. Here," he said, taking out a business card, turning it upside down, and scribbling his name diagonally across the back. "Hold on to this. If you ever need me, use it."

Lenny considered. "Okay, I will. But this is just between you and me."

"Absolutely," Senior Younger, Jr., said with a satisfied grin. "Maybe they'll learn they can't push an old man around." And with that, Lenny began to push him once again toward the House Office Building.

Chapter Six ⟩ goes to pg.

"Well, what do you think?"

Miriam measured her words carefully. "I'm not sure what to tell you, Dickie." His draft of *Daylight and Mankind* sat between them.

"You don't like it!" he exclaimed with a hurt look.

"I didn't say that, Dickie," she said, hoping to avoid a statement that might compromise Dickie's self-destructive bent. "In fact," she hesitated, "it's very well written in spots."

"But do you see what I was getting at?"

She smiled. "I think I do."

"I was trying to tie the universal daylight saving time issue to basic values," he said. "To things the average person can understand. The point is to get the legislation moving and to create a national coalition, right? I mean, it's not what I believe, but this is more important than what I believe."

Out of the mouth of babes, she thought. Miriam looked at him and, for an instant, saw her own reflection. She came to Washington from Cleveland with a journalism degree six years ago, but did not truly arrive until she learned what Dickie appeared to have learned already—that what she believed didn't matter. She had gotten a job with an advertising and public r lations firm where she Xeroxed and stapled for a year and a half until a friend called about a researcher's job with the Senate Science and Engineering Committee.

She came to Washington with her own beliefs, of which she was quickly cured. After a year with the committee she had remade herself. She gave up searching her soul for what was right and substituted searching the public for trends. In fact, so had most of the people she knew, in one way or another. The only difference she could see was that the sane ones were aware of what they were doing, and set their beliefs aside in the hope that they would one day be reunited with them.

She regarded Dickie critically. He was enthusiastic and hardworking, and eager to please. She enjoyed having somebody try to please her. Men, in general, rarely did, out from under the gun of matrimony and reproduction. Of course, he was also bumbling, and his ambition was often clumsily transparent. But in his own way, she had to admit he was nice.

The thought snapped her out of her contemplation. Nice. That was the problem: she'd had it with nice. Miriam had once been nice, but she gave up nice the way she quit smoking, forsaking its pleasure for the clinical benefits of nicelessness. She was thirty, unhappy with the flat trajectory of her career, discontent with her life. There was a time she had squandered herself on helpfulness while everyone around her helped themselves. She had been a victim of nice, and neither Dickie nor anybody else could entice her to put the nice monkey on her back again.

"Well, regardless of what you believe," she told him gently, "it's very forceful. It really goes right after the reader."

"Do you really think so?" he said, clinging to her approving tone. "Then what should I do now?"

"Dickie," she said, measuring him for the blow, "I think you're at the point where you ought to circulate your draft and get some reactions."

"To whom should I circulate it?

"People whose reactions you want." Bang! she thought. In a

few minutes Dickie would put *Daylight and Mankind* in Hugh's hands. Hugh wouldn't be able to escape the fact that Dickie was out of control. Miriam would be ready. She would suggest making him her research assistant. She could put him to work on the equipment-that-doesn't-work tax credit, compiling lists of supporters, keeping her file of newspaper clippings. Hugh would have to agree. Dickie's essay would convince him that the daylight saving program was a minefield. It would be a masterstroke.

"I've got to run. I'll see you later. Bye." She walked away, the damage done. He called after her to thank her again.

But days and then weeks passed, with no evidence that Hugh had read it. Dickie, moreover, was continually busy. He called his list of interest groups and trade associations. His calls were not returned at first, since nobody knew who he was and, therefore, everybody knew he was unimportant. But occasionally he got the chance to corner an association representative and present him with the plan for universal daylight saving time and how it would affect his industry, product, service, or interest. By the end of their discussions, the representatives were forced to agree that there might be some connection between the two. The more he did it the better he got at it.

Dickie also assembled a presentation for Hugh and the A.E.I.O.U. He would begin by discussing their goals, and then explain in detail the progress he had made preparing notes for public consumption, and selecting fora (not forums, he reminded himself again to correct Hugh). Then he would hit them with his best idea—having Senator Moss submit the bill in a sundown ceremony on the day clocks were turned ahead this spring. How proud they would be of him—Miriam, Hugh, Chance and Collins, even Senator Moss himself, if he ever got to meet him. His delight at this prospect encouraged him to work even harder. Soon, he thought. It would happen soon.

*   *   *

And then the day arrived for which Dickie and Miriam had both prepared. Dickie was at his desk, going over a list of his newest friends and contacts when the phone rang. "Of course, I'll come right in," he said. This was it! He grabbed his notes and scampered into Hugh's office.

"Sit down, Dickie," was all Hugh said.

Dickie sat down in eager anticipation. Hugh took a folder out of his desk and opened it. Dickie waited for the right moment to begin his presentation. "You've been working on the universal daylight saving time issue, haven't you?" Hugh asked.

"Yes, that's right, Hugh. Remember our meeting with the A.E.I.O.U.? You asked me—"

"Yes, I remember that meeting, Dickie. But I wonder if you do. Can you tell me what you've been doing since then?"

Dickie could not see how his presentation would fail to impress him. "Well, after we met them, you told me to get a feel for the situation, to lay some groundwork, write some notes, develop arguments, that sort of thing."

"I certainly did say that," Hugh interjected. "What do you think that means?" Dickie was prepared to answer when Hugh swept a magazine out of his folder and held it in front of him like a torch. "Does it mean this?" he asked.

"Well, I don't know," Dickie said, uncertainly. "What is that?"

"Take a look!" Hugh growled, and threw the magazine into Dickie's lap. Hugh had a strange way of bestowing laurels, Dickie thought.

The masthead had two bull's-eyes at either end. Between them, in bold letters, was printed

MODERN WEAPONS
The Magazine for Modern Americans

Dickie was confused. He never had seen *Modern Weapons* magazine before. He scanned it quickly. On the back cover was an advertisement for a chewing tobacco depicting four hunters skinning a large animal. The front cover featured a paragraph printed inside a black-bordered box. A line printed across the top said PRINTED AS A SERVICE TO THE READERS OF MODERN WEAPONS MAGAZINE.

Dickie was about to flip to the table of contents when he saw the title. "Daylight and Mankind" by Senator Luther A. Moss (R.-Fla.).

Dickie looked up at Hugh in ecstasy. "Well, how about that!" he exclaimed. "Somebody actually printed it!" He held the magazine at arm's length to fathom it in its entirety. "Boy, Hugh, this is really great. Wait until the A.E.I.O.U. sees this! And I bet Senator Moss is really going to be pleased." Despite his excitement, he could not help but notice that Hugh had turned a deep shade of crimson. He began to get the impression that something was wrong. "Hugh, excuse me for asking, but is something the matter?"

Hugh shuddered slightly. "Dickie, give me that magazine."

"Sure, Hugh. But we ought to make copies—"

"Shut up!" Hugh shouted, startling Dickie. "Did you write this?"

"Of course I did, Hugh. It's what I wanted to show you."

"How the hell did it get in *Modern Weapons* magazine?"

"Well, I can't take credit for that, Hugh. *Modern Weapons* was not one of the magazines on my list."

"What list? You had a list?"

"Well, I had no idea what magazine to send it to. So I went down to the Library of Congress reading room and asked to see the five most influential magazines they had. *Foreign Realities* was one, and *Policy Agenda* was another."

Hugh erupted. "Dickie, how could you possibly take it upon yourself to send out an article under Senator Moss's name?"

"But that's what you told me to do! You said to develop arguments and to select some fora. And by the way, Hugh, it's *fora*, not *forums*. The plural of *forum* is *fora*. So I did. I tried to take account of Senator Moss's political situation, you know, establish a national base for his ideas. So he could be president one day. Isn't that what Senator Moss wants?"

"I asked for groundwork for a bill, Dickie, not an inaugural committee. Senator Moss doesn't need you to give him a national base, and he certainly doesn't need articles in gun magazines! Didn't it ever occur to you to circulate a draft?"

"But that's exactly it, Hugh! Miriam said that I should circulate it and I said, who should I circulate it to? So she said I should circulate it to people whose reactions I wanted. That's why I mailed it to—" Dickie stopped. "That wasn't what she meant, was it?" he said quietly.

"She meant me!" Hugh shouted furiously. "She meant give it to me!"

"I'm terribly sorry, Hugh. All I was trying—"

Hugh banged his fist on the desk and made Dickie jump. "Don't you think Senator Moss's enemies are going to take those reprints and use them against him? Can you imagine what they'll say, Dickie? That he's a crank: a gun nut! That he's against disco music!" He was by now out of his seat, leaning over his desk, flushed with emotion.

Dickie sat, his eyes tearing, as he had sat before Dr. Horton a few months ago, and realized he was at yet another way station, bearing the cross of his ineptitude. But now it was even worse. This time he had let down not only himself, he had let down Senator Moss, Dr. Horton, Hugh, Chance, Collins, and, most of all, Miriam. "I'm so sorry, Hugh. I'd never do it again, honestly."

"Dickie, you're separated from the committee as of this morning. Moreover, the committee is going to sue you for fraudulently misrepresenting the committee in general and Senator Moss in particular. Our lawyer will be in contact with you. Do you understand?"

Dickie nodded, although he had missed most of what Hugh said, with the exception of understanding that he was being fired and sued. This was all the more disappointing because Dickie knew people sometimes sued their bosses when they got fired, but Hugh, by suing him first, had taken away this only conceivable avenue of redress. But then again, he lacked the guts to sue Hugh anyway, especially since Hugh was absolutely right—he had messed up again.

"I understand," said Dickie. "I enjoyed working here, Hugh, and I'm sorry."

"I'm sorry, too," Hugh said, without looking up. "Have all of your things out by noon."

"Of course," Dickie said. He turned and walked out, leaving his status as a scientist-patriot behind him.

Chapter Seven

Dickie made his way back to his desk. It was every bit the shambles he was, covered by stacks of transcripts, journals, inserts, lists, records, papers, and submissions. He looked at his in-box. It overflowed forlornly into his out-box. He sat motionless for several minutes. He had nothing to do and nowhere to go. He was nobody.

"Dickie? Are you all right?" Miriam asked. "You haven't moved since I came in."

He sighed and looked down at the floor. "Hugh fired me."

Miriam sat forward, excited by the news. He had not been made her research assistant, granted, but she was not one to split hairs. "Dickie, what happened?" she asked, as she pored over his crushed countenance, much as the army studied the remains of Hiroshima. He was more than a broken man. He was a successful experiment in bureaucratic preemption. She had done it to him before he did it to her.

"Hugh fired me," Dickie repeated to the only sympathetic soul he knew. "He said that I wasn't supposed to promote the daylight saving time legislation. He said that I was supposed to keep it to myself. He didn't want any articles or magazines or national constituencies. He didn't want any of that."

"But that's so unfair," she said, quickly disavowing herself of her own advice. "How were you to know?" She now wanted to get away from him as gracefully as she could. "Dickie, I'm so sorry. But you can always go back to geophysics," she said, prepared to remand him there for eternity.

"No. They fired me before I left. And now I've been fired here. I don't know where to go now."

She held her breath and looked down at the floor. She had not realized the extent of Dickie's situation. Rather than a visiting scholar, he was a visiting vagrant. Oh, well. "I'm really sorry for you, Dickie. If there's anything I can do, let me know."

"Maybe you could talk to Hugh."

"I don't think so, Dickie," she said, backpedaling. "Talking to him could only make it worse."

"I guess so," he said dejectedly, failing to see how it could be worse.

"But if there's anything else, just call," she said softly.

He looked up again. "Do you have any ideas about another job for a geophysicist in Washington?"

"I'm afraid I really don't know about that. But if there's anything I can do, let me know." She squeezed his forearm, got up, and left the room quickly. Dickie leaned back and sighed. Circulate it, he thought to himself. How was he supposed to know something like that? Miriam was right. It seemed so unfair. But there was nothing he could do.

"Excuse me," someone said, a moment later. Startled, Dickie turned and saw a man in his fifties, thin-framed and of modest height, with dark eyes and a pencil mustache on a bony face. He carried an army-green duffel bag and a brown suitcase, and wore a denim jacket that seemed too big for his small frame, Western boots, and a red woolen watch cap over a shaved head.

"Can I help you with something?" Dickie asked.

"Yes," said the man. "I'm looking for Dickie Vanderhaltz."

"I'm Dickie Vanderhaltz."

"So you're Dickie Vanderhaltz!" the man said, pausing to admire the man associated with the name. "Pleased to meet you," he said as he extended his hand. He spoke with an intent expression but a restrained tone, his lips barely moving. "My name is Laslo Schang. I am the editor and publisher of *Modern Weapons* magazine."

"Oh no," Dickie moaned, letting his despair get the better of him. "Are you the man who published—"

"*The Daylight Manifesto*, yes I am," the man interrupted. "I changed the title. Here." He produced a pamphlet from the pocket of his denim jacket. It had the title on the front cover in gilded letters, and below it, *reprinted from* Modern Weapons *magazine*. It looked like a fancy piece of work. "You've really touched a nerve." He spoke quickly and efficiently. "It's a complete success. Our entire movement thinks so."

"Movement? What movement?"

"We have a subscription list of about sixty thousand people, and a newsstand readership of maybe fifteen thousand more," Laslo said. "Have you ever seen *Modern Weapons*?"

"Well, yes, five minutes ago. It had Senator Moss's article in it. I just got fired for that," Dickie said indignantly.

"Yes, I know. I called Senator Moss's office this morning. Some young Harvard type, who had no time for a principled naturalist like me," he said, with a sneer, ignoring Dickie's ignorance as to what a principled naturalist might be, "disavowed its contents completely. He told me it was written by a committee staff member who was going to be dismissed and that there would be court action. So I asked who the author was and they told me it was you."

"But I didn't send you that article."

"I know, but you did mail it to an editor of *Foreign Realities*. Fortunately, one of my readers works in their mailroom. When he saw your essay and realized its importance, he redirected it to me. Which is just as well. These Eastern establishment types don't see things as clearly as you do. But there are plenty of people out there, Dickie, who do."

"There are?" Dickie said, surprised. "I had no idea that saving financially troubled electric utilities was that popular."

"Saving what?"

"Saving financially troubled electric utilities. Like the A.E.I.O.U."

"What is the A.E.I.O.U.?"

"The Association of Electric Investor-Owned Utilities. They want universal daylight saving time in order to increase the demand for electricity. You see, electricity—"

Laslo interrupted him. "They think that that's going to save their antiquated carcasses?" He shook his head in disgust. "Characteristic of regulated management. It's like the caribou. If you don't subject them to the risk of the hunt, the weak ones will breed."

"What?"

"It's nature's way," Laslo explained, to his own satisfaction.

Dickie, however, hadn't followed him at all. "They said that having universal daylight saving time creates greater demand for electricity, which will assist those electric utilities—"

"Forget electric utilities," Laslo said, dismissing them with a quick wave of the hand. "Thousands of people wrote to us about your article. This has nothing to do with electric utilities. It's about a new credo, one that you've provided. I've never seen such a spontaneous outpouring."

"From my article? And I lost my job for it," Dickie mumbled, incredulously.

"Oh, forget about that," Laslo said. "Not only are you going to get your job back, they're going to give you a raise, I assure you."

Dickie shook his head.

"Here. Let me show you something. This bag," Laslo said, opening his suitcase, "contains petitions in support of the Universal Daylight Saving Time Act, and a notebook with names of Daylight Committee members and local Daylight Committee organizations in forty-six states. Within six months," he said, emphasizing each word distinctly, "I can promise you 350,000 active, working *principled naturalists*."

Dickie watched Laslo Schang as an infant might watch television, absorbing the signal without having the vaguest hint as to its meaning. "Principled naturalists?"

"Absolutely. *Daylighteers*."

"Daylighteers?"

"Good, isn't it?" Laslo said, not sensing Dickie's deeper confusion. "Daylight saving time supporters—Daylighteers."

"I see," Dickie said, rummaging through the petitions. "Where did you find all of these people? You must have over 100,000 names."

"I didn't find them. They came to me. They just pulled this postcard out of the magazine and mailed it in." Laslo handed Dickie the insert he'd placed in the most recent issue of *Modern Weapons*.

YES! I'm tired of watching our society move away from nature. It's time for principled naturalists everywhere to set the clock forward and our country straight! Here's my name and address, and a contribution to get the ball rolling!

"And here," Laslo said, tossing the duffel bag into Dickie's lap, "is $400,000 in cash collected with the postcards, from petition drives, from sales of the pamphlet. And this is all within a few weeks. My readership is highly motivated. Can you imagine what we'll be able to do in six months?"

Dickie leaned forward and opened the duffel bag. It was filled with stacks of twenties and fifties, rubber-banded and worn. Dickie had never dealt with much cash, but he knew that a duffel bag full of it was better than a duffel bag full of anything else. He tried to take it all in. The man had names, organizations, lists—forty-six states! He had put together a mass movement to promote universal daylight saving time around the same article that Hugh had fired him for writing. He had a national constituency in his suitcase.

"Now, we've got a lot to do," Laslo continued. "First, we're going to have to go talk to your boss. And we've got to get my lists on computers. And we need to get our people together and build our program." Dickie wondered what the rest of the program might be, but decided not to ask until the issue of his unemployment was resolved. After all, when writing the article, he had intended to trigger a national response, and now he had it. He had no idea why Laslo agreed so vehemently with his ideas about having daylight saving time all year—maybe the man was a lunatic—and had even less of an idea as to how Laslo could find 350,000 principled naturalists, whatever a principled naturalist was. But he did not care, so long as Laslo had lists, money, and momentum, and was willing to apply them to letting Dickie be a scientist-patriot once again.

"All right," Laslo said, grabbing the suitcase and duffel bag. "Let's go see your boss, what's-his-name."

"Hugh Brock," said Dickie, getting up from his desk.

"Whatever," Laslo said. Dickie walked out the door and down the hall to Hugh's office, leading Laslo, but following him just the same.

Hugh was reviewing the witness list for the next hearing on the equipment-that-doesn't-work tax credit when Elsie let herself in. "There are some people outside—"

"Not now," Hugh said sharply.

"It's Dickie Vanderhaltz, and he's got someone with him," she said quickly, content to have gotten that much out.

"Who? A lawyer?" Hugh sneered.

"Do you want to see them?" she asked.

"Sure, show them in," Hugh said, "and I'll show them out." He walked to the front of his desk as Elsie walked out and folded his arms imperiously. It was his power position: they were no match for him.

The door opened again and Dickie entered, accompanied by a small, bald man in an oversized denim coat with a flinty glare. Hugh was taken aback by the man, who seemed oddly dressed for a lawyer and an unlikely associate for Dickie. Nonetheless, he quickly took control of the conversation.

"What are you doing back here? If it's about the conversation we had, I don't see any reason to continue it," he said preemptively. "My decision is irrevocable."

Laslo stepped in front of Dickie and extended his hand toward Hugh. "Hello, you must be Hugh Brock," he said politely.

Hugh looked at Laslo, startled by his presumption, and shook Laslo's hand perfunctorily. He returned his attention to Dickie. "Dickie, your separation from the committee is final. I'll contact your fellowship program and, if they think it appropriate, they can find you a new situation."

Hugh stopped at that point and congratulated himself on his generosity. He started around his desk to sit back down, fully expecting them to leave, when Laslo spoke up. "Mr. Brock," he said, "my name is Laslo Schang."

"That's very nice, Mr. Schang," Hugh said dismissively. "I hope you don't intend to insert yourself in the matters of this committee. Are you, perhaps, a lawyer representing Dickie?"

"No," Laslo answered with a laugh, amused at being mistaken for anything as meaningless as a lawyer. "I'm the publisher of *Modern Weapons* magazine," he said.

Hugh stopped in his tracks and turned a deep shade of crimson. "Do you mean . . . this garbage?" he said, picking up the magazine on his desk.

"Leaving aside your characterization, yes," Laslo responded crisply.

Hugh's fury built to a stormy crescendo. "You! Who the hell are you? What business do you have publishing that goddamned piece? Well, I'll show you how things are done around here. No release was signed for that article and no letter of submission with Senator Moss's signature exists! You had absolutely no authority to put that piece into print! None whatsoever! Doesn't that bother you?"

Laslo chuckled. "Things don't bother me," he said. "I bother other things."

Hugh was oblivious to his message. "No self-respecting journalist would do this!"

"Actually," Laslo said calmly, "only journalists lacking in self-respect wouldn't publish something they wanted to publish. We self-respecting journalists don't share their problem."

Hugh sputtered. Laslo's logic escaped him, as did his own remaining composure. "Mister, I am going to put your gun nut magazine out of business. And as for you, Vanderhaltz, you little quisling, you'll be sorry you were ever born," Hugh shouted.

Laslo snatched his duffel bag from the floor and dropped it on Hugh's desk. "Did you call me a gun nut, Mr. Brock?" he asked, with an intense stare. "Suppose I told you I had a .45 Browning self-loading automatic weapon in this duffel bag and that I am perfectly indifferent as to whether I continue this conversation or blow your brains out. Would I be a gun nut then?" He reached for the zipper of the duffel bag and both Hugh and Dickie gasped as their hands flew into the air. "But, of course," he continued with a small smile, now that he had Hugh's full attention, "I don't. I only want to impress upon you that it would be foolish to dismiss the people I represent as gun nuts. The point isn't guns, Mr. Brock. The point is politics.

"As the publisher of *Modern Weapons* magazine, I've been searching for a new approach to the issues of American life," Laslo expounded, as Hugh and Dickie slowly dropped their hands to their sides, realizing that their lives were not, after all, in danger. "People who are interested in guns have strong feelings about our society. They care about the preservation of family, the brood." He sighed gently. "Let me tell you something. You don't really appreciate the importance of family until you've shot a female adult in the wild and seen the look in her little ones' eyes. That convinces you."

"Mr.—"

"Schang, Laslo Schang," said Laslo, extending his hand once again.

"Mr. Schang," Hugh went on, ignoring the hand. "I can assure you that Senator Moss opposes gun control, but I do not see why you are in my office, taking up my time."

"Well then, Mr. Brock, let me show you." Laslo stepped forward and reached for the duffel bag on Hugh's desk. Hugh stepped back rapidly, his hands starting into the air, as Laslo unzipped the bag, turned it upside down and allowed its contents to spill out onto Hugh's desk. Hugh looked down at the mound of bills, fifties and hundreds piled in disarray. He was speechless.

"Four hundred thousand dollars," Laslo said. "All of it legal. I have the receipts."

"But, where," Hugh attempted to ask, "how—"

"My readership is a political group, Mr. Brock," Laslo explained. "Until now, their point of view has gone unarticulated. Dickie's essay said plainly and simply what we all had been feeling for years: it's time to get our society back to nature's guiding principles. And I'm not talking about tree-huggers. I'm talking about principled naturalists.

"Principled naturalists sent me this money from all over the country, people who read *The Daylight Manifesto* and were moved, people who want Senator Moss to be a champion for principled naturalism and nature's way. I've got lists of them in every state. The only question is, will Senator Luther A. Moss lead them, or will somebody else?"

Hugh sat down at his desk and looked at the pile of cash in the middle of it, his head aswirl with questions. What the hell was Schang talking about? Could he be serious about this absurd philosophy of his? Had Dickie's ridiculous essay really generated this kind of reaction? It all seemed impossible, but you can't get more possible than money, he thought. Actually, it made little difference what he thought. With his duffel bag in tow and his membership lists and state organizations in place, Laslo Schang, whoever he was, could write his own ticket. Hugh sighed and gazed again at the cash. Maybe it was legal, maybe it wasn't.

Maybe he had been wrong about Dickie, maybe he hadn't. Maybe Dickie's queer little friend was crazy, maybe . . . well, no, he was crazy, no question about that, but a big pile of money can make such distinctions seem small.

"What do you want?" he asked, finally, with an air of concession.

"I'd like the three of us to walk over to Senator Moss's office and have a little talk."

Hugh considered, and then dialed the senator's number.

Laslo stepped back and rubbed his hands together. "There you go," he said. "Now we're getting somewhere."

Chapter Eight

By the mid-1970s, the mid-Florida land boom stalled. Just when a new wave of money was needed to perpetuate the Ponzi scheme to broaden the pyramid base while thrusting all participants toward the peak, interest rates rose, the economy soured, and tourism fell off. The mid-Florida boom collapsed under the weight of the overbuilding that occurred in anticipation of the boom that would be triggered by the overbuilding. The belt from Tampa to Daytona Beach began to leak money, first in trickles, then in spurts.

Into this morass stepped Luther A. Moss, a young mid-Florida real estate lawyer who had been watching the crash with great appetite. He was a Florida State University law graduate who played golf expertly and looked well dressed in a Ban-Lon shirt. He was tall and well proportioned. He was not good-looking, but he was formidable-looking, with a long, straight nose over thin lips and a jutting chin. He was clever enough to see an opportunity in the making. After several phone calls to banking connections he was on a plane to Bahrain. After several days in Bahrain he was on a yacht to Qatar. After several meetings in Qatar, he was on a plane to Tampa, this time the guest of the plane's owner, an oil-soaked cousin of the ruling family, who represented most of the money in his country. "The Kuwaitis and Saudis own Miami," Luther A. Moss told him at forty thousand feet, "but the Qataris own nothing. The question is, will the Qataris be represented in Florida or will they be left behind?" The urgency of the situation was immediately clear to the Qatari. It was essential they be positioned in the Florida real estate market, as a counter to rival positions emanating from the Persian Gulf, and as a sound investment, given the realities of interest rates, exchange rates, and other economic factors. Luther A. Moss had no idea what these realities were, but merely citing the realities' existence proved as powerful an incentive as understanding them.

The Qataris took Tampa by storm, enjoying its oppressive heat and ample beach, and opened their wallets. Within a few days they had purchased enough real estate to get most of the worst cases off the death list, and they then invested an extra $60 million in the Texas Rangers baseball team, which they promptly moved to Orlando. And so the new money got in, the old money got out, and the Qataris got box seats by the third base dugout where they rooted for the Orlando Rangers, a name that was freely translated to them as the Orlando Bedouins.

To a base of vanity and ambition, Luther A. Moss suddenly added prosperity, power, and connections. He was made the Florida Chamber of Commerce's Man of the Year, became a member of boards of directors, and provided his legal services, which were no better than those he had always provided, at a tenfold increase in price. He enjoyed being Man of the Year, Businessman of the Year, and the Man Who Saved Florida. He enjoyed luncheons with businessmen, bankers, and university presidents, and dinners with the old-line families of Jacksonville and the recreation kings of Miami. He toyed with running for governor, but considered the governor's daily administrative responsibilities distasteful. It would have to be the Senate, and, at the first available opportunity, it was.

Senator Luther A. Moss enjoyed the leisurely gravity of the

Senate, knowing that crises were occurring daily and that, if one didn't feel like addressing them, they would reappear tomorrow, each retaining the same crisp urgency it had had the day before. He enjoyed the fellowship of friends from his party and colleagues from the other party. He knew that what helped businessmen make profits was good, what didn't was bad and, whatever it was, it had to be forthrightly explainable to a Sunday School class. He served his constituency's interests well, supporting tourism, the space program, the citrus industry, and the real estate interests that he had once saved and now represented. He did not write much legislation and found voting a chore, but he knew how to use his staff to protect Florida's national labs, national parks, interstate highways, pristine environmental areas, oil and gas industries, commercial interests, mass transit systems, small businesses, and endangered species. He found that being a senator was a natural extension of being a real estate lawyer. It relied on the same abilities: drinking while remaining conversant, getting along with people disliked by one's wife, getting mad only when its histrionic value was high, and keeping a stiff left arm through your approach to the tee.

Art Mack, Senator Moss's administrative assistant, had served Senator Moss since he had taken office. He was sixty years old but could have been older. He had no ambition of his own, an overwhelming sense of loyalty, and a desire to serve, a constellation of personal qualities that Senator Moss appreciated. Senator Moss listened to him, because he knew that Art would not bother the senator unless it was in the senator's best interest. So it stood to reason that if Art Mack was waiting for Senator Moss when he arrived at his office after a breakfast meeting, and if Art Mack stopped Senator Moss from going into his office, that Senator Moss would ask him why.

"Because something strange is going on in there," Art replied.

"What are you talking about?" asked Senator Moss, his topcoat in one hand and his briefcase in the other.

"Hugh is in there and he's got two guys with him. One, I

think, is the science fellow from the National Association for Physical Science. Hugh called you about him a month or so ago. Something about daylight saving time."

"That's right. He was going to use him to get money out of the A.E.I.O.U."

"Right. Five hundred thousand dollars."

"Has something gone wrong?" A secretary took Senator Moss's coat and briefcase.

"I'm not sure. Hugh won't tell me anything, as usual. But I've been getting these strange phone calls from trade associations, interest groups. They're calling to express their support for something called universal daylight saving time. People we never heard from before—athletic shoe manufacturers, barbecue equipment makers, fast food restaurants, landscaping and lawn care industries. They tell me they're behind us one hundred percent and want to know if there are any fund-raising tickets they can buy."

"But we're not having a fund-raiser."

Art Mack nodded. "I know. At first, I dismissed it, too, but it's happening too often. I swear, if we had some kind of Daylight Political Action Committee or something, we could have put together $500,000 in the last few days. Somebody's out there working these guys, and process of elimination says it has to be that fellow."

"What fellow?"

"The science fellow. It has to be somebody over at the committee, but if it was Hugh he'd have told you about it, and if it was any of the regular staff, Hugh would have taken credit for it." His logic was impeccable. "Hugh said he was going to use the fellow to blow some smoke. I bet you the guy slipped the leash."

Senator Moss grimaced. "Success you didn't plan for is bad, Art." The senator drew a large breath. "Okay then, who's the other guy?"

"I have no idea."

"Okay, come in with me." Art followed Senator Moss into his office. The office was spacious and high-ceilinged, its walls covered with photos of Senator Moss with various dignitaries, constituents, world leaders, children, and animals. On one wall was a magnificent blue marlin, frozen forever in mid-leap. The young blond man who Art suspected was the science fellow and a man in an oversized denim jacket sat on a sofa. Senator Moss looked them over: the short one looked too smart and the blond one not smart enough. Hugh sat in a chair near Senator Moss's desk. The two men rose quickly when Senator Moss opened the door, and Hugh followed them to their feet.

"Hello everybody," Senator Moss said as he strode to his desk. "Hello, Hugh," he prompted.

Dickie watched Senator Moss with awe. He was bigger than Dickie had expected, more vital and forceful. Dickie was afraid of him instantly. Dickie looked at Laslo, who sat beside him, completely unaffected, and wondered why he had decided to trust him. He then heard Hugh say his name.

" . . . whom I've mentioned to you," Hugh was saying, "the geophysicist from the South Florida Institute of Technology who's been working on the daylight saving time project." Dickie stepped forward and extended his hand to the senator.

"I'm pleased to meet you, Senator," he said nervously.

"And, Senator, this is Laslo Schang. Senator Moss," Hugh told Laslo, who stepped forward briskly.

"My pleasure, Senator," Laslo said confidently.

"Nice seeing you, too," Senator Moss said. "Okay. Why don't you tell me why we're here, Hugh?"

"Well, Senator, a good deal has happened since we last spoke about daylight saving time. Dickie and I met with representatives of the A.E.I.O.U., and discussed their plan to institute daylight saving time all year long. We agreed to study the matter and consider the possibility of action."

"Yes, I remember, you were going to stall these guys while we took their money."

Dickie's eyebrows shot up. He looked to Laslo, who must have heard it as well, but was too busy taking in every word and gesture to react. Dickie turned back to the conversation.

"So, what happened?" the senator asked.

"Well, the bottom line is that a major article on the subject has been published under your name in a . . . " he paused and considered, "surprisingly large magazine."

"How did an article get published under my name if you, Art, or I didn't know about it?"

"It's hard to explain—"

"Try me, Hugh," Senator Moss said.

Dickie stood up abruptly and faced Senator Moss. "I wrote it, sir. I mean, Senator."

Senator Moss looked at Dickie and then turned back to Hugh. "Hugh, did this guy send out an article under my name while you thought he was playing with himself at his desk?"

"Well, yes, Senator," Hugh said quietly.

"And do you have a copy of the article?"

Hugh dug into his briefcase. "Give me a moment—"

Laslo stood up, pulling Dickie back down onto the sofa as he did so. "Senator Moss, may I shed some light on this?" Everybody was startled to hear Laslo interrupt.

"Who are you, again?"

"My name is Schang, Senator, Laslo Schang. I'm the editor and publisher of *Modern Weapons*, the magazine that published Dr. Vanderhaltz's article. Here's a copy of it." Laslo flipped a *Manifesto* onto Senator Moss's desk.

"Well then, the first thing you could shed some light on is how the devil you got your hands on—"

Laslo was about to answer when Hugh interrupted. "I've taken care of that, Senator, let me assure you. I've told Mr. Schang that he and his magazine can count on a fairly drawn-out court proceeding and one of the worst legal experiences that anybody in his line of work has ever had. Mr. Schang has no letter of transmission, no letter of receipt, no agreement to compensation, no right to publish."

"Is that true, Mr. Schang?"

"Senator, I have something much better than those things." Laslo reached for his duffel bag. "This bag," he said, as he unzipped it and dumped it on Senator Moss's desk, "contains $400,000 from contributions, and sales of Dr. Vanderhaltz's article. The money was collected in the space of a few weeks. Cash, with receipts and records, no contribution larger than $500. The suitcase contains lists of people who've signed universal daylight saving time petitions, joined organizations, or sent in money. There are over 100,000. Daylighteers, we call them, and we've got them in forty-six states."

Senator Moss looked at the money overflowing his desk. He looked up at Laslo, who unflinchingly returned his gaze. He looked at Dickie, who was worried that Senator Moss would send them all to jail. He looked at Hugh and, finally, he spoke. "Offhand, Hugh, you'd have to say that Mr. Schang does have something better than a letter of transmission, wouldn't you?"

"Senator," said Hugh, trying to maintain his composure, "this man is a lunatic. He's publishes a magazine for gun nuts. He goes off on psychotic tirades about principled naturalism, whatever that means, and he insinuated that he was going to kill me in my office today."

Senator Moss and Laslo studied each other. Laslo smiled first. "I've been called worse."

Senator Moss smiled delightedly at Laslo's panache. "Mr. Schang, can you explain yourself?"

He might as well have asked a snake if it could eat bunnies. Laslo was off to the races. Society was decaying, he said, because it had come loose from its natural moorings. It wasn't possible to restore the literal realities of nature because man had changed all that. But it was possible to allow affluence and progress to blend with the principles of nature, to practice principled naturalism as opposed to literal naturalism. Laws that protect animals from predators do not help the animals, they simply make them too numerous, changing only the vehicle of their death from predation to starvation. Similarly, laws to protect those predated in the economic and social sphere only change the manner of their misery, not its level. Senator Moss listened, captivated. It sounded good for profits and could be explained to a Sunday school.

"But what does this have to do with the A.E.I.O.U.?" he asked.

"I wouldn't know, Senator," said Laslo.

"I suppose not. Perhaps my counsel can shed some light on that for us."

Hugh clenched his teeth and weathered Senator Moss's sarcasm, knowing anything he said would only inspire further humiliation.

Senator Moss got up from behind his desk and looked out at the East Lawn of the Capitol. He paused a moment to savor the view. "No? Well, stop me if I have any of this wrong, Hugh, but I get the following impressions. First, you snookered some electric utility representatives about a proposal for universal daylight saving time. Then you got yourself young Vanderhaltz to do the grunt work and keep us looking busy. Vanderhaltz goes out and writes an article that ends up being published in *Modern Weapons*, operated by Mr. Schang here—"

"Laslo, please," Laslo said pleasantly.

"—of course, Laslo, who promptly uses the article to raise $400,000 in legal money and produces a list with over 100,000 names on it and local organizations in forty-six states. An article you didn't know about. Have I got this right so far?"

"Senator, I know it sounds like—"

"I know how it sounds, Hugh. Now, did I leave anything out?"

Art spoke up from his corner of the room. "Well, there's the phone calls and the fund-raising tickets."

"Why that's right, Hugh. Did you know we're getting phone

calls from trade associations and interest groups who want to buy tickets to our universal daylight saving time fund-raisers?"

"They do? Really?" Dickie, excited, couldn't help but ask.

"Do you know something about this, Vanderhaltz?"

Dickie's enthusiasm drained under Senator Moss's glare. "Well, yes I do, Senator. I called those groups, visited some of them, too. I was only trying to put together a coalition, you know, a national organization that would tie universal daylight saving time to some common themes and some basic values and then get those themes and values associated with you," he blurted, parroting Miriam's advice. Senator Moss laughed in quiet amusement.

"Did you hear that, Hugh?" he said. "Your science fellow is out putting together a national organization dedicated to my name recognition. What are you doing for me, Hugh?" Senator Moss hissed. "You can't be running my committee, because all of this is happening in my committee, and you don't know about it. You can't be coming up with new ideas for me, because the only ideas I hear in the room are from a man you have decided is imbalanced—no offense, Mr. Schang."

"Laslo, please."

"And you can't be out there building a national organization for me, because your science fellow is doing that. You want to hear the list, Hugh? Do you want to hear whom he's contacted?"

Hugh looked down at his feet. "No, I don't, Senator."

"Good. Read him the list, Art."

Art Mack pulled out a sheet of paper and began reading. "The National Association of Athletic Equipment Manufacturers. The National Footwear Association. The Association of Athletic Equipment Retailers. The American Barbecue Institute. The National Franchise Store Committee. Americans for Tennis. The National Association of Athletic Facilities and Health Spas. The National Association of Fast Food Restaurants. The American Automobile Committee . . ." Art continued to read the list while Senator Moss sat back and watched Hugh squirm in his seat. Dickie's jaw dropped as he watched Senator Moss hang Hugh out to dry. Hugh had been the most powerful person he knew in Washington, and Senator Moss was toying with him like a cat with a cornered mouse. Laslo watched Senator Moss with admiration as Art ran down the list: not only was Senator Moss stripping the bark off of Hugh, he was now having somebody else do it, leaving him free to sit back comfortably and enjoy it. It impressed Laslo deeply. He realized that he had underestimated Senator Moss, and resolved that he would not do so again.

"Okay, that's enough, Art," Senator Moss said suddenly. "All right people, we have some catching up to do. Art, make sure you get all of this. First, Hugh is going to keep his title as staff director, but he's going to handle the administrative end only. Until he can find something else. Schedules, hearings preparations, bookkeeping. And whatever else Dickie tells him to do. Got it? Second, Dickie is appointed special counsel and gets whatever he wants. He's in charge."

"But Dickie's not a lawyer, Senator," said Art.

"Who cares? It's my committee, and I could make a tuna the special counsel if I wanted to." He turned to Dickie with a solicitous tone. "Will you need some help, Dickie?"

Dickie stammered as he tried to think. "Well, yes, some help would be nice, I think so."

"Who's over there to help out?"

Dickie only had to think for a second. "Miriam!" he replied.

"Which one is Miriam?" Senator Moss asked over his shoulder.

"Cute number, late twenties, dark hair," said Art. "Miriam Moskowitz."

"Who cares? Miriam Moskowitz it is," Senator Moss said. "She's Dickie's now.

"Third," Senator Moss continued, without missing a beat, "we're going to form a National Special Committee on the Daylight Issue. I'm the honorary chairman. Conrad Scott will be the chairman. Then we'll go get the people off Dickie's list of groups and have a Special Committee meeting. Laslo, your Day-lighteers will be one of the constituent members of the Special Committee. Art, you're the committee secretary. Sit down with Dickie and get going."

He rubbed his hands together as if saving the best for last. "Okay. Finally, I want a press conference announcing the formation of the Special Committee. A big one. I'll speak, Scott will speak, Laslo here will speak."

Art Mack glanced nervously at Laslo. "Are you sure about this?" he asked Senator Moss as subtly as he could. Senator Moss saw him look toward Laslo but nodded decisively.

"Absolutely. Now, is that everything?"

"May I say something, Senator?" Laslo offered.

"Absolutely, my friend."

"Dickie here has been operating on fairly meager compensation and he's being asked to take on some serious responsibilities. Particularly if he's going to be special counsel."

"I get you, Laslo. Hugh, double Dickie's salary. And Art, have the Special Committee pay Dickie a $25,000 consultant's fee."

Dickie was flabbergasted. "Why, thank you, Senator," he stammered. He looked worshipfully at Laslo, who had delivered everything he had promised.

"Good." Senator Moss paused and reflected. "This daylight saving time thing is controversial, you know. There are a variety of Florida interests that may be hurt by this kind of proposal, so we're going to have to make an effort to bring as many of them into the tent as we can. But we're going to risk it," he said, gazing out the window again, "because this is a winner. I can feel it."

He turned and looked at Laslo. "You're an interesting man, Laslo. All I ask is that you remember the first rule of politics: make new friends, keep the old ones." Dickie was delighted to hear that the rule he knew was the right one. He wished that there had been a quiz.

Senator Moss issued some final observations for Art and, in another few minutes, the meeting was over. As he left, Dickie was again in a daze. He had been fired, defrocked as a scientist-patriot. But Laslo then appeared just as the angel appeared to Joseph in the desert, leading Dickie to a new name and a new destiny, raised to a greater glory. Laslo seemed to see what was going to happen before it actually happened: Dickie only saw what happened after it happened to him.

Dickie considered the many things he had to do. It was a good thing Miriam was there to help him.

Miriam! His thoughts suddenly turned to her. Every shred of advice she had given him was heaven sent: the article, the trade associations, building a Daylight Coalition, Senator Moss's motives and instincts, all of it. Dickie's pulse quickened as he thought about all he had to tell her. And then, of course, he'd have to sit down with Laslo and find out what had just happened.

Chapter Nine

MEMORANDUM

To: All Committee Staff
From: Art Mack
        Office of Senator Luther A. Moss
Subject: Committee Staff Changes

As many of you know, there has been a new initiative coming out of our committee concerning legislation to promote universal daylight saving time, conducted by Dr. Dickie Vanderhaltz. We will be placing heavy emphasis on the daylight issue during this session of the Congress.

Given this change in emphasis, Senator Moss has asked me to bring a number of staff changes to your attention. First, Hugh Brock will divest himself of policy guidance responsibilities, but will remain on staff to facilitate an administrative transition. Second, substantive matters, issue development, and policy formulation will now be done under Dickie Vanderhaltz, who will assign priority to the universal daylight saving time issue. All staff members seeking guidance on committee policy will report directly to him. These changes are effective immediately.

Miriam was stunned. Everybody was stunned, but only Miriam could really grasp what had happened. Dickie had not only survived his firing but was being put in charge of the entire circus! But how? Dickie must have convinced somebody, most likely Senator Moss himself—although how Dickie had access to Senator Moss was beyond her—that he had a world-beater issue on his hands. Despite her machinations, despite everything she thought she knew about politics in the bureaucratic jungle, he had come out on top. She shuddered. What if he chose to get rid of her? All her work, her plans, her momentum—gone. She sighed. It if it had happened to anybody else, she'd have thought it fair.

Her phone rang. "Yes?" she said softly.

It was Elsie. "Dickie wants to see you."

She hung up and began to walk slowly down the hall, convinced this trip into Hugh's office—Dickie's office now—would be her last. Despair and resentment overcame her. She had tried to be nice to people once and was screwed for it. So she tried to be manipulative and was getting screwed for that, too.

She entered Dickie's new office and saw him rummaging through Hugh's desk, playing with whatever he found—Hugh's letter opener, Hugh's date stamp, Hugh's Rolodex—like an infant king. He looked up and gave her a sheepish smile.

"Isn't this something?" he said, making a sweeping gesture around the room.

She collected herself for one last play. "Dickie, I don't know what you're thinking or what you intend to do." She braced herself for the painful crawl across the floor. "But before you do anything, there are a few things I want to say."

"Well, there are a few things I'd like to say, too, Miriam."

"Please, Dickie," she begged. "Let me—"

"No, no, no," he insisted. "You sit down right there." He

pointed to the seat he first sat in when he met Hugh several months before. She dutifully sat down. "Miriam, I know what you're thinking. You're wondering what's going to happen to you."

Damn you, she thought. "Yes, Dickie. I'm wondering about what's going to happen to me."

"Well, let me say right at the outset that I'm not the kind of guy who forgets what the people around him have done."

"Dickie, please forget what I did. I just want to go about my job and be of service to the committee."

"No, Miriam, the work you were doing has come to an end."

"Dickie, please reconsider."

"No, that wouldn't be right. Not after all you've done."

He got up from his chair and paraded around to the front of his desk, just as Hugh would have done. "The fact is that if you hadn't helped me the way you did, then I wouldn't have this job."

Her forlorn expression suddenly transformed into confusion. "You wouldn't?"

"Of course not! Without your advice there would have been no *Daylight Manifesto*, no Daylighteers, no Special Committee, none of it. Miriam, I owe it all to you."

Her teary eyes dried instantly. "What are you talking about?"

He smiled a deep, gooey smile. "So much has happened since yesterday I don't know where to begin," he said, and it all came out in a confused tangle: Laslo, the article, the money and lists, how Senator Moss pushed Hugh out and made Dickie the special counsel.

Miriam's countenance changed as quickly as the tropical sky after a hurricane. "Let me get this right. This fellow—what's his name?"

"Laslo. Laslo Schang."

"He raised how much money?"

"Four hundred thousand dollars. And that's just for starters."

"But, *Modern Weapons*. I mean isn't it just a magazine for gun nuts?"

"Shh! Don't ever let him hear you say that! It's not about guns. It's about principled naturalism versus literal naturalism, about the relationship between nature and man."

"What does that mean?"

"I don't know. But you'll see, believe me."

"And he's got a name list—"

"As long as your arm," Dickie interrupted. "Forty-six states."

"And trade associations are actually—"

"Art's been getting phone calls from all over town. People are dying to get on the bandwagon—"

"And Senator Moss made you special counsel?"

"That's right." Dickie gleamed.

"And what about Hugh?"

"You got the memo. He'll keep his title for a while. Let him save some face."

"Where are you going to put him?"

"Out in the galley. He can always squeeze another desk in there."

"You're not going to put him in with me?"

"Of course not! I want you to have that entire space to yourself. You could even get some new furniture, maybe some new plants. You'll want something like that for your new job."

"My new job?"

He rubbed his hands together gleefully. "Yes, your new job. You're going to be deputy special counsel for the entire committee!"

For the slightest instant she was dumbstruck, but only for the slightest instant. She jumped from her seat and threw her arms around Dickie's neck. "Thank you, Dickie," she chirped, "thank you!" She squeezed him and then quickly drew back from this compromising position. "I'm sorry," she blushed.

"That's okay," said Dickie, equally embarrassed.

"Deputy special counsel!" She repeated the title to herself. She had heard of counsels, deputy counsels, chief counsels, special counsels, assistant counsels, but never of deputy special

counsels. Still, it was more than she had expected or had a right
to expect.

Dickie exhaled deeply, enjoying the happiness he had brought
to her. "Well," he said, "we've got plenty of work to do. What
were you working on?"

"The equipment-that-doesn't-work tax credit," she said wearily.

"Well, tell Hugh to do that."

"Okay, I'll take care of it," she said, eagerly preparing herself
to push Hugh around.

"And then, we have to organize a committee."

"What kind of committee?"

"Senator Moss wants us to organize a National Special Committee on the daylight issue, with all the groups on our list. Senator Moss will be honorary chairman, and Conrad Scott—he's
one of these utility guys—will be chairman. And we're going to
have a big press conference to inaugurate the Special Committee. A really big one. Call Art and get the list of organizations.
We want all of them there. And lots of reporters, television,
newspapers. Can you do all that?"

She grinned at him. "You bet I can. When do you want it?"

He stopped. It was his first decision. "How long does it take
to set up one of these things?"

"It depends. If we have to put lists together, it might take a
few weeks, even a month. How about the fifteenth?" she suggested.

"Good idea," he agreed, savoring his first decision. "We'll
have it on the fifteenth. Okay, then. Let's get going."

"I'll get right on it, Dickie," she said. Had she been told those
words would ever escape her lips, she would have laughed in disbelief. But Miriam knew there was no point in searching good
luck for flaws, or bad luck for justice. Everything she had wanted
was going to be hers, but only because she had missed her guess
at every turn.

So what? She saw no point in pondering her good fortune. A
day ago Dickie had been an inept, naive, self-aggrandizing fool.

Now he was her meal ticket. He obviously had the uncanny ability to defy bureaucratic gravity: when he fell, he fell up. Just as she had once vowed to ruin him, she now vowed to keep him happy. Deputy special counsel! She made a mental note to send out for new business cards. She started toward the door, then stopped and turned. "And thank you again, Dickie. Let me know if there's anything else you need."

He smiled as she walked out. He sat down and turned his chair so he could look out the window at the Capitol. So much had happened. He was special counsel of a major Senate committee. He was a power broker in a national political movement. His salary had just skyrocketed and he was enthroned in a magnificent office. Why then, was his concentration fixed solely upon the moment when Miriam Moskowitz had thrown her arms around him?

Chapter Ten

Wyatt Industries was the largest employer in Walcott Falls. It was built in the 1920s, and employed a thousand people making bolts and fasteners for the region's light manufacturers. It went broke in the 1930s, and was modernized as part of the war production program during the 1940s. It established a global presence in the 1950s, and was a model for labor-management cooperation in the 1960s. It was taken over by a hotel-based conglomerate in the 1970s and was the subject of a failed leveraged buyout in the 1980s. It was then bought by a turnaround artist in the 1990s and, after a massive retooling, now employed two hundred men and women making bolts and fasteners for the region's light manufacturers. It was considered a raging economic success story.

Buddy Youngblood saw Wyatt Industries not as a forge or factory or a place where men and women toiled and through this labor brought home sustenance to their families, but as a chain link fence with only one convenient gate through which workers passed regularly and, therefore, an ideal site for a photo opportunity. It would be the perfect place to put Congressman Wheezle in front of some voters, "real, live people" as Buddy often called them.

Congressman Wheezle had been enjoying his usual breakfast of coffee and cigarettes when Lenny and Jeff Monge picked him up to drive him to the foundry. Buddy was there when they arrived, directing a handful of cameramen and positioning the long-range microphones. His purpose that chilly morning was to capture campaign footage of Congressman Wheezle greeting the seven A.M. shift.

"We're just about set up," Buddy said as they approached. He led Congressman Wheezle to the gate. "I want you standing here so the sun comes across you front right." He positioned Congressman Wheezle and took a step back to admire his work. "Perfect," he said self-approvingly. "Now, when the workers come and shake your hand, give them each a couple of good pumps, but don't look at your hand. Look them in the eye. Let them find your hand." Congressman Wheezle nervously puffed a cigarette and nodded. "Good. Now, you," he commanded Lenny. "Step up here and shake Congressman Wheezle's hand so we can see how it looks in the lens. Just like a real person."

Lenny walked over to Congressman Wheezle and offered him his hand. Congressman Wheezle absentmindedly offered Lenny his hand in return. "No, no," said Buddy. "Come on, Ezra, shake his goddamned hand. And don't look down. You're the congressman. Let him look down. Try it again.

"Good, good," he commented as he watched them shake hands a second time. "Now talk to each other. Good. How is this?" he asked his crew. They nodded and mumbled in various affirmative ways. "Good. Let's get with it."

Buddy took a position behind a cameraman, and watched as the foundry workers began to file past Congressman Wheezle. Lenny stood next to him and watched as well.

"I'm Ezra Wheezle," Congressman Wheezle said to each one as he shook their hands.

"Yeah, sure," said the first.

"Hi, Mom!" another said to the cameras.

"You running for something?" asked a hefty woman, moving quickly past Congressman Wheezle's outstretched hand.

"What about the trade deficit?" asked an older man wearing a union pin.

Congressman Wheezle answered, though surprised to be asked a substantive question. "I stand for free trade and fair trade," he said.

"What about imports of bolts and fasteners?" the man asked.

"Blatantly unfair," Congressman Wheezle replied. "An American firm that sold at those prices would go broke. There's no question foreign governments are subsidizing their producers. My position is that we should keep their subsidized bolts and fasteners out of our market until the subsidies stop, and we can have a free market again."

Buddy waited behind the camera, silently willing Ezra to present him with a usable sequence. The man with the union pin walked on and a man with a bushy mustache and a woolen jacket approached. "What about our schools?"

"Our children need schools that are second to none," Congressman Wheezle responded.

"Get off it, our schools suck," the man said, pulling back his hand.

"But we need to make them second to none," Congressman Wheezle responded.

"With what, a wish?" the man said. "Why can't there be money to fix the schools? The ceilings are falling down, for Chrissakes."

"I've always supported more money for schools," Congressman Wheezle asserted.

"And a fat lot of good it's done us," the man said. "And what about drug treatment? There isn't a single place in this city a person can walk in and get drug treatment if they need it."

"I find that shocking," said Congressman Wheezle.

"Your being shocked doesn't do anything to improve the situation."

"We're going to fight and win the war on drugs," Congressman Wheezle said.

"Yeah, right," the man said. "And what about day care?"

Congressman Wheezle began to wonder how he was going to shake this guy. "Well, day care is a very important service," Congressman Wheezle said, as other voters walked past them.

"Yeah, I know. My wife works and it's very hard to find. So what's your position?"

"Well, that's an issue that will have to be handled here in Walcott Falls."

"Yeah, but you're the congressman, for Chrissakes. You got influence, you know a lot of people. There must be something you can do."

"All I can say is that the people of Walcott Falls deserve day care services that are easily affordable and readily available."

"Jesus," the man fumed, "don't you think people ever get tired of double-talk? People out here work hard, they need help, and all they get is double-talk. You're all the same. The hell with you," the man said, dismissing Congressman Wheezle angrily and striding through the gate.

Congressman Wheezle wiped his face with his hand, and then offered it to the next person coming by. "Hi, I'm Ezra Wheezle."

Buddy made a small fist in the air as the man stormed away. "Was that a great sequence, or what?" he asked Lenny with satisfaction. "Did you see the look of concern on that guy's face, like he meant what he was saying? And Ezra nodding, saying things right back to him? I mean, it was just like they were interacting! We'll lose the sound, run a narration, and cut it before the guy walks away. That's a day's work right there."

Chapter Eleven

The hearing room of the Science and Engineering Committee was wooden-paneled, with a vaulted ceiling and portraits on the walls of senators who were once chairmen of the Science and Engineering Committee but were now dead. A sweeping curved table held a collection of microphones, wires, plugs, meters, and other electronic paraphernalia.

The room was already half full when Dickie and Laslo entered. They were surprised to see so many young people, neatly dressed, with blue blazers and knitted ties, flannel skirts and makeup. They looked like a reunion of Junior Achievement, not the way that Laslo imagined Daylighteers to look. Dickie strained to recognize somebody, anybody, when he saw Miriam approaching him.

"Well guys, what do you think?" she said, showing off her work.

"Miriam, this is wonderful," he gushed. "Where did these people come from?"

"Oh, I called a couple of local campuses, college Republicans. You know, a few hundred dollars can keep a Young Conservative Club in newsletters for a whole semester."

"You mean you rented these people," Laslo said testily.

"Laslo, look at it this way," she said. "It's nature's way. Does an animal join the pack unless the head male allows it to feed?" she said, anticipating Laslo's perspective. She had been paying attention since he had returned to Washington from his home base in the Everglades.

Laslo couldn't help but agree. "I see your point," he said.

"Besides, like you said, Dickie, universal daylight saving time is going to be very popular among college students, since they don't get up before nine o'clock anyway."

Dickie did not recall making that point, but it was a good one and merited remembering. The room was filling up quickly and the noise level rising. Miriam excused herself and left, approaching a severe-looking young man and showing him her pocket watch and the schedule on his clipboard. Dickie looked toward the door, where he saw Art Mack entering with Conrad Scott.

Dickie and Laslo made their way across the room. Art introduced them to Scott, a large man in his mid-sixties, with an air of self-satisfied prosperity about him.

"We'd better get started, Dickie," Art said. He led them to the podium, where he started making introductions. "Ladies and gentlemen," Art began, "we are here to announce the formation of the National Special Committee on the Daylight Issue. My name is Arthur Mack, and with me today are Dr. Dickie Vanderhaltz, special counsel to the Senate Committee on Science and Engineering, on leave from his professorship of geophysical science at the South Florida Institute of Technology, and Mr. Conrad Scott, the chairman of the board of Florida Heat Steam and Light, and chairman of the Association of Electric Investor-Owned Utilities." Polite applause greeted each name.

"Senator Luther A. Moss will be here shortly. Senator Moss is deeply committed to the adoption of universal daylight saving time, and the goal of the Special Committee is to bring the fight from Main Street, U.S.A., to Pennsylvania Avenue." There was more applause now, as the audience slowly put itself in the festive mood required for media events.

"It is now my pleasure to introduce to you our first speaker, Mr. Conrad Scott."

There was more applause as Conrad Scott ambled to the podium. "I want to thank you for allowing me to be here this afternoon," he said majestically, as if the crowd had something to do with the decision, "as we launch the National Special Committee on the Daylight Issue." More clapping was heard at the mention of the Special Committee's name. Dickie looked about the room and saw Miriam make a small slashing motion over her throat to a pimply man with horn-rimmed glasses. The man put his hands at his side and the applause quickly faded. "Today, we fire the shot heard 'round the clock, beginning our national campaign for universal daylight saving time.

"The goal of universal daylight saving time is to increase the convenience of American life, just as the nation's electric investor-owned utilities do every day. There are people out there who say that the utility industry supports universal daylight saving time because it will benefit us. That is preposterous. Universal daylight saving time is not about electricity, or electric utilities, or the very real regulatory threat to our nation's electric future. Universal daylight saving time is about our modern way of life and the kind of country we are. The time that was read in the Roman hourglass and the Babylonian water clock should not be the time we read on the LED display of a digital watch. That's why we're here, and that's why we are going to make universal daylight saving time the law of our land."

There was excited applause: few had expected emotional peaks from an electric utility executive. Dickie was clapping enthusiastically along with everyone else, when he turned and saw Laslo's scowl. Dickie would have asked him what was wrong, but he was afraid to ask Laslo anything when he wore his carnivorous expression.

"Did you know he was going to say that?" Laslo demanded.

"Say what?"

"Didn't you hear that crap about our modern way of life? There's not one iota of principled naturalism in that man's body. I'm going to go up there and denounce their literal naturalist rear ends," Laslo said as the applause died down and Art prepared to introduce him.

"Laslo! Please! You can't do that," Dickie pleaded, but Laslo was already out of his chair and on his way to the podium. Dickie wished that Miriam was on the podium with them, so that she could do something.

" . . . Mr. Laslo Schang, the publisher of *Modern Weapons* magazine, the magazine for modern Americans."

Laslo stood at the podium. After a moment spent looking out at the audience, he began.

"I'm very pleased to be here among supporters of universal daylight saving time. And there are more of us than people think. In the two months since the publication of *The Daylight Manifesto*, nearly a quarter of a million Americans have become Daylighteers, supporters of both principled naturalism and the daylight movement." He spoke calmly and quietly, but forcefully. "Daylighteers support principled naturalism because we believe in both the power of nature and the power of man. Our adversaries—the literal naturalists, the bunny clutchers, the deer dung counters, the antigrowth fanatics—want to drape their banner of pristine nature, of literal naturalism, over the coffin of our society. Daylighteers support universal daylight saving time because we seek to conserve not some nostalgic fantasy of nature, but nature's basic laws—enterprise, risk and balance, and the preservation of the species through the brood." Miriam's hired marchers, who didn't know what Laslo was talking about but nonetheless didn't like deer dung counters and instinctively supported free enterprise and the brood, let pour a torrent of enthusiasm.

"But our struggle goes deeper than that," Laslo continued, his cadence quickening as he pumped the well of emotion. "I want to know, how many people here today are happy with the kind of society we have? How many of us believe that we truly live according to the principles of nature? Can anyone be proud of what our nation has become?"

There was a befuddled silence until a man in the center of the crowd bellowed out "You bet we are!" and suddenly there was more applause, then a chant began from the back of the room: "U.S.A.! U.S.A.! U.S.A.!" It grew in strength with each repetition. Laslo tried to outshout the crowd and correct their dangerously wrongheaded thinking, but they were out of control. "U.S.A.! U.S.A.! U.S.A.!" they insisted.

But if their noise was uproarious, it became almost deafening when the committee room doors swung open and Senator Moss strode into the room with the smile that salvaged the Florida real estate market. He walked up to the podium and patted Laslo on the back. "That's enough, Laslo, you were great."

Laslo wanted to continue, but he realized that he had been played. Senator Moss turned to the crowd as Laslo returned to his seat. As the noise ebbed he started to speak.

"As all of you know, we're not going to move forward unless we move forward together, Daylighteers and electricity consumers, all of us. The fact is we're after universal daylight saving time because we want to change the fundamental habits of the American consumer. Let me tell you how much this could mean to some of you. Convenience stores would sell an extra two billion dollars worth of goods under universal daylight saving time. We foresee an increase in the sales of barbecue goods by over a billion dollars. A billion dollars just for moving the little hand back an hour. An additional ten million rounds of golf, including greens fees, balls, tees, clubs, bags, and sportswear. One hundred thousand new tennis rackets a year. One million new pairs of running shoes. The prospect of—and let me emphasize that this is a rough estimate—an extra one billion fast food meals. How many tons of organic chemicals are needed to mix one hundred million additional thick shakes? How much timber will be needed to produce sixty million new golf tees? How much cloth goes into ten million new pairs of sweatsocks? Yes, universal daylight saving time is going to help sustain the economic recovery now under way in the Hoak-Honeycutt administration."

There was a burst of applause, in which Dickie, Art, and Laslo participated, Dickie with enthusiasm, Art with indifference, and Laslo with bitterness and suspicion. They listened and applauded, applauded and listened, as Senator Moss went on for some time. Miriam, who stood in the back of the room throughout, regularly checked her watch.

Senator Moss waved to the crowd as cameras went off around him. Conrad Scott then started toward the microphone. "A group of us, representing the A.E.I.O.U.," he began, "have gotten together and asked me to present you, Senator Moss, with this token of our appreciation." He reached into the breast pocket of his suit and extracted a long jewelry box. "Senator Moss, on behalf of the nation's electric investor-owned utilities, it gives me the greatest of pleasure to present you with this gift commemorating the beginning of our campaign to right America's clocks."

He flipped open the lid of the jewelry box and in it sat a gold watch. The crowd gave up a drawn-out "oooh!" as if they were admiring the prizes on a game show. "The inscription says, 'To Senator Luther A. Moss, the champion of universal daylight saving time.'" Every manner of individual stood and cheered. "Moss! Moss! Moss!" they chanted, as Senator Moss flung his arms into the air like Pavlov's sainted bitch, transposing himself into a Y-shape at the sound of his own name.

Conrad Scott laughed and raised his giant paw to obtain order. "Now, before I actually give Senator Moss this watch, there's one last thing I want to do." He held the watch up and pulled out the adjustment mechanism. "If I can get this to work . . . there. I'm going to . . ." there was the first gurgling of laughter ". . . that's right . . ." anticipation of his comedic stroke swept through the room ". . . turn it back one hour!" A tsunami of applause drenched the crowd, as Senator Moss put on the watch and listened to it with a vaudevillian stage motion. Conrad Scott then grabbed Senator Moss's watched wrist and thrust it into the air, allowing the crowd to exercise their delirium one last time. From the back of the room, Miriam could not tell if together they looked like a man with a pet gorilla or a sportsman dangling a fishing trophy.

Dickie and Laslo pushed on into a hard spring rain, walking down Constitution Avenue. Dickie huddled in his coat against the weather, his chin jammed into his chest. Laslo walked along with him, erect and relaxed, his nostrils savoring each crisp breath. But not even the cold rain could dampen Dickie's sense of triumph now that the Special Committee had begun to meet, a few weeks after the press conference.

"Boy, Laslo, this is amazing. First the press conference and now actual Special Committee meetings. I just can't believe it."

"I don't see why I should find lobbyists going to meetings unbelievable, Dickie. It's like being impressed with lemmings rushing into the sea. It's what they do."

Dickie knew better than to disagree with Laslo, given Laslo's uncanny knack for being right all the time. Still, he could not share Laslo's cynicism. "Laslo, a few months ago you were looking for a manifesto and I was writing an essay. Now we've got the Special Committee, we've had a major press conference, we've had committee meetings, we've formed subcommittees—"

Laslo took Dickie's arm and stopped him. "Dickie, I've been watching what's happened here very carefully. We had membership lists, cash, an entire national organization. Somehow, our assets have become the Special Committee's rather than our own. Damn, Dickie, I should have seen it all along. Imagine a real estate lawyer putting one over an old swamp man like me," Laslo snickered mirthlessly.

"What are you talking about, Laslo?"

"Dickie, Moss has us in a trap. The Special Committee is a

sham. If Moss were eager to have universal daylight saving time, then the first thing we'd see is a bill. But there is no bill, is there?"

The rain was beginning to trickle down the back of Dickie's neck, and he hoped that the right answer would get Laslo walking again. "Sure, Laslo, but Art is chairing a drafting committee—"

"Oh, there'll be a bill one day, but what kind of a bill will it be? Moss wants to see who's stronger—us, or the hamburger and track shoe people. They don't really care about universal daylight saving time. If they could just reset their cash registers, they wouldn't bother with the clock. Why, probably not one of them has read *The Daylight Manifesto!*" Laslo said, sneering.

"We need to control the Special Committee, Dickie," he continued, "and we need a bill soon." Dickie nodded, in the hope that nodding would move the conversation along and get him out of the rain. "We've got to grow. We've got to start pushing for the other things we want."

"What other things? What else should we want?"

Laslo looked into space, and suddenly his eyes widened as if he beheld the Promised Land. "We need . . . a convention!"

"A convention?"

"Yes! Why didn't I think of it before? We'll have a national convention of Daylighteers, all of them, from everywhere. Put them all in the same place and put together a national program, a national agenda for principled naturalism. It's nature's way. When the herd is threatened, it gathers together for strength. It's so obvious."

"But what about Senator Moss?" asked Dickie. "What if he won't go along with it?"

"We'll have the convention in Florida," Laslo said simply, "and we'll make Moss the keynote speaker. A convention of a national movement looking to him for leadership? In his home state? He can't say no to that, now can he?" Dickie smiled. He was always happier when Laslo asked easy questions.

"Now, of course, we're going to need a place to have it, some registration procedure, publicity, an agenda, some more speakers. But we can come up with those. You get Miriam on it right away." Laslo nodded to himself, the rain pouring off his shaved head and dripping off the tip of his nose. "We've got plenty of work ahead of us. But at least we won't have to worry about a keynote speaker." He threw his head back and, for the first time in Dickie's recollection, laughed a deep, rolling laugh.

Chapter Twelve

Assembling the mailing list for the Daylighteers' national convention was easy, but getting responses proved difficult, given the Daylighteers' propensity for living in remote locations and their suspicion of mail in general, often leaving it unread save for their biweekly copy of *Modern Weapons*. Nonetheless, the responses began coming in, and in great number. But, while the Daylighteers were difficult to convene, they offered the compensating advantage of being able to hold their convention virtually anywhere, since the average Daylighteer's idea of comfort was a tent, a camper, or the back of a pickup.

Laslo chose Marshport, a town of fifteen thousand people situated on the perimeter of Lake Okeechobee and the Okaloacoochee Slough of the Everglades, as the site. Miriam pointed out that Senator Moss's natural habitat was a more urban one, but Laslo insisted that only an environment that graphically illustrated nature's principles would do. Moreover, Marshport had a modern high school and community center that had been financed through a grant secured by Senator Moss himself, which made the location all the more appealing.

Meanwhile, the Daylighteers' momentum grew. They attracted dedicated zealots of Esperanto, antivivisection, survivalism, breast feeding, and gravity boots. The national press began to run stories. Local Daylighteer chapters popped up across the country. Small towns held special Daylight Days, in which municipal offices and school systems would set their clocks ahead for one day. Features about the National Special Committee on the Daylight Issue, accompanied by sidebar interviews with Senator Moss, were printed in the *New York Times* and the *Washington Post*, and in Sunday newspaper magazine supplements. The *Wall Street Journal* adopted the cause in support of investor-owned electric utilities, but delighted in the eccentricity of the principled naturalist movement, allocating it its front-page feature column, complete with an illustration of Laslo. Miriam's intuition that universal daylight saving time would sweep the imaginations of college students, who did not care if the sun did not rise until nine since they didn't either, proved correct. They poured out in large numbers for Daylight rallies, carried Daylight petitions, held seminars and campus teach-ins about the issue, and formed a national youth support group called Young Americans for Fitness. Universal daylight saving time appeared on the television news, first on cable, three months later on the networks.

Laslo knew that Senator Moss's allegiance to the Daylighteers was a pragmatic rather than philosophical one, but as long as the Daylighteers grew in numbers and power, pragmatism would be as good as ideological purity. He also knew that the truce within the Special Committee, between his interests and the business lobbies, was at best temporary. If the two sides embraced, it was only to keep each other's arms occupied.

Dickie had some idea of the forces that operated around him, but like any other idea that Dickie had, it was poorly formed and susceptible to the influence of the last person to whom he spoke, which was usually Miriam. Having turned her file of clippings on the equipment-that-doesn't-work tax credit over to Hugh, Miriam now devoted herself to protecting Dickie from everyone, including himself. She served Dickie as aggrandizingly as she had once undermined him. She had no trouble identifying

Dickie's interests. First, the Special Committee had to remain intact, bathwater to be preserved for the baby. Second, Dickie had to satisfy Laslo that he was a principled naturalist at heart, since Laslo's incomprehensible faith in Dickie was Dickie's ace in the hole.

But, more importantly, she realized that if Laslo's plans actually worked, and she had to admit that, so far, they had, she would become a hot political property. So it was worth playing up to Laslo, even though he was probably little more than certifiable. Laslo, in turn, recognized Miriam's attitude, but tolerated her because she helped to perpetuate the appearance that Dickie was in charge, and because her competence made up for Dickie's obvious limitations.

Finally, Miriam had to mediate between Senator Moss and Laslo. Senator Moss believed that Laslo was a powerful, shrewd, and brilliant crank. As long as Senator Moss thought Laslo was under control, he would go along with the activities of the Special Committee, and their prolific marriage of convenience could continue.

And if this unlikely mix of interests made the road to the Daylighteers' national convention a bumpy one, the trip itself was worse. Laslo had arranged for Senator Moss, accompanied by Dickie and Miriam, to fly from Washington to Tampa to a small airstrip near Marshport. From there, they would be driven to the docks on Lake Okeechobee, where Laslo had secured a large powerboat capable of traversing the swamps. Laslo would then boat the senator, Dickie, and Miriam to the docks at Marshport. The senator would arrive out of the swamp, the brackish, reedy home of nature's principles. The Daylighteers would love it.

Miriam, Dickie, and the senator, however, did not. The trip was harrowing. The flight to Tampa was bothered by rough weather. The Cessna that met them at Tampa had engine trouble, nothing serious, but enough to provide Senator Moss, Dickie, and Miriam with several unpleasant moments. Dickie and Miriam weathered the ordeal well, but Senator Moss had attended a luncheon that afternoon that left him too full of béarnaise sauce, and was in danger of leaving his hosts' hospitality in the lurching airplane.

It was late afternoon by the time the Cessna landed in Marshport and the trio drove to the Marshport docks. Laslo waited, as promised, next to an impressive powerboat. He waved in a businesslike manner to Dickie, who escorted Senator Moss and Miriam to the pier. Laslo took their bags and tossed them into the boat's hold.

"How is everybody?" he asked.

"We've had an awfully tough afternoon," Senator Moss said, breathing deeply.

"Bad ride down?"

Senator Moss belched. "I'll be all right. Just give me a moment to settle my stomach."

"No problem, Senator. How about you folks?"

"We're fine, thanks," Miriam said.

"Good, then we can be on our way." Laslo got into the boat and reached out for Miriam's hand. "You first."

Miriam climbed in, followed by Senator Moss and then Dickie. Miriam sat in the co-pilot's seat, and Dickie and Senator Moss took the stern, where the bucking motion would be less pronounced. Laslo leaned back and eased the throttle of the speedboat forward. The bow reared as they took off into the swamp. Dickie liked the idea of riding in speedboats, but not with a nauseated Senator Moss. The boat hurtled into the bogs with a violent lurch.

Laslo thrust his face into the wind and yelled over his shoulder. "Senator, I bet that for as long as you've represented this state, you've hardly had the chance to appreciate it for what it is." Senator Moss leaned forward in his seat, trying to hear Laslo over the roar of the powerboat's engines and the rush of the wind.

"What's that, Laslo?" he asked.

"This is how nature meant South Florida to be, Senator. Just the cypress and the swamp. Look at those hombres over there," he said, tossing his head toward a family of alligators on a mud bank. "Magnificent animals," Laslo continued. "But let me ask you this, Senator. Are alligators, coyotes, predators of all sorts, going to be safe from the literal naturalists?" He shook his head sadly. "It all goes back to the one issue, doesn't it? Are we going to waste our time trying to preserve every bunny in the woods like the literal naturalists want, or are we going to fight to allow the coyote, the mountain lion, and the alligator to maintain nature's balance as it was ordained in principle long, long ago?"

Miriam shot Dickie an exasperated glance. She could not decide if Senator Moss looked uncomfortable because he wanted to throw up, or because Laslo appeared ready to harangue them for the entire trip.

"In fact," Laslo continued, seemingly indifferent to Senator Moss's discomfort, "I think it's time we started developing a principled naturalist program that goes beyond universal daylight saving time."

Miriam and Dickie looked at Senator Moss anxiously. Senator Moss rocked in the bucking boat, waiting for his nausea to subside. Dickie, anticipating the question Senator Moss would have asked, had he had the ability to open his mouth with confidence, said, "What do you have in mind, Laslo?"

"Dickie, principled naturalism can be applied to a wide range of social problems that are still lying around waiting to be solved." He snorted as he reflected on the ease of solving them. "For example, the government actually spends billions of dollars every year on disaster relief! Can you believe that? The government actually spends money to help people when hurricanes or tornadoes or floods strike and they become the victims—" He paused suddenly and smiled. "You know, that word—*victims*—has a whole range of connotations, doesn't it? I mean, that's exactly what the literal naturalists want us to think—that if a tornado comes and destroys your house, then you're some kind of victim."

"What would you call it?" Miriam challenged him.

"I'd say that you *experienced* a tornado, I'd say that you were the *recipient* of a tornado, but to say you were a *victim* of a tornado is to make a value judgment about nature, isn't it? We have to root out this idea that if something natural happens to you, you're a victim. If we're going to have emergency loans for farmers whose crops are destroyed by frost, then why don't we have emergency taxes for farmers whose crops are nourished by sunshine?"

Dickie nodded. It was beginning to make sense to him.

"So disaster relief has to go," Laslo said decisively. "And another thing is this budget deficit."

"What about the budget deficit?" Dickie asked.

"I'll tell you," said Laslo, glancing quickly back at Dickie and Senator Moss as he raced the powerboat over the marsh. "What is a budget deficit? It means that there isn't enough of whatever it is to satisfy everybody's needs. Will you grant me that?"

Miriam stared back at him blankly from the co-pilot's seat.

"Okay. Now every winter you'll see the smaller mammals, like mice, or shrews, even some deer, foraging in the wilderness because there isn't enough food. Now, how does nature resolve the situation?" He looked at Miriam and Dickie, but neither volunteered an answer.

"Well, I'll tell you what it doesn't do. Nature doesn't have all the mice and the rabbits and the squirrels sit down at a meeting and decide they're all going to eat 10 percent less, or that they're going to freeze the amount they eat so they only eat as much as they did last year. What actually happens is that some of them starve and some of them don't. That's nature's way. It's random, like a lottery. The solution to the budget deficit is to use nature's principles. You have a random drawing—a lottery—and the losers have to pay off the national debt and the winners get to walk away."

"You've got to be kidding," Miriam said.

"That's nothing," he dismissed. "Let's talk about something really important. Animal trapping."

Dickie had been trying to listen to Laslo but was growing more concerned about Senator Moss's discomfort, which increased each time the boat skimmed off the face of the water and landed with a resounding *whop!* on the surface once again. Senator Moss's cheeks ballooned in and out, and his face slowly began to reveal most of the colors of the flag.

"Laslo, maybe we should slow down a bit," Dickie prompted, trying to outshout the engines.

Senator Moss suddenly rose. "Laslo," he said haltingly, rocking back and forth as he tried to walk forward, one hand on his stomach and the other cupped to his lips, "Laslo, it's important that I make my position clear to you before we arrive." He suddenly lurched and started toward the rail. Dickie rose to grab him, but Senator Moss waved him off. "I'm perfectly happy to come to your convention," he continued, "and I appreciate the support of the Daylighteers. But I can't in good conscience give you the carte blanche you're looking for. There are simply too many interests to balance, and yours is only one of them."

"Are you saying you won't support us?"

"I do support you, but you have to understand my situation," said Senator Moss, who suddenly stopped short and started toward the rail again.

"Goddamn it, Laslo!" Miriam shouted. "Slow this boat down! Senator Moss is going to be sick." Laslo reached for the throttle and started to pull back on it, but, unfortunately, Senator Moss could take no more.

"Oh no," he gurgled, lunging back to his seat in the hope that he could direct his nausea away from his suit and, perhaps, from Dickie. But as he lurched, Laslo spotted a bog in the speedboat's path and cut the wheel. The boat suddenly bucked, sending Senator Moss caroming toward the stern and then over it—head, then chest, then knees, then feet, into the swamp's brackish water. Dickie jumped up to grab him but succeeded only in swatting at his calves as they toppled over the gunwale and disappeared into the splash.

Laslo turned in his seat. "What the hell was that?" he asked. Senator Moss was bobbing in the boat's wake, coughing up water, thrashing his arms and legs.

"Stop the boat!" Miriam screamed. "Stop the boat!"

Laslo pulled the wheel to circle back. "There's a line coiled under your seat, Dickie. Get it out to him, right now," he said with surprising urgency. "There's 'gators out there."

Dickie grabbed under his seat for the rope and leaped to his feet. Laslo had already turned the boat and was circling back. Senator Moss reappeared from one of his submersions, only fifty feet away. An accurate throw would drop the rope on top of him. Dickie spread the coils of the rope across his palm, preparing to throw, when he noticed a smaller and more gentle wake proceeding in the senator's direction.

"Laslo," he said, with alarm. "There's something out there . . ." But there was no need to continue. The waters plowed up around Senator Moss. A long green snout emerged, and a large scaled body followed it. There was a violent thrash and a short sudden scream. Up and then down the green body reared, taking Senator Moss with it. There was a swirling eddy where a moment before had been Senator Moss's flailing arms and legs.

Miriam shrieked. "Laslo! An alligator's got Moss!"

"Probably more than one," Laslo noted, drawing a tighter circle. Dickie looked at the rope, wondering how he could use it to save Senator Moss. Senator Moss bobbed back above the surface, struggling for air, only to retreat into the swamp again as the alligator repositioned him in its mouth. Dickie threw the rope out to him the next time he surfaced, but as he did, the senator was dragged down once more. Something like "Help!" came from the senator's struggling form, but the water cut the word back letter by letter until he emitted just a gargling sound and then nothing more.

"Laslo!" Dickie shouted. "What are we going to do?"

"A gun! You've got to have a gun on the boat, Laslo," Miriam said.

"Yes, I do," Laslo said pensively, "but getting shot might not be any less painful than getting eaten."

"No, the alligator, Laslo!" she insisted. "Shoot the fucking alligator!"

"Shoot the alligator?" Laslo asked, astonished. "For doing what nature made him to do? I can't see that."

Miriam clutched Dickie by his shirt and spoke clearly and commandingly. "Dickie, Moss is going to die. We've come too far, Dickie, we can't let him die!" Dickie turned from her, sucked in a deep breath, and put his foot on the gunwale of the boat, readying himself to go in after the senator, when he felt a hand on his arm. He turned and saw Laslo looking at him sternly, shaking his head.

"Don't do it, Dickie," Laslo said. "It's suicide."

"Shut up, Laslo," Miriam shouted, wresting Dickie's arm from him. "Do it, Dickie!"

He was ready. "I've got to save him!"

"He's gone, boy, there's nothing to save." He looked at Dickie sternly. "It's nature's way."

Dickie was dumbstruck. It was nature's way. It was what he described in *The Daylight Manifesto* and what Senator Moss and Laslo and all the Daylighteers were fighting for. It was the basis for Senator Moss's national movement. But now nature's way had claimed its champion. The idling engines filled Dickie's ears as he struggled for the right thing to think and say. His lower lip trembled. Miriam was trembling, too.

"What are we going to do, Laslo?" Dickie said. "What are we going to do?"

"Well, we're going to head for shore and see if the park rangers can't fish something up." Laslo stood calmly, staring out at the water's surface as if he were assessing the weather for a day of bass fishing.

"But we don't know if Senator Moss is really dead."

Laslo shook his head. "False hope doesn't serve any of us, Dickie. At least he didn't die in a hospital. He didn't die surrounded by doctors who couldn't save him or grieving relations who couldn't wait for him to die. He died," he looked up and spread his arms, "here."

Dickie sat down in the boat, his world quickly coming to pieces. His absent gaze fell upon the water—please, he thought, please. He folded his hands tightly and prayed for Senator Moss, unable to think of anything else to do. And, just then, as if in response to his prayers, Senator Moss's hand punched through the surface in a frantic wave.

"Laslo! Dickie!" Miriam cried. "Look!"

Tears came to Dickie's eyes and relief overwhelmed him. The hand lurched down into the water again, and then popped back up, fingers spread wide.

"He's alive!" Dickie cried. "Laslo, he's alive!" Laslo threw his hands cleanly across the wheel and the throttle to pull up alongside him. Dickie leaned over the side of the boat as it neared Senator Moss, his fingertips extended toward his hand, closer now, closer . . . there! He grasped the hand and pulled with all his might.

And tumbled back into the boat. The arm ended at the shoulder, a twisted stick of gristle and sinew, dripping with blood and swamp water, nothing more. Dickie held it up, expecting to see the man at the other end. But there was everything but the man—the college ring, the wristwatch, the shirtsleeve, the cuff link, the suit sleeve—and then no more. In his dying gesture, Senator Moss was doing what he had done throughout his life—shaking hands. Shaking hands as he had in shopping centers, at Jacksonville fund-raising dinners, on the Senate floor, in real estate transactions, in county party meetings, in Qatar, at campaign whistle stops, at factory gates, in the third base dugout of the Orlando Rangers, on Chamber of Commerce podiums, in White House prayer breakfasts, in Senate party caucus meetings, shaking hands as he had done since the day he first joined the Wawahatchee County Chamber of Commerce and began his climb to the Capitol. He died as he lived, pressing the flesh, leaving the instrument of his amiability, with its uncalloused palms and manicured nails, behind him. Dickie turned pale and felt the world begin to spin as he shook the lifeless hand in front of him. He was ready to keel over when he was jolted by the feeling of the arm being yanked from his grip.

"Give me that thing, Dickie," Laslo said. He popped the ring from its finger. "Give this to his wife," he said as he put it in Dickie's hand. "The rest goes to the matador, Dickie. The ears and the tail." He flung the forearm into the water. It floated for a moment and then sank into the swamp.

Laslo took a deep breath and nodded. "The animal earned it."

Chapter Thirteen

There was silence in the boat as it continued on to Marshport. Laslo had marked the spot where Senator Moss had disappeared with a buoy, but he knew that the body wouldn't be found. He stared straight ahead as he guided the craft through the marshes. Miriam sat next to him in the co-pilot's seat, gazing ahead, tranquilized by the sunset. Her breathing was deep and her skin warm when only a few minutes before she had been gasping and shivering. She found herself hoping that the boat ride would never end, that she could ride along forever with the sun in her face and the engines drowning out every other noise. But her mind kept wandering back to Senator Moss. Her disbelief that he was dead rapidly gave way to a host of new and unanswered questions. What was her relationship to Dickie now? And to Laslo? Who would fill the vacuum that Senator Moss left behind, as a senator, as the chairman of the Science and Engineering Committee, as the chairman of the National Special Committee on the Daylight Issue?

Dickie sat in the back of the boat grasping the seat cushions beneath him to prevent himself from sharing Senator Moss's fate. He realized that the chain of events that had propelled him from unheralded mundanity to renowned mediocrity had beshattered by Moss's death, but he did not, of course, know how. He could not see a way to emerge from this predicament unscathed. Having a U.S. senator die in your care was probably one of the worst things that could happen to you, he reasoned. "He stood up to throw up and he fell over the side," he mentally rehearsed for the hordes of detectives he imagined waiting for him. "He *stood* up to *throw* up and he fell over the *side*." He repeated it to himself until it acquired a rhythm.

They continued in silence until they could see the Marshport docks ahead. Dickie leaned forward and shouted over the roar of the engines. "What are we going to tell them?"

"Just what you saw," Miriam said.

"Don't tell them anything," Laslo interrupted, calm but insistent. "Let me take care of it."

Dickie was prepared to let Laslo take care of it, but Miriam obviously was not. "Let you take care of it? Like you took care of Moss?"

Laslo glowered. "What do you mean by that?"

She returned his fierce expression with one of her own, but when she opened her mouth to tell him what she meant, the sound she heard was that of a marching band blaring out the opening phrase of "The Washington Post March." Miriam, Laslo, and Dickie turned and looked ahead to the dock. A large crowd had gathered there, with flags, trucks, banners, and a high school marching band that had just begun the program. They could see more of the crowd as they drew closer. It was enormous. The band grew louder as they approached, and they could see a sign extended across the dock's pilings: WELCOME SENATOR LUTHER A. MOSS.

Dickie gulped. "Laslo, what are we going to do? What are we going to tell people?"

Rather than answering, Laslo pulled the throttle and circled the boat alongside the dock. A delegation walked down the pier toward the spot where the boat would be tethered. "Listen," he said quickly, glancing at Dickie and Miriam. "Just because Moss wasn't at both ends of the boat ride doesn't mean that we forget about why we're here. Just let me do the talking and later you can do anything you like."

"Laslo," Miriam insisted, "the death of a senator is subject to a federal investigation." New waves of fear rippled through Dickie. "We have to report this to the F.B.I. as soon as possible."

"Well, that won't be a problem. The head of the F.B.I. regional office is at the convention right now," Laslo said as he edged the boat up against the dock.

Laslo cut the engines. A group of men approached the boat with expressions of eager anticipation. The head of the delegation surveyed the occupants. "Laslo! Hey, Laslo, old man! Where's Senator Moss?"

"Hello, Tom," he said, reaching up and clasping the hand of the president of the Florida Daylighteers. "How are things here?"

"Just fine, Laslo," the man said with a smile. "But where's Senator Moss? Is something wrong?"

"Nothing's wrong, buddy," Laslo said, bounding up onto the dock. "Nothing at all."

"But where's Moss?"

"A little logistical problem, Tom. The senator . . ." Laslo paused and glared intimidatingly at Dickie and Miriam, " . . . stopped for lunch. In the meantime, let me introduce you to some people," he said, turning to Dickie and Miriam as they climbed out of the boat. "Folks, this is Tom Sewell, president of the Florida Daylighteers. Tom, this is Miriam Moskowitz, who works for Senator Moss, and this," he said, moving next to Dickie and extending an arm around his shoulders, "is Dickie Vanderhaltz."

"Dickie Vanderhaltz?" Tom asked. "*The Daylight Manifesto* Dickie Vanderhaltz?"

"One and the same," glowed Laslo.

"Well, this is truly a pleasure." Tom grinned. "I carry r

everywhere." He reached into his back pocket and produced a copy of *The Daylight Manifesto*. "Can I ask you to autograph it?"

"Now listen, Tom," Laslo interrupted, taking him by the arm and walking him away from the dock. "I've got a little problem on my hands. Nothing important, mind you, but just a few things that Dickie, Miriam, and I have to work out. Where do you think I could find Bill Reese?"

"He's up at the bar in the hotel, the last I saw him."

"Okay. We're going to have a word with him. Why don't you get one or two of your boys to unload our stuff and take it up to our rooms?"

"Sure, Laslo. But what about Senator Moss? Everyone's expecting him."

"Just tell everybody that they're going to have the surprise of their lives tonight, how about that?" He smiled. "Let me go see Bill and I'll meet you later, okay?"

The F.B.I. man sat at the bar in front of a martini. He was in his fifties, but trim and athletic. He and Laslo shook hands, and Laslo quickly got down to business.

"Look, Bill, we've got a real problem on our hands. Senator Moss is dead. He fell out of our boat and was dismembered by a 'gator."

Bill Reese put his drink down on the bar, instantly serious. "Are there any remains? What the hell happened?"

"I can draw you a map, Bill, and I've got a radio buoy at the spot, but you're not going to find more than table scraps. All we saw was an arm. Dickie here got his ring for his wife."

"Dickie? Dickie Vanderhaltz?" The F.B.I. man asked. Dickie nodded. "Well, I'm very pleased to meet you, sir," Reese said, shaking Dickie's hand enthusiastically. It reminded Dickie of his last contact with Senator Moss and he began feeling queasy. "Let me see the ring, Dickie," Reese asked. "The murder of a senator is a federal offense," he went on, as Dickie handed over ̣e ring. "Even though I don't think that there's a murder here, ̣circumstances warrant a full investigation. But all you have to do is be responsive at the inquest and everything will turn out fine." He gave the ring back to Dickie after looking at it.

Miriam spoke up. It seemed to her that she was responsible for Senator Moss's interests, especially in the obvious absence of anybody else who would be. "How can you be so sure we'll be exonerated?"

"Well, you didn't do it, did you, ma'am?"

"You're the regional director of the F.B.I. You just gave the only existing piece of evidence in the death of a United States senator back to a prospective suspect."

"I did?"

"Yes," Miriam insisted. "The ring."

"Oh, shoot, Miss Moskowitz. This is Dickie Vanderhaltz. If you can't trust Dickie Vanderhaltz, then——"

"How can you be so sure we're not criminally involved in Senator Moss's highly unusual death?" she persisted.

"What's unusual about it?" Bill Reese said, shrugging. "I don't know where you're from, Ms. Moskowitz, but down here, any fool can tell you that if you fall out of a boat in a swamp, you stand a good chance of being eaten by an alligator, even if you're a United States senator."

"There has to be an investigation."

"Well then, I don't see a problem, because there will be." Bill Reese considered the matter closed. He looked at his watch. "It's six o'clock right now. Laslo, what's the plan?"

"I don't know yet," Laslo sighed. "But we'll think of something."

"Well, I'll have to take statements, but that can wait. First, I'm going to call the regional office and have them dispatch an agent. And I guess I have to sequester you until we take your statements."

"Sequester?" asked Dickie.

"Now don't let me upset you, Dr. Vanderhaltz. It's just a formality. There's a room behind the stage at the community center. I'll have dinner sent to you there. With a little luck, we'll be able to get a preliminary statement out of the way before this evening's events. I'd go ahead and do it myself, but the other agencies are going to want one, so we might as well wait. You all stay right here, while I make some calls." He ambled over to a pay phone in the bar and made three or four calls.

Miriam watched him, growing ever more ill at ease. She didn't like any of this. She didn't like being at a convention of cranks, law enforcement personnel, and right-wing college students. She didn't like being associated with the death of a U.S. senator. She didn't like the way Laslo had the complete cooperation of the F.B.I.

And, she didn't like Laslo. The more she thought about it, the more she didn't like Laslo from the word go. She might have gone along with him, but she didn't like the way he suddenly appeared and took over the show, the ease with which he was able to manipulate Dickie, or the way he chewed up Hugh, even if Hugh's being chewed up didn't bother her at all.

She didn't like the bizarre philosophy through which Laslo viewed the world. She didn't like his intuitive political acumen, his understated manner, or his overstated Machiavellianism. She didn't like the way Laslo maneuvered Senator Moss into a boat and then out of it. She didn't like the one-in-a-million way Senator Moss died. And she didn't like the question to which she kept returning.

Had Laslo killed Senator Moss?

Maybe Laslo thought Moss was going to distance himself from Laslo. Maybe Laslo thought that he would be better off with Moss out of the picture. And maybe he was capable of setting the whole thing up.

Did he engineer the entire convention as a ploy to get Senator Moss to take this strange travel route? Or did he engineer the entire movement as a ruse to have a convention as a ploy to take Senator Moss into the swamps and to his death? Dismemberment by alligators, she thought, was too convenient. Were they planted? Had Laslo orchestrated the powerboat, the swamp, the convention, the travel route, the alligators and the F.B.I. into Senator Moss's murder, just as he had orchestrated Dickie, the A.E.I.O.U., universal daylight saving time, *Modern Weapons*, Conrad Scott, and Senator Moss into a mass movement? Had he manipulated everybody he met in Washington, people he instinctively felt superior to if not despised, by playing to their inflated sense of self-importance and their insatiable ambition? Or was it only her guilt that projected Laslo as the ringmaster of a circus of foibles? Was it her shame that she, like everyone else around her, had such insatiable ambition that she could be brought into a scheme or a trap with ease, and that her hopes for power and glory made her as predictable as Dickie's naïveté and opportunism made him. She peered quickly into her own makeup and then quickly turned away.

When the chief of the county police, the commander of the local National Guard, and the regional bureau chief of the F.B.I. left the room behind the stage, Dickie, Miriam, and Laslo were alone for the first time since they had arrived. Dickie looked around, nervous and pale, exhausted from his ordeal. He looked at Laslo, who was lost in thought. He looked at Miriam, who leaned against the wall, biting her fingernails.

The silence and uncertainty were too much for him. "Well," he whimpered, "what are we going to do now? There are thousands of people out there in that hall who are waiting to hear Senator Moss. What if the police think we killed Senator Moss? We could be tried for murder!"

"We're not going to be tried for murder because nobody murdered anybody," Laslo said. Laslo glanced at Miriam, who returned his look with a cold stare. "What is it?" he challenged. "Do you think that Senator Moss was murdered?" he asked her.

"I don't know if you killed Senator Moss or not," she answered.

"You were there. He fell out of the boat. How could I have killed him?"

"Maybe you lured him onto the boat just so you could push him into the swamp. Maybe you wanted Dickie and me along just to make it look good."

Laslo's expression hardened. "That's a lot to do, isn't it?"

"But you're the guy to do it, aren't you?" she shot back.

He smiled modestly: there was no disputing that.

"After all," she pressed on, "it looks like you've got the entire law enforcement establishment at this little party of yours."

"It takes more than a chief of police to get away with killing a senator, young lady," Laslo responded.

"Come on, Laslo. You've got the regional F.B.I. chief serving you dinner."

"Miriam!" Dickie exclaimed. "You can't believe that Laslo would actually kill Senator Moss! It's not possible!"

"Why not?"

"Because there would be an investigation."

"Maybe. It really depends on whether there are witnesses with stories to tell."

Laslo leaned against the wall, entertained by the speculation. "You may be right, young lady," he chuckled. "But you haven't told me *why* I would kill Senator Moss."

"Because you knew that Senator Moss was going to use the Daylighteers, then sell out daylight saving time to further the interests of the Special Committee and the utility guys. Come on, Laslo, you've expected that from the start."

Dickie had never heard talk this blunt about Laslo. He fearfully walked over to Laslo and looked into his eyes.

"Laslo, did you kill Senator Moss? Did you plan this whole thing?" Laslo silently returned his stare. "Laslo, answer me."

Laslo gazed into Dickie's eyes for a long moment. "No, I didn't, Dickie." He then turned to Miriam. "And that's the truth," he said, approaching her. "I didn't kill Senator Moss. There was no need to. I had him where I wanted him, right here, at the convention. I was going to force-feed him the Daylighteer program in public. When we got back to Washington we would have gotten our bill." He shook his head and laughed. "Why kill a posturing little puppet like Moss when he was still worth something left alive? It would be like harvesting a plow animal."

She sighed deeply. "Laslo, I don't know if I believe you."

"But you were right there," Laslo snarled, starting to become uncomfortable. "You know I didn't kill anybody."

She looked at him and snickered. "Perhaps so, Laslo. But in our system, we let twelve of our peers decide that. It all depends on who says what. The way I look at it, I get to decide if you killed him or not."

"You're bluffing," Laslo snapped.

"Okay, Laslo," she deadpanned, "let me show you how it works." She walked to the door and banged on it. "Officer!" she called. The state trooper opened the door immediately.

"Something wrong, ma'am?"

She looked over her shoulder at Laslo. He was frozen in his tracks. His eyes darted between her and the trooper.

"Miriam," he said, almost in a whisper.

"See what I mean?" She smiled at him, and then turned toward the trooper. "Excuse me, officer. Do you have a cigarette?" she asked.

"Yes ma'am, I do," he said, pulling a Lucky Strike out of his shirt pocket and offering it to her.

She let him light it and dragged deeply. "Thanks," she said, as the trooper closed the door behind him. She blew a cloud of smoke toward Laslo. "There, you see? There's a squadron of F.B.I. agents right outside. Dickie's and my deposition looks pretty big from here." She took another drag of her cigarette. "You'd make an interesting defendant, don't you think?"

"You're trying to frame me!"

She chuckled. "And it's not proving very difficult, is it?"

Laslo got her point. Who would have thought the little minx had it in her? "Okay, then, young lady. Where do we go from here?"

She had his undivided attention. "Look at things my way for

a minute, Laslo. Our immediate problem is that we've got a crowd out there that needs a speech, and I know that I'm not going to give it to them. Then, when we get back to Washington, we've got a National Special Committee on the Daylight Issue without a chairman. No senator, nothing. Who's going to sponsor your legislation now? Who's going to shill for you and keep me and Dickie in groceries?"

"Well, who's next in seniority on the Science and Engineering Committee?" Dickie asked.

"I'll tell you who," she answered, without taking her eyes off of Laslo. "Somebody who won't be taken in as easily as Moss was. Somebody who's a little more impervious to Laslo's quick cash. Particularly now that the last guy who took Laslo's money was eaten by an alligator. Does everybody see my point?" Everybody saw her point and thought it was a good one. "We've got to have a senator in our pockets to keep this thing going, Laslo, because if this thing doesn't keep going, we're all headed home. So this is the plan." She paused and crushed the cigarette under her heel. "We run Dickie for Senator Moss's seat."

"We what?" exclaimed Dickie.

"Do you get it, Laslo?" she prodded, ignoring Dickie's gulping noises. "We go out there and announce that Dr. Dickie Vanderhaltz, native son of the Sunshine State, famed geophysicist from the South Florida Institute of Technology, author of *The Daylight Manifesto*, father of the movement for universal daylight saving time, handpicked by Senator Moss before his death to be the special counsel of his committee, is going to run for Senator Moss's seat to continue the great unfinished work of bringing principled naturalism to the public forum, and whatever the hell else it is you say. It's a natural. They'll eat him up out there. Maybe when we get him back to Washington the other members of the Special Committee will back us. After all, they think Dickie's one of them, no thanks to you. We'll hit them all up for money and maybe we'll shake any other candidates out." She looked at Dickie and Laslo, who stared back at her, dumb-founded.

"Miriam," Dickie pleaded. "It doesn't make any sense!"

"It's too late to start worrying about making sense now, Dickie," she said. "Now we're only in it to win. Look, if we win the Republican primary, and we've got a shot at it," she continued excitedly, "then the national party is going to have to carry us if only to keep President Honeycutt from losing Florida to Don Green. First, of course, we have to get to the governor, since the governor gets to appoint a successor to fill the office until the election. If we can get the governor to appoint Dickie, and keep the Special Committee behind us, we'd be a shoo-in. We'd have money, support, and the powers of an incumbent. It would be a cakewalk from there."

"I don't know," Laslo contemplated. "Do you really think this boy could pull it off? And what if the governor doesn't appoint him?"

"I don't know, but it's the only shot we've got. We'll worry about everything else when the time comes. Right now, we've got to put Dickie up there in front of that crowd and announce his candidacy."

Laslo was unused to hearing good ideas from other people, but he was smart enough to recognize one when he heard it. "You're right," he said with a look of determination. "Let's do it."

"Laslo, what the heck are you talking about?" Dickie moaned. He walked into a far corner of the room, his hands on his head, and whirled toward Laslo and Miriam. "I can't run for the Senate. I can't run for any office! I just can't!"

"You're over thirty and a citizen, aren't you?" Laslo said. "Miriam's perfectly right about this. You've got to do it," he said, as if explaining a law of nature.

"I'm not going to do it," Dickie said, drowning in fear. "I'll go test minerals in a laboratory. I'll go be a rig hand for a seismic crew. I don't know what I'll do and I don't care. But I'm not running for office and I'm not making a speech in front of all those people out there."

Laslo strode across the room and backed Dickie against the wall.

"You listen to me," he said. "This little girl has it right. You're going to get your ass out there on that stage and you're going to give my people a speech. You're going to make Daniel Webster look like a cigar store Indian. I'll introduce you and tell them that Moss got boxed on the way over and at the end of your speech you're going to announce that you're running for Moss's Senate seat. Now get yourself together. You read me?"

"Like heck I will!" Dickie shouted. "I'm not doing anything of the sort. I'm not going to tell anybody about principled naturalism, or man and nature, or about preserving the brood, or any of your other insane ideas." He threw his hands up and turned away. "Why did I ever listen to you? I could be back at S.F.I.T. right now and out of harm's way if you hadn't come along," he moaned, forgetting that he couldn't. "Forget it, Laslo, because I'm not going to do it."

"All right, that's enough!" Miriam said, stepping in. "Laslo, get out of here," she ordered. "Now."

"What the devil—"

"Just get out of here and stand out there with the trooper until I tell you otherwise. Do you understand?"

"All right," he said, "but I'll be right there by the door." He glowered at Dickie as he left.

She turned to begin her pitch, but Dickie beat her to the punch. "I don't care what you say, I'm not going out there in front of all these weirdos and announcing I'm running for anything."

"Shhh," she said softly, and put her hand over his mouth. When he had quieted, she took her hand off his mouth and laid it on his chest. "Look, I don't know what gives with you. When you got to Washington you made an ass of yourself hoping to be somebody. There wasn't anything you wouldn't do.

Now you're being offered the grand prize and you're going to turn it down." She came closer to him, as close as she had ever been. "I don't know if you've ever wanted something, Dickie, but I want something. I want to be somebody. That's what I want. And you're going to get it for me." She reached up and pulled his head down toward hers. He resisted, but at the first touch of her lips he was converted. He slid his arms around her waist and drew her firmly against him. She looked up at him with an expression he'd never seen before. "You're going to do this for me, aren't you?" she asked, as she rubbed her hips against him.

"You can't do this to me, Miriam. Please."

"You're going to go out there, aren't you?"

A magnificent sensation spread from his groin. He sighed deeply.

"You are, aren't you?" she cooed. "It's going to be you and me, Dickie, isn't it?"

"Yes, yes," he agreed, releasing himself to the feeling.

She kissed him again and slid her hands in front of her. She could feel him tighten in surprise when she began to unbuckle his belt.

"What are you doing?"

"I'm going to show you what's in it for you, Dickie," she said. In a moment his staff was waving in the air, guided by her dexterity.

"Miriam!" Dickie gurgled.

"Close your eyes," she whispered. She was at work in an instant. He leaned back against the wall, trying to keep from toppling over her. He thought of a girl he had spied undressing through a window in high school, and an eight millimeter black-and-white film he once had seen at a stag party. In a moment he gave out a small cry and she gently put him back as she found him. He realized that his underwear was going to be uncomfortable for the rest of the evening, but he was still in love.

"Take a deep breath," she told him.

"I've taken a couple deep breaths," he said, panting.

She straightened his clothing and smoothed his chest with her hands. "Get yourself together now," she said.

"Okay," he responded.

"You can do it," she whispered to him. "Just imitate Moss, like he was at the press conference, but remember the thing Laslo said on the boat. Predators, disaster relief, budget deficits; do you remember?" He nodded quickly. "And if you run out of that, go back to the article you wrote. Remember, this crowd came to hear a speech they agree with. Nobody's going to debate you."

He nodded like a prizefighter between rounds.

"And apologize to Laslo."

"But did Laslo kill Senator Moss?"

"How should I know? Probably not."

"And he's not going to kill us?"

"He's not going to kill us, Dickie. And if he *was* going to, you'd want to stay in the public eye."

"You mean you said all that just to scare him?"

"That's right, Dickie. I did it for us."

"Okay," he muttered.

"Are you ready?"

He wanted to say no, but it was too late. He nodded. She walked to the door and opened it. Laslo was standing across the corridor. He looked in to see Dickie composing himself, and knew the answer immediately. "You're going to do it?"

"Yes," Dickie said, "and I'm sorry about what I said."

"Me, too," Laslo said, extending his hand, and they shook hands like recalcitrant children. Dickie walked past him, out the door and toward the stage. Miriam started after him when Laslo stepped in front of her.

"What the hell went on in there?" he asked firmly.

"Not what you think." She glowered at him and followed Dickie down the hall.

Chapter Fourteen

Buddy Youngblood led Congressman Wheezle, Jeff, Lenny, and the Message Concepts production crew to the base of the Capitol on a sunny summer morning. "Okay, everybody," Buddy said. "Let's run through this thing once so we all understand what we're supposed to do, okay? This is a thirty-second television spot for Congressman Wheezle. Congressman Wheezle will run up the Capitol steps and there'll be a narrative voice-over. When he gets to the top he says a few lines, and that's it." He beckoned an assistant who carried a looseleaf notebook. "Here's the script for the voice-over. It goes like this:

'*You get up early in the morning and fight for yourself and your family. Ezra Wheezle gets up early in the morning and fights for you. You're fighting to keep your job. Ezra Wheezle is fighting to help you keep it. You're fighting to keep your taxes down. Ezra Wheezle is fighting to keep them down, too.*

'*If you were in Congress, would you fight for anything different? Ezra Wheezle doesn't think so, and that's why Ezra Wheezle's a congressman . . . so you don't have to be!*'

"Got it?" he asked Congressman Wheezle. "Now, by the time we get to the slogan, you'll be at the top of the Capitol steps and facing the camera inside the door. Our friend—What's your name?" he called to the cameraman.

"Chuck," the cameraman said.

"Ezra, our friend Chuck here is going to be inside the door of the Capitol. When you get to the top of the stairs, stand right there and say your lines to the camera. Do you remember the lines, Ezra?"

Congressman Wheezle scratched his head.

"Goddamnit," Buddy mumbled under his breath. "Can somebody give Congressman Wheezle the lines, please?" he shouted.

" 'You deserve three things in a congressman. You deserve—' " one of the crew responded.

"Right, that's it," said Congressman Wheezle, interrupting. *"'You deserve three things in a congressman. You deserve a congressman who's dependable, who'll be there in Washington representing you, so that you don't have to be. You deserve a congressman who's familiar, who's been a congressman for a long time, someone you've had a chance to get to know. And you deserve a congressman who's convenient, who won't take up too much of your time with complicated issues that he's supposed to understand instead of you. That's why I'm your congressman. So you don't have to be. So vote for your congressman, Ezra Wheezle, on November 5.'"* He looked at Buddy. "Is that right?"

"That's perfect," gushed Buddy. "Absolutely perfect. Okay, just a walk-through, this time, everybody." Lenny and Jeff watched the camera crews move into place. Congressman Wheezle waited at the base of the Capitol steps in the direct morning sun, his forehead beginning to grow moist.

"Okay, everybody," Buddy's voice came over a bullhorn. "Are we ready? Are you ready up there at the top of the stairs?" A production assistant standing next to him, his ear to a walkie-talkie, nodded. "Are you ready back there?" A man with a portable camera on his shoulder nodded from behind Congressman Wheezle. "Are you ready, Congressman?" Congressman Wheezle patted his hair into place and then nodded. "Okay then, let's walk through . . . now."

He clapped his hands and Congressman Wheezle took off up the Capitol steps with surprising pep. The man with the portable camera trotted behind him. Buddy read the narration over the bullhorn for timing. Congressman Wheezle reached the top of the steps and delivered his lines, a bit self-consciously, but competently just the same. Buddy listened through a small earphone on his headset that gave him a direct feed from the camera at the top of the steps. "That's not bad," he said to nobody in particular. "Send the congressman down here and maybe we can print one."

"What did you think?" he asked Lenny as Congressman Wheezle came down the steps.

"The idea is fine, Buddy, but I wonder if Congressman Wheezle is up to running up steps all morning."

Jeff interrupted him. "Lenny, why don't we let him judge what he's capable of doing?"

Congressman Wheezle came down the steps and approached Buddy. "How did that look?"

"It looked fine, Congressman. I'd like you to move a little quicker, but it was just fine." He rubbed his palms together with enthusiasm. "I think we ought to tape one now, if you don't mind. Are you ready?"

Congressman Wheezle looked at the cigarette he had just lit, took a quick drag, and put it out. One of Buddy's assistants mopped Congressman Wheezle's brow with a handkerchief and the camera crew took their places. "Okay, everybody," said Buddy. "This one's for real." Congressman Wheezle took his position at the base of the Capitol steps, Buddy gave the cue, and off he went again. When he was about halfway up the steps, the sun disappeared behind a cloud, and the cameraman shooting down at Congressman Wheezle waved his hands at Buddy.

"Shit," Buddy muttered. "The lighting's all wrong." He turned on his walkie-talkie and spoke. "Send him back down and let's wait for this cloud to pass." Lenny and Jeff watched as Congressman Wheezle started back down the steps, this time a little slouched.

"That was fine, Ezra," Buddy said with a smile. "We'll be done before you know it."

"Good, good," Congressman Wheezle said, his breathing a little strained, sweat starting to dampen his shirt.

In a few minutes the sun emerged from behind the clouds. "Is everybody ready?" Buddy asked. He looked around and saw everyone in place. "Okay then, Congressman, let's roll."

Congressman Wheezle again set out up the steps, now churning like a locomotive. His face grew ever more red and his brow ever more furrowed. He reached the top step and looked into the camera. "You deserve three things in a congressman," he said, his lungs pulling in as much air as they could between phrases. "You deserve a congressman who's dependable, who'll—" He suddenly stopped and looked up with an expression of frightened confusion.

"—who'll be there in Washington representing you, so that you don't have to—" a woman with a script prompted.

"—who'll be there in—" Congressman Wheezle began again, only to stop short once more.

"—who'll be there in Washington representing you, so that you don't have to—" the woman repeated.

"—who'll be there in Washington—" he said, suddenly bringing his shoulders forward.

"—representing you—" the woman prompted.

"—representing me—"

"No, you! Representing you!"

"Fuck," Congressman Wheezle muttered as he felt his insides swarm into his throat.

"—representing you, so that you don't have to—" the woman again prompted, but Congressman Wheezle did not respond. Instead, he clutched his chest with a look of desperate agony and began to fall backward, at first slowly, then, catching his heel on the ledge of the top step, he tumbled, spinning off the steps on his back until his heels flipped over his gaping scarlet face and then his face over his heels. End over end he fell, bouncing off landings and railings, losing momentum and then regaining it on the downhill straightaways, until he landed at the base of the steps, coming up heads in the final toss, his bulging, strangled face staring up at the now cloudless sky.

Lenny was the first of the group to move from where they stood frozen in place and rush to Congressman Wheezle's side. He ripped open Congressman Wheezle's shirt and pressed an ear to his chest.

"Get an ambulance!" he shouted.

"Shit!" Buddy Youngblood threw his headset to the ground, shattering it in rage. "Shit! Shit! Shit!" he pressed on with his thinking. "Don't panic!" he cried. "There's a phone in the production truck. I'll call an ambulance from there. Jeff, come with me. We've got to get ahold of Rollo," he said. "Lenny, stay here and wait for the ambulance." With that, he dispersed the crew and went to the truck, leaving Lenny with the smoked and pickled body he once had called "sir."

Lenny had always planned for the day when he would no longer depend on Congressman Wheezle for his livelihood, but he was unprepared for it when it arrived. He had always assumed the old man would hold out long enough for Lenny to springboard to his next job. Standing outside of Congressman Wheezle's hospital room, he strained to think of what he might do now.

He was interrupted when the elevator door at the end of the hospital corridor opened and Rollo Plank, the Speaker of the House, emerged. The Speaker stormed down the corridor, trailing Jeff, Steve Lowry, and Buddy Youngblood behind him.

"Okay," The Speaker said to announce his arrival. "What the hell is going on here?"

"He's had a stroke," Lenny said, motioning to the door of Congressman Wheezle's room.

"Is he alive or dead?"

"He was alive fifteen minutes ago."

The Speaker sucked air. "Okay, everybody follow me and keep your mouths shut." The Speaker pushed the door open and walked in. Congressman Wheezle was surrounded by doctors and nurses, some preparing hypodermics, others watching screens that monitored Congressman Wheezle's vital signs. His eyes were unopened and his body inert.

"All right," commanded The Speaker as he moved toward the bed. "What's going on here?"

A doctor with wire-rimmed glasses turned to the nurse and extended a clipboard toward her. "Hold this," he said, then stepped forward to take The Speaker's arm and lead everyone out of the room.

"How is he?" demanded The Speaker in the hallway.

"May I ask your relationship to this man?"

"Never mind who I am, what's wrong with him?"

The doctor with wire-rimmed glasses did not really care who the man was, so long as he could be prevented from interfering with medical procedures. "He's got some broken bones and some internal bleeding, but fortunately, he was already uncon-scious by the time he began to fall, so he was limp enough to avoid the degree of trauma normally associated with this kind of accident. But he's had a stroke, a bad one. A very bad one."

"Is he going to live?"

"The short answer is yes." The Speaker exhaled with relief. "But I'm afraid it might not be that simple," the doctor cau-tioned. "There's a question of his motor and mental functions. The flow of blood might have been impeded long enough to in-flict serious injury to parts of the brain. It's a real possibility, I'm afraid, one that we have to face."

"But he's going to live?"

"As I said, I think so," the doctor said. "But—"

"I understand," The Speaker interrupted.

"Very good. Now, if you don't mind, I'm needed inside." The doctor went back into the room, leaving everybody in silence, waiting for The Speaker's reaction.

"We're going to lose his goddamned seat," The Speaker roared as he punted a chair down the corridor. "You stupid dipshit."

He glared at Buddy. "Why the hell did you have a sixty-four-year-old man running up the Capitol steps?"

"It was his idea," pleaded Buddy, pointing to Jeff. "He told me Ezra was capable of doing it."

The Speaker whirled at Jeff and grabbed him by his shirt. "I ought to put you in the bed next to Ezra!"

"But, Mr. Speaker!" Jeff bleated, as The Speaker wrapped both his hands deeply in the furls of Jeff's suit and lifted him off the floor.

"Rollo!" shouted Buddy Youngblood.

"Mr. Speaker!" cried Steve and Lenny, as they tried to pry him off his victim.

"Get off of me!" The Speaker spat as he dropped Jeff and stepped away from him. Jeff retreated down the corridor and The Speaker whirled and pushed open the door to Congressman Wheezle's room in a frenzy.

"Doctor!" he shouted into the room.

The doctor reemerged with a look of annoyance. "Sir, if you don't mind, we're busy saving this man's life."

"Who's in charge here?" The Speaker demanded, ignoring the doctor's protests. "I need to see whoever's in charge right now."

"I'm sure that the chief of medicine is very busy," the doctor replied.

The Speaker reared and glared. "Do you know who I am?"

The doctor had seen intrusive and demanding relatives before, but was nonetheless galled. "No," the doctor challenged. "Should I?"

"I'm the Speaker of the U.S. *Fucking* House of Representatives!" he hissed. That was enough to get the doctor in wire-rimmed glasses to call the eighth floor. In moments, the chief of medicine arrived, a middle-aged man with a clinical demeanor.

"Mr. Speaker, I'm very pleased to meet you," the chief of medicine said. "Unfortunately, I hear there's some sort of problem."

"There's no problem at all," The Speaker said, taking the

chief of medicine by the arm and leading him down the hall. He led him into the first room he came to. Inside, a man lay motionless in bed, amid a maze of tubes.

"There's somebody in this room," the chief of medicine noted.

"Hey, buddy," The Speaker shouted toward the man. There was no response. "Don't worry, he can't hear us. Now look. Do you know who you've got in the next room?"

"No, I don't."

"Congressman Ezra T. Wheezle, and he's just had a massive stroke."

The chief of medicine nodded. "Well, I can assure you he'll be given the best of care."

"I know he'll be given the best of care," The Speaker said. "But this situation can have significant repercussions. You can imagine that, can't you?"

The chief of medicine nodded again.

"Look," said The Speaker, sensing that the chief of medicine might be a compliant soul. "I don't want this to get out for a while. It would be very bad politically. Do you follow me?"

"It might be very hard to contain this kind of thing," said the chief of medicine.

The Speaker's face took on a contemplative look. "Let's consider what that would mean. There's something I want you to imagine."

The chief of medicine looked uncomfortable. "What is that?"

"Imagine," The Speaker said, "an entire building full of Medicare and Medicaid payment auditors whose jobs, for the rest of their lives, will be to investigate the submissions from this hospital and any other hospital that ever employs you. Every form, every voucher, every expense claim."

"That's blackmail!" blurted the chief of medicine.

"That's good government," corrected The Speaker. "Cost

control. The public's very concerned about cost control, Doctor. Do you follow me?"

"I do follow you, Mr. Speaker, but—"

"That's fine. So what's it going to be?" The Speaker asked.

"Whatever you want," the chief of medicine said.

The Speaker smiled his most opulent smile, opened the door, and stuck his head out into the corridor. "Steve!" he commanded, and Steve Lowry entered the room.

"Yes, Mr. Speaker?"

"The chief of medicine of this hospital has graciously agreed to help us out with any information problems that may arise regarding Ezra's stroke. I want you to stay with him for the next couple of days and help him through any difficult situations."

"Yes, Mr. Speaker."

"No one is to know what has happened to Ezra," The Speaker said, addressing Steve Lowry but looking at the chief of medicine. "If word does get out that Ezra's here, we say he's in for tests."

He turned to Steve. "The doctor says Ezra might have some long-term brain damage, maybe zeroed out completely."

"That's not at all uncommon in this kind of accident," the chief of medicine offered.

The Speaker stared the chief of medicine back into silence and then continued. "It's too late for a new candidate, Stevie. If Ezra doesn't wake up in a day or two, we're cooked. I don't want one word of this out until we know what we're doing. Got it?"

"Yes, sir."

"Okay, fine." He paused to check his watch. "It's not noon yet. I can still get my ass over to mass. Remember our deal, Doc," The Speaker said, and bounded out of the room. The door shut behind him, leaving the chief of medicine with The Speaker's assistant.

"Hi there," Steve beamed at him, extending his hand. "My name's Steve Lowry."

Chapter Fifteen

The aide to the governor of Florida was a young man named Skip Fletcher, the second most powerful man in the state.

"You don't think that Luther," the governor's aide said, referring to the late Senator Moss, "was actually going to let this daylight saving time business happen, do you?"

"I can assure you he was going to do exactly that," Laslo said. "He was going to do so by the time the presidential campaigns got under way."

"That's impossible."

"That's not the point," Miriam interjected, summoning all of her political skills. "What about the nomination? We're ready to play ball with your people, and we have something very substantial to offer," she said, trying to sound confident.

"You have something to offer, all right." Fletcher laughed. "You've got ten thousand gun nuts."

Laslo glared, but controlled himself. "Twenty thousand in Florida alone," he said.

"Gee, that's swell. What are you going to do with them? Have a parade?" Fletcher asked, contemptuously.

"Now, wait," Miriam said. "Forget about the gun nuts. We've got a strong set of local organizations that could be very helpful to the statewide ticket. There would be no question about our loyalty to the governor and the state party organization. We've demonstrated our fund-raising capability."

The governor's aide held up his hand to stop her. "Let me lay this out as clearly as possible. The governor is not going to appoint this man in front of me, whose name, I am told, is Dickie Vanderhaltz, to the Senate. The governor does not support universal daylight saving time. The governor supports the hotels and tourist attractions in Miami and Orlando and Palm Springs, because the hotels and the tourist attractions support him. Hotels and tourist attractions write big checks. You write pamphlets."

"We've got a national organization that can raise millions!" Laslo snapped.

"The Republican National Committee is a national organization that can raise millions, too, Schang. Which do you think the governor prefers?"

Miriam continued, businesslike. "Does the governor know whom he's going to appoint?"

"He's going to appoint Medwin Rojas, the majority leader of the State Assembly."

"But Rojas was planning to run for governor," Miriam said.

"Right, and the governor thinks that makes him a very good candidate for the Senate," the governor's aide said. He glanced at his watch. "Let me end our meeting with some advice." He gave them a patronizing smile. "Stay the hell out of this election. Right now, you're a crank group on a roll. If you get involved in this election, you're going to be a crank group on a slab. Your membership will stop paying dues. They'll stop reading your newsletters and attending your weird little conclaves. They will pick some other religion. Where will you be then?"

He leaned back in his seat and softened his tone. "You look like three intelligent people," he said, taking liberties with his impressions. "Go home and do something else. Or stay and work in Medwin's campaign, and you might get something out of it when he wins. But for heaven's sake, don't run against Medwin in the Republican primary. You'll be eaten alive."

Miriam could see that Laslo was fuming, and spoke before he could do something damaging. "I appreciate your time, Skip," she said, suddenly rising. "We're going to think about your advice."

"Good." The governor's aide smiled. "You won't regret it."

Dickie, Miriam, and Laslo went out onto the streets of downtown Tallahassee. The sun immediately seared through their clothing. "Look, there's a luncheonette across the street," Miriam said. "At least it's air-conditioned. Let's go sit down and figure this out."

It was mid-morning, between the breakfast and lunch rushes, so the luncheonette was empty. They collapsed into a booth in the rear, dropping briefcases and newspapers on the table in front of them. A demoralized silence hung about them.

"Well, I'm out of ideas," Miriam finally said.

Dickie did not need to announce that he was out of ideas. He was crushed with disappointment as well. Now that Miriam had seduced him into desiring it, the nomination had been plucked from his grasp.

"There must be something," Laslo said.

"We've got zilch to offer the governor, Laslo," Miriam replied. "The governor is not going to appoint Dickie to Moss's seat. Unless somebody else has anything to add, it's over."

"Why?" challenged Laslo. "Because the governor won't cooperate with us?"

"Yes, Laslo," Miriam said, exasperated. "You can talk about nature until you're blue in the face and you won't be able to change it. This is politics, Laslo, not *Wild Kingdom*."

Laslo rose to the challenge. "You may know something about politics, young lady, but let me teach you something about survival. Size doesn't guarantee survival. Power doesn't guarantee survival. Adaptation is the key to survival, the ability to find a niche in the scheme of things." He became more animated and certain of himself as he spoke. "That's how we got this far, don't you see? We had found our niche with Senator Moss. If we're going to thrive, then we've got to find a new niche." He stopped and his eyes seemed to focus far, far away.

"The environment abounds in niches," he continued. "Just because some little toady tells me he's uninterested in the burgeoning national movement for principled naturalism doesn't mean we're doomed to wither and fail." He was on his game again: Dickie and Miriam could both sense it. "Have you forgotten what we've accomplished in a few short months?" Dickie and Miriam were quiet now, giving Laslo the mental space he needed. "There is a niche for us," he assured them. "There's a niche for every species. All we have to do is find it, and we're going to. It's right underneath our noses, I tell you." And with that, his gaze alit on the newspaper that lay on the table, underneath his nose, exactly where he had predicted it would be. His eyes opened wide. "In fact," he said triumphantly, "it's right here."

He reached across the table and drew the newspaper closer. Across three columns at the top of the front page, the headline read:

COL. CODY CLARK TO SPEAK HERE TONIGHT
Evangelist/Consultant on Florida Tour

Chapter Sixteen

Thirty-odd years ago, Col. Cody Clark was an ordinary accountant seeking his M.B.A. in night classes, when his unit in the Army Reserve was dispatched, through bureaucratic error, to the tiny Antillean island of Castillaneta for the purpose of its liberation. He was glad to be assigned to such a wholly unanticipated locale, but was subsequently appalled to find out the mission involved securing the airport in Castilla, the tiny capital city, in the face of several battalions of communist troops said by military authorities to be stationed there and prepared to fight to the death. His unit was then to advance from the airport to seize and hold the island's two other points of strategic interest—the seat of government, formerly known as the Hilton, and the local franchise of Club Desire, a holiday encampment for American singles seeking chance sexual encounters.

A feeling of ever-constricting tightness gripped Col.—then, of course, only Corp.—Cody Clark's chest as a helicopter bore him to his rendezvous with history, and it is not hard to imagine the extent of his relief when he landed on the airport runway to find, rather than communist insurgents, only the ground crew and local constabulary, all deep in their midday sleep.

The airport thus secured, Corp. Cody Clark's unit opened a

lane to the beach, an easy task in the absence of any resistance save a gentle sea breeze. They were met by American landing craft bearing vehicles of every size, weight, and disposition, each carrying fresh troops into the nonexistent fray. The on-the-scene commanders dispatched a platoon to advance on Club Desire, where, intelligence reports suggested, several hundred vacationing Americans were being held hostage. Corp. Cody Clark was assigned to this detail, much to his glee, for he had considered vacationing at a Club Desire and would now have the chance to see one close up.

There were no communist insurgents holding American tourists hostage at Club Desire, as there were none anywhere on the island. In fact, Corp. Cody Clark's detail found little more than a calypso band and a few lethargic waiters carrying cocktails to the vacationers sunning on the beach. The commander of Corp. Cody Clark's unit, however, was unconvinced by these tranquil appearances and ordered his men to spread out and patrol the perimeter of the club in search of the enemy.

Corp. Cody Clark would have liked to lay down his gun and spend the rest of the invasion gazing at half-naked bodies, but was sent off into the nearby piney woods to search for insurgents. He had walked for ten minutes through peaceful groves of trees, leaving the beach far behind, when he saw a small shack in a clearing. He wet his lips pensively and considered the situation. With a grim sense of duty he maneuvered stealthily toward the shack, choosing an angle of approach that would not allow him to be seen from any of its small windows. He came up to the hut and cocked an ear. He heard a clumping sound inside, as if furniture was being moved, and then the sounds of voices, or at least one voice, speaking Spanish. Spanish, he thought, biting his lower lip as he considered the language's subversive implications.

He crawled around the corner of the shack. A few broken-down stairs led up to the door, ever so slightly ajar. He heard the Spanish voice again, and noted a second sound—not words, but a low moaning.

A sense of urgency overtook him. He looked about him. There was no one else there, friend nor foe. He reached to his belt and removed his service revolver, cocking it as slowly and deliberately as he could. Crouching low, he sprang up the steps.

He burst into the room but didn't process what he saw until he awoke a day or so later, because a moment after he saw it he was lying unconscious in a pool of his own blood. But when he finally got to see what he saw, what he saw was a young female American tourist atop a creaking cot, her eyes rolled up into her head, nakedly straddling one of the club's waiters, a young man of local origins, also naked save for a medal celebrating the virgin birth of the Mother of the Savior. She was bobbing up and down on him, her jiggling breasts dripping a mixture of perspiration and tanning oil. The waiter cried out at the interruption and, the instant he did, the young American woman saw Corp. Cody Clark, stopped her movement, reached for a sandal lying next to her, quickly and deftly snatched it up and hurled it right between Corp. Cody Clark's eyes.

Cody Clark thought he saw a girl with big breasts fucking a local, and wondered how this could be, amidst an insurgency, but suddenly some kind of flying object hit him in the face and sent him bouncing out the door and backward down the broken steps, jarring his right arm and setting off his service revolver, which delivered its charge squarely into Corp. Cody Clark's crotch with a loud crack.

The young American girl and the waiter scrambled to their feet and out the door to Corp. Cody Clark's side. She fell down on her knees, her hands pressed tensely against her face, as the waiter examined the situation, aghast.

"Madre!" the waiter exclaimed, his face paling with comprehension. "Thees man hahs bean chot in the deek!"

It was not an exact diagnosis, but it was as close to the mark as the errant bullet itself. Corp. Cody Clark awoke the next day in an army hospital. He was not the only casualty of the invasion—there were several cases of sunstroke and a number of severe hangovers—but he was certainly the most serious. As his consciousness slowly rekindled, he became aware of both the terrible discomfort in his groin and the group of men that hung over him.

"Corporal Clark," one of the men said loudly. "Corporal Clark, can you hear me?"

Corp. Cody Clark nodded as he tried to clear his head.

"Good," said the man. Corp. Cody Clark blinked. The man was in a general's uniform. "How do you feel, Corporal?"

"I—I'm okay," he said. His throat was dry and sore.

"Then you're okay," the general repeated approvingly.

"No," Corp. Cody Clark said as the pain in his groin resumed stabbing at him. A series of tubes ran in and out of his crotch. He tried to reposition himself, to lessen the pain, but a second man lurched forward to stop him.

"Please, Corporal," said the second man, a doctor. "You've sustained a serious injury and any sudden movements are going to be extremely painful."

"Jesus!" he moaned, regretting his sudden movement and slumping backwards in extreme pain. "What's happened to me?"

"Nothing that can't be overcome with therapy," the doctor said, patting his arm consolingly.

"What—what does that mean?"

"Don't you worry about that now," the general said sternly. "We've apprehended the insurrectionist that did this to you, let me assure you. And we're going to see to it that your valor in battle is recognized."

"What are you talking about?" Corp. Cody Clark moaned groggily, remembering. "There was this girl, she was fucking a waiter."

"A terrorist," the general spat. "It's not enough that they want to destabilize every freely elected government in the hemisphere, they have to victimize a defenseless American woman in the process."

"But she was on top."

"Spare me," the general said. "The young woman gave us all the details." He laughed. "You don't suppose that an American girl would run off to a shack in the woods to roll with a local like that, do you?" He smiled knowingly. "No, she gave us the whole story. You're a hero, young man."

Corp. Cody Clark felt sorry for the waiter but felt sorrier for himself as a sharp pain stabbed his groin. "Can I have something for the pain?"

"In a minute," the general said. "First, I have something very important to discuss with you. Later this afternoon, the President of the United States is coming to see you."

All of the men around Corp. Cody Clark's bed nodded admiringly.

"Me?" he said, startled by the news into sitting up.

"That's right," a man in a well-tailored blue suit said. "The president wants to thank the brave men and women who participated in the liberation of this island."

He grimaced as a bolt of agony seared through him. "Why? Why's he coming to see me?"

"Because you've been injured."

Corp. Cody Clark almost doubled over at the reminder. His groin felt as if it were on fire. "Jesus," he moaned. The doctor stepped in front of the man in the blue suit and gently eased him onto his back again. "Jesus!" he said again, and winced at the pain. "Do I still have a dick?"

"Technically? No," the doctor said.

"Look!" the man in the blue suit interrupted. "The president is going to be here in a few hours."

"But what about me!" Corp. Cody Clark pleaded. "What about my dick? Can't I have something for the pain?"

The man in the blue suit whirled toward him. "Could you just forget that for now?" he spat. "In a few hours you're going to meet the President of the United States. You can worry about your dick later!" He turned to the doctor and the general. "Would you excuse Corporal Clark and me for a moment?" he asked graciously, and they promptly complied. He turned back to Corp. Cody Clark, all formality gone. "What's your story, Clark? An accountant studying to be an M.B.A., right? Well, what do you think meeting the president is worth? Huh?" he prompted. "A bedside visit from the President of the United States? Well, I'll tell you. You're going to be a national hero."

Corp. Cody Clark's head swam. "What do I have to do?"

The man in the blue suit smiled. "Just meet him, really. Let him thank you for liberating the island, and for capturing that insurgent."

"What insurgent?" Corp. Cody Clark asked between winces.

"That fellow in the shack."

"I think it was a waiter fucking that girl."

The man in the blue suit smirked. "He was part of a network of insurgents that had infiltrated Club Desire, prepared to seize it as part of a larger plan to replace the government. By the way, don't say 'fuck' to the president."

Corp. Cody Clark groaned. "Fuck! I've got to have something for the pain."

"Okay," sighed the man in the blue suit. "But only if you'll do as we say."

"Anything," Corp. Cody Clark said, and so the pain went away and the president arrived in its place. Meeting the President of the United States eventually proved to be magic for Corp. Cody Clark. After his discharge, he was passed among the president's social circle, the hero dinner guest, and was sent out to speak on patriotic occasions. Even his business school professors treated him better, allowing him to earn his degree without the laboriousness of attending class or taking exams. All doors opened to him upon his graduation, but Corp. Cody Clark found that the best market for a warrior–business consultant was among the religious right wing, white people with small minds and stiff hair who appreciated a nice-looking man who had given the nation his all (or at least his most important part, although they were spared the specifics) and could help them with their finances.

Corp. Cody Clark, who did not much care whom he knew so long as they could get him ahead, appreciated them as much as they appreciated him. He developed a clientele amongst their number and started to work various Pentecostal themes into his business consulting. And, as he found sincerity to be an effective sales tool, he came to believe the things he said. He began appearing on Christian television stations, touting a Heavenly Buy List of undervalued stocks on the New York Stock Exchange, and explaining the biblical origins of his favorite economic proposals. "As you sow, so shall you reap, the Good Book says," he told them, "and yet there are those who would take the capital gains that are the fruit of the investor's labors and tax them away at the same rate as is taxed the wages that are rendered unto Caesar. Is it any wonder that the vineyards and the fields of our industries do not multiply when they are denied the full measure of their worth?" After a while, he came to believe it.

His public ate it up. He served on corporate boards and preached in public prayer gatherings. He used his television show as a springboard for even greater success. He was promoted to the rank of honorary colonel in the National Guard, turning down a general's rank to create an illusion of modesty, and to preserve the alliteration in his name that he found so appealing. He became a one-man empire and his coffers grew even fuller. He could do anything he pleased.

"I can do anything I please," Col. Cody Clark told Laslo. "Why should I want to be president?"

He was having his hair cut in his hotel suite when Laslo, Dickie, and Miriam came to see him.

"Well, Colonel," said Miriam. Wouldn't you like to be president?"

"I never considered it," Col. Cody Clark said as he began to. "What does it pay?"

"It's not exactly the money," Miriam said, "as much as it is, well, the prestige of the thing, the opportunity to lead the country." She was confused, unprepared to explain why being president was desirable.

"Well, that's all well and good." Col. Cody Clark nodded. His barber lifted his hands until Col. Cody Clark's good-looking, fiftyish head stopped moving. "What else does it get me?"

Miriam's eyebrows fluttered as she tried to think of what might appeal to him. "Well, there's an awfully large amount of, uh . . . goodwill that you can generate in that kind of position. You get lots of exposure, publicity, that kind of thing."

"I get that now," Col. Cody Clark said matter-of-factly. "And isn't it a lot of work?"

"Oh, no," she insisted. "Not at all. It's really only as much work as you want it to be."

"I suppose," Col. Cody Clark said, unconvinced.

"There's a house thrown in, too."

"Still, I don't quite see myself—"

"Now wait a minute," Laslo said, jumping in, much to Col. Cody Clark's surprise. "I'm surprised that a man as formidable as yourself is looking at this in conventional terms."

"What do you mean by that?"

Laslo focused his eyes on him unflinchingly. "I'll give it to you in one word. Cost-sharing. If you run for president, the government will pay you to promote yourself."

"It will?" he asked with a tone of pleasant surprise.

"Yes," Miriam nodded, following Laslo's lead. "Tax free."

"But I don't pay any taxes as is."

"Sure, right now you pay no taxes as a religious institution, and that's fine. But if you qualify for matching funds, the federal government will give you a new dollar for each tax-free dollar you raise."

"But I could raise millions of dollars if I wanted to."

Laslo nodded. "Of course you can. So can we, frankly. But there's lots more where that comes from. Our Principled Naturalist Omnibus Salvation Act has features in it that are going to attract plenty of new money. Big money." He leaned toward Col. Cody Clark and spoke confidentially. "What if tornadoes and hurricanes were no longer classified as natural disasters?"

"What do you mean?"

"Exactly that. What if they weren't classified as disasters? Think about how much money insurance companies would save. And how grateful they'd be."

Col. Cody Clark considered this point. "That's very interesting," he said, waving the barber away.

Laslo reeled him in like a sport fish. "If you run for president, your money makes money. So what I propose is symbiosis— what you might call a joint venture, I suppose. Let's ally our political associations. You support Dickie's Senate candidacy and we'll support your presidential campaign. We'll raise our funds through your organization and they'll immediately earn a return of 100 percent. We'll split the return with you. From an economic point of view, it can't miss. And, of course, there's the issue of introducing each of us to the other's following. You know, there are plenty of principled naturalists out there, all of them with portfolios."

Col. Cody Clark's brow furrowed. "I follow you."

"If you follow me, you agree with me," Laslo said evenly.

"Is what you're proposing legal?"

"It sounds legal. Besides, that's really a matter for the lawyers, isn't it?"

"And I don't have to win, do I?" he asked.

"Not if you don't want to," said Laslo.

"Do you think I could win?"

"I think you could make a fortune."

"Is there any other way to win?" Col. Cody Clark asked with a smile.

An hour later they were on their way out of Col. Cody Clark's hotel suite, a presidential candidate in hand. Miriam watched the numbers light up in descending order as the elevator took them to the lobby. "It's going to be hard to get him on the ballot in all fifty states, you know," she said.

"As long as he's on the ballot in Florida," Laslo replied.

"But he's got to raise money in each state to qualify for matching funds."

"Don't worry," said Laslo. "We'll raise it."

Dickie gaped at the two of them. "Does this mean he's going to run for president? I mean, did we just talk him into it?"

Laslo turned to him. "Yes, that's right."

His incredulity got the better of him. "How do you think of things like that?"

"Oh, you know how it is, Dickie," he said. "Adapt or die."

Chapter Seventeen

Congressman Rollo Plank (D-Oh., 10 C.D.), the Speaker of the House, was an imposing man of immense vitality and insatiable appetites. He was from Ohio and carried this burden proudly on his square shoulders, in the sprawling expanse of his wide ass, in the lumpy nose that led him into everybody else's business, and in the cocky swagger with which he moved all of these assets about. He grew up in Columbus, and at an early age became fixated on the two-story statue of Big Buckeye—the football player who stood atop the hamburger stand opposite the main gates of Ohio State University. He grew to feel an overpowering desire to be Big Buckeye, to be larger and more powerful than everybody and everything around him. He committed himself to a youthful training regimen that included weight lifting, calisthenics, and field practice, and, when he had done all of that, beating his head against a wall until the reeling and blurry sensations were at their peak and then reciting the multiplication tables.

By the time he reached OSU, he had mastered this ability, and he became the captain of the Ohio State University football team. As he left daily team practice at Buckeye Stadium, he would stop in the concrete runway and violently smash his helmeted head into the wall. His teammates, however weary, would gather to watch as he inflicted these blows upon himself while he recited perfectly the contents of their playbook. "35DA. Fall back, look for middle linebacker. Guard stunts left. Keep middle linebacker to my left. Trail halfback for fumble recovery. 35DB. Same play, right." Coaches would lecture freshmen: "Do you see Plank? Are you watching? Do you think he's ever going to forget what he's supposed to be doing out there?" His fellow Buckeyes could only nod in amazement.

When he arrived in Washington, Congressman Plank found the Congress was an institution that would reward handsomely a person with the ability to recite football plays while reeling from blows to the head. His talent served him well in floor and committee proceedings, and in soliciting support and favors from his colleagues. It also attracted the attention of the previous Speaker, who cultivated Congressman Plank with a series of important assignments, culminating in his appointment as majority whip. When the previous Speaker chose to retire, the caucus found itself weary of a life without punishment and yearned to be pushed around a little in the interest of the common good. Congressman Plank was the obvious choice. "Rollo," mused the chairman of the Committee on Spending. "Nothing throws the guy. He could recite the numbers of every outstanding bill while you beat him on the head with a hammer." That was the kind of respect that Rollo Plank commanded.

The Speaker enjoyed being the Speaker. He liked the prestige of his position and the gamesmanship of politics, but most of all he liked pushing people around. He would meet the recalcitrance of any member hesitant to join the fold with a fierce glare and a hunch of his huge shoulders, bending his towering 260 pounds around them with a menacing innuendo that was inevitably rewarded by submission. He enforced party discipline with relish, furthering the legislative interests of those who were loyal to the leadership and thwarting those who weren't.

*   *   *

The Speaker sat in the conference room in his inner office in the Capitol. Before him were Steve Lowry, Buddy Youngblood together with an unknown associate, and Fred Coleman, who represented Senator Don Green, America's Friend, the Democratic candidate for president. The Speaker reached over to a side table and retrieved a crystal decanter and a set of glasses. "Who's for a drink?" The Speaker asked, raising his hand at the wrist to demonstrate the right response. Everyone at the table declined. "Fine then," said The Speaker, pouring himself two fingers of single-malt Scotch and draining them. "Who's for another?" he boomed and repeated the process. "Okay," he grunted. "Let's go."

Steve Lowry explained to the group what they already knew. Ezra Wheezle was in bad shape. He was yet to wake up, and if he did, he probably would not know the difference. "That leaves us with the issue," Steve Lowry continued, "of what to do about the race in the Pennsylvania Fourth C.D. There's not much time left and Ezra was in a dead heat despite thirty-odd years in office. Any new candidate we send in is going to lose ground, and affect the vote all across the ticket. It could mean a ten-point swing in the presidential election in that district. Do you know what a ten-point swing in that district means in votes?"

Fred Coleman nodded. "About twenty thousand votes," he said.

"President Hoak himself only won the state by fifty thousand votes," Steve Lowry said.

"What are we going to do?" Fred Coleman said in despair.

The Speaker took a moment to enjoy Coleman's helplessness, then said, "What we're going to do is field a candidate. Now, as to whom, I think the choice is obvious." The choice was by no means obvious, so everybody turned to The Speaker to find out who the obvious choice was. "We're going to run Ezra Wheezle."

"But you can't run Ezra Wheezle," Fred Coleman whined. "He's in a coma."

"Well, that's the kind of personal attack we can expect from the opposition," The Speaker said, "but we owe it to his constituents to stress the positive side. A record of three decades of service. Distinguished legislator, a man who fights for his district. Seniority. Familiarity. Dependability. Convenience. Frankly, he retains all the advantages of incumbency, even in a coma."

"But how are you going to build a campaign around a man who's lying in a hospital bed like a vegetable?"

The Speaker raised his hand for silence. "That's a more pressing issue, and that's why I've asked Buddy Youngblood from Message Concepts, the campaign consulting firm, to be here." He motioned toward Buddy and the man sitting with him. "Buddy, would you mind taking over?"

"I'd be pleased to, Rollo," he said, rubbing his pudgy palms together. "First, I'd like to introduce my associate, Dr. Fabian Hostetler, a professor of perceptual mechanics at New York University and director of political psychology research at Message Concepts. Fabian and I have been giving some thought to this problem and we think we have a solution. I'm going to let him do the explaining, Rollo, if you don't mind."

The psychologist was a tall man with a stiff posture and glasses, with hair divided into small mounds on either side of a center part. He smiled briefly and rose to insert a videocassette in a VCR beneath a television on a rolling cart before speaking. "My work in perceptual mechanics shows that it is possible to arrange an array of perceptual inputs in a pattern that allows the nucleus of cognition to be diverted from the ostensible center acquired through socialization, or in some cases, mere repetition." He set the machine and looked up at The Speaker.

"This is an ad for a man who was elected to the State Senate in Nebraska last year. There was something special about his campaign." He turned the tape on. "Watch the perceptual mechanics in this television spot. It opens very nicely, no hint of what it's about." The first scene was of small animals skittering about the forest floor, scavenging acorns. "Now notice how straightforward the message is."

The narration began. *"Do politicians sometimes seem small to you? Do they seem preoccupied with their own survival instead of yours? Do they seem unable to solve their own problems, let alone our country's?"*

"Now, watch this sequence," Dr. Hostetler interrupted. On screen, the camera's eye started to rise, tracking the majestic trunks of the hardwoods. Orchestral music swelled in a long crescendo until the camera reached the canopy of the trees, just in time to capture the sight of an eagle spreading its wings and taking flight.

"Some politicians don't view the world from ground level," the narrator's voice resumed as the camera followed the soaring eagle. *"Some politicians think their job is to see the whole landscape, to expand their vision and challenge our imaginations. The question is: who would you rather have represent you?"* The eagle banked as the question was posed, and in a final close-up landed in its nest once again. *"Donald Stafford wants to be your state senator,"* the narrator concluded, *"and he can be, with your help. Vote for him on November 7."* With that, the tape ended and the screen erupted into a blizzard of gray static.

"Now," Dr. Hostetler said, "think for a minute about what you just saw. What was conspicuously absent?" Puzzlement came over the faces at the table. "The candidate!" the psychologist exclaimed. "Where was this man named Stafford? What does he look like? What does he sound like? Is *he* in a coma? This ad conclusively proves that you don't need the candidate to run a campaign. The only thing the candidate contributed was his name, and that's all that counts, since the name is all there is in the voting booth. The candidate behind the name is superfluous. In fact, a candidate can sometimes do best by not being seen or heard. This is particularly true for an unpopular candidate, or in our case, a comatose one. Showing him only reminds voters that he's in a coma, which is usually perceived as a negative."

"Perhaps we could we get an actor to stand in for him, deliver his speeches," The Speaker suggested.

"No, not an actor. But you can use stand-ins, someone who stands *for* him. A human version of the eagle in the ad. Somebody who's believable, trustworthy, and capable of inspiring confidence. Especially back in the district."

"Hey, wait a minute," Buddy Youngblood interjected. "There's a kid in Ezra's office, a local kid, good-looking, solid citizen. And—get this—he's a local hero. When he was a kid, he saved a girl from drowning at a community picnic. While Ezra was giving a speech, no less. Jumped into a raging river, the whole thing, just like a movie."

"Lenny Keeler!" Steve Lowry exclaimed.

"Keeler, that's it," Buddy agreed.

"And you would actually put this kid on the stump?"

"Why not?" Dr. Hostetler replied. "We'd coach him, of course, but he'd probably do just fine. He'd bring word from Congressman Wheezle to the voters, sort of a messenger from the bedside of the great man himself."

The Speaker reached out and poured himself another drink as he thought. Finally, he said, "I like it. Let's go make it work."

"This is the most off-the-wall thing I ever heard," Fred Coleman protested. "No matter how good a campaign you put together you can't run a vegetable for Congress!"

"Nonsense," said The Speaker, banging back his drink with a satisfied smack. "You can run anyone for Congress. That's what makes this country what it is today."

Steve Lowry stepped into the anteroom of Congressman Wheezle's office and unfolded a piece of paper. "I'm here to read a statement regarding Congressman Wheezle's medical condition," he said to the assembled group of reporters. "Congressman Wheezle is out of danger and it is anticipated that he will soon speak to you. Nothing has happened to change any political plans on Congressman Wheezle's part. Congressman Wheezle is ill, but he is not uncomfortable, and he does not intend to withdraw from the race. Specifically, the rumors that Congressman Wheezle has had a heart attack are untrue. Future statements will provide greater details on these matters, within the bounds of respect for Congressman Wheezle's personal dignity and that of his family." He looked up from his paper. "Are there any questions?"

The first reporter wanted facts. "Is Congressman Wheezle in a coma?"

"I've already read our statement," said Steve Lowry coldly, "and described Congressman Wheezle's medical condition."

"But is it true that he's in a coma?"

"As our statement indicated, we do not intend to give out any further medical details out of respect for Congressman Wheezle's personal dignity and that of his family. As the statement also indicated, Congressman Wheezle is out of danger and we anticipate that he will speak to you soon. And as we further said in our statement, nothing has happened to change Congressman Wheezle's political plans."

The second reporter was more accusing. "Is it true that Congressman Wheezle is unconscious?"

"Please, I don't want to—"

"Is it true—"

"The questions you're asking are very personal—"

But the second reporter was insistent. "Can you verify that Congressman Wheezle has not said as much as a word, nor opened his eyes, nor given any other sign of life since his accident?"

"As our statement said, Congressman Wheezle is ill, but he is not in danger, he is not uncomfortable, and he does not intend to withdraw from the race. I don't see what's to be gained by going over whatever the personal details of his illness might be."

The reporter from television was contentious. "Is Congressman Wheezle a vegetable?"

"I find that question to be demeaning to Congressman Wheezle."

"It wasn't meant to be demeaning to Congressman Wheezle."

"Well, that's how I find it," Steve Lowry snapped. "Next question."

"But what if Congressman Wheezle has the same qualifications to be a congressman as a tossed salad or a baked potato?" asked a reporter from a political journal.

"I'm not going to dignify that question with an answer."

"But is it true?"

"Next question."

The fourth reporter probed. "How do we know that Congressman Wheezle is alive?"

"I just read you his statement, didn't I?"

"But anybody could have written that statement."

"I find it hard to imagine that anybody on Congressman Wheezle's staff would take it upon himself to write a press release and sign Congressman Wheezle's name to it without Congressman Wheezle's approval."

"But did you?"

"I did not write this press release."

"Who did?"

"It was written by a member of Congressman Wheezle's staff."

"Who?"

"I don't know offhand."

"Did Congressman Wheezle dictate it?"

"You'll have to ask him."

"When will we be able to ask him?"

"As the statement indicated, soon."

"Then you refuse to confirm that Congressman Wheezle is unable to speak to us now?"

"I didn't refuse to confirm that. I refuse to refuse to confirm that."

"Can we send in a pool photographer for one shot of Wheezle?"

"Congressman Wheezle is ill and deserves a rest."

"Just one picture."

"Congressman Wheezle is ill and deserves a rest."

"Come on," whined an older reporter in a brown corduroy sport coat. "They took a picture of Eisenhower in his hospital bed."

"Eisenhower had a heart attack. As Congressman Wheezle's statement makes clear, Congressman Wheezle has not had a heart attack. I don't see any parallel whatsoever."

"Then what's wrong with him?"

"Congressman Wheezle is ill, but he's not uncomfortable. I won't otherwise comment out of respect for Congressman Wheezle's family."

"But then how do we know that Congressman Wheezle didn't have a heart attack?"

"The statement makes it very clear that Congressman Wheezle has not had a heart attack."

The television reporter bristled. "Can we ask if there are any other illnesses that Congressman Wheezle doesn't have? Maybe we can narrow it down to the one he does have."

"I'm not here to play games with you," Steve Lowry said peevishly. "Are there any other questions?"

"Can we speak to Congressman Wheezle?"

"Would you like me to take a sick man and drag him out of his hospital bed just so you can take pictures of him and ask him how he's feeling?"

"Then you will confirm that Congressman Wheezle is gravely ill. Can we quote you on that?"

"You can quote me as saying that Congressman Wheezle has served in the Congress of the United States with great distinction for over thirty years and that he merits reelection by the people of the Fourth Congressional District of Pennsylvania in the most absolute terms. You can quote me as saying that Congressman Wheezle has distinguished himself as a legislator and a statesman and that he is not going to allow any minor medical setback to obstruct him from providing the people of the

Fourth Congressional District with the kind of representation they deserve."

"But what's wrong with him?"

"I've already answered that," Steve Lowry snapped. "Next question."

Chapter Eighteen

But you *have* to advertise," Miriam explained as patiently as she could. "That's what campaigning is all about. Getting the word out."

"But I already get The Word out."

"Not The Word. The word."

"Oh." Col. Cody Clark rubbed his chin pensively. "I don't like this at all. All advertising means is expenditures. If you ask me, we'd be better off just keeping the campaign money, from a dollars-and-cents point of view. The government's going to match every dollar I bring in. That's a pretty good business right there, and nobody's done a lick of advertising yet. The power of God is at work."

"But you have to get a certain percentage of the national vote to qualify for the matching money," she persisted.

"You do?" Col. Cody Clark was disconcerted. "Nobody said anything about that."

"Relax," Miriam said. "You've just about got it sewn up. If half of your regular television audience votes for you, you'll have it easily. But a presidential election provides you with the opportunity to reach groups that don't read your newsletters or watch you on television. And frankly, Dickie is in this election to win, and our association with you makes sense only insofar as you help us to promote both his candidacy and yours. That's why we've been diverting our campaign funds to you."

Col. Cody Clark nodded solemnly. "I see your point. I suppose that I'm not above some advertising." He pondered for a moment. "Okay, we'll give them advertising. We'll tell the people that God is our Father and our Banker, and He wants us to be saved and He wants us to be solvent. That's what we'll tell them."

Laslo had been listening and now spoke up. "I'm with you, Colonel, but I can't help thinking you're distracting yourself with this salvation and solvency business. Frankly, while it sounds good, if you can't find it in the principles of nature, then it's not worth finding."

"I appreciate your view, Laslo," Col. Cody Clark said, "but I'm hard pressed to see the connection between the financial world and nature—squirrels, bunnies, that sort of thing. What's the point?"

"The point is nature's principles," Laslo answered with the slightest touch of frustration. "Nature teaches us how to govern society through its examples."

"Perhaps," Col. Cody Clark said, taking up the challenge. "But the Lord tells us how to manage our lives and assets. Jesus tells us to throw our bread upon the water and it will return to us increased manyfold, implying a dramatic rate of return. And with prudent asset management, Jesus fed the multitudes with one fish and one loaf. That is what Jesus tells us about investing. What does nature say?"

Laslo wrinkled his brow for a moment, and suddenly a look of clarity came over him. "Well, in nature, the equivalent of financial assets are caloric assets, and all animals store caloric assets when they carry their embryonic young. If we wanted, for example, to increase the amount our society saves, we could apply that principle. It's obvious, once you think about it. When do people save? When they expect a child. That's why it's called a nest egg, right?"

Col. Cody Clark was overcome with a look of realization. "Why, that's exactly right! It's the unborn child, isn't it? The unborn child is the key to savings!"

Laslo smiled. "When you look at it in terms of nature's principles, I suppose it is," he said.

"Of course! That's exactly the point! We're talking about the financial life of the unborn child! Parents save for their unborn children, but they're denied the full benefits of tax provisions related to savings and portfolio decisions because the law doesn't recognize the fact that their unborn child is a person!"

"What are you talking about?" Miriam asked.

"Yeah, I don't get it," Dickie added, relieved that someone else was as confused as he.

"The financial rights of the unborn!" Col. Cody Clark said excitedly. "All of the estate and gift tax provisions are geared to the born child, which discriminates against the unborn child. Think of it. What if the parents of unborn children could give their unborn children gifts, or establish estates for them? They'd be able to transfer assets that create significant tax liabilities away from themselves and create tax-free trusts for the unborn child."

Dickie was still confused. "Can an unborn child have an estate?"

"Why not?" asked Col. Cody Clark. "If an unborn child is a person, then why should that person's temporary inability to sign a piece of paper prevent him from having assets? I think we're on to something here, Laslo, my friend," he said, beaming in satisfaction at this new vision of the ways of the Lord.

Lenny walked nervously through the corridors of the Longworth House Office Building until he reached the office of Congressman Senior Younger, Jr. A middle-aged woman sat in the anteroom. She looked up at him as if surprised to have a visitor. "Can I help you?"

"I'm here to see Congressman Younger."

The woman's surprise quickly gave way to her instinctive desire to let no one near the congressman. "Is he expecting you?" she asked, confident of the answer.

"No, he's not. But he gave me this," Lenny explained, and handed her the business card the congressman had given him when they met in the tunnels beneath the Capitol. She turned it over and saw Senior Younger, Jr.'s, signature, upside down and diagonal. Her expression changed, as if he had just said the secret password.

"I'll see if he's available for you," she said politely and dispatched herself to the inner office. She was only gone a moment when she returned to usher him in.

Senior Younger, Jr., was sitting in the center of the room in his wheelchair, a newspaper strewn over the blanket in his lap. He smiled when Lenny entered. "Lenny, my boy," he said, reaching up for his hand. "It's wonderful to see you." He tapped the chair next to his with his cane. "Sit right here. Thank you for those files you sent over. They're whipping my rear end back in Idaho with this equipment-that-doesn't-work tax credit, you know. Some Coalition for Economic Directions, or something like that, has been funneling money into my district for door-to-door work and television spots, and they keep on hitting me on that issue. I'm twenty points down and dropping," he said.

"I'm sorry to hear that. But if those files didn't help, what can you do?"

"Plenty," Senior Younger, Jr., said, snapping his cane before him as if to smite an imagined foe. "I'll show those scoundrels. As soon as I figure out my secret plan they're going to be sorry they fooled with me, I promise you." He coughed into his fist and drew back into his chair. "They're not going to put me in a home," he said with quiet determination. "But what about you?" he asked, gracefully changing the subject. "Tell me why you've come."

"I need to talk to you about Congressman Wheezle."

"Ezra! I heard he's in the hospital." He shook his head. "What happened?"

"He had a stroke when he was filming a campaign commercial. He's in a coma and they don't know if he'll ever wake up."

Senior Younger, Jr., rubbed his chin as he considered this news. "That's never good," he concluded. It never ceased to amaze him when the catastrophes that should have been his happened to everybody else. But it would be impossible to live to 114 without feeling like that somewhere along the way.

"Yes, but as if that's not bad enough, they're going to keep it a secret."

"A secret? That's a big secret to keep. Who's running Ezra's office?"

"Steve Lowry from The Speaker's office. And Buddy Youngblood's handling the campaign."

"And what's your part in this?"

"Well, I'm supposed to go to Walcott Falls and make appearances for him. I really don't know what to do. He's in a coma. It doesn't make sense."

"It doesn't make sense because you're trying to make sense of it," Congressman Younger said with sudden peevishness. "It doesn't make sense if you think that elected representatives ought to be able to think, speak, and stay awake through most of the day. Hell, I'd only give myself, say, one and a half out of three on that score. But it does make sense if you think about how desperate Rollo is to hold on to Ezra's seat. You're from Ezra's hometown. Name another candidate who's as well known as Ezra back there."

Lenny thought for a moment. "I guess I can't."

"You see? He's really the only possible candidate. Ezra's got everything. A voting record. Name recognition. Long-standing relationships with key constituencies. He's a natural, even in a coma."

"But what should I do?" Lenny asked. "It doesn't seem right. What should I do?"

Senior Younger, Jr., turned to him, startled. "Why, whatever you want to do, of course."

"I suppose I was hoping you'd have some advice."

"Okay, then," Senior Younger, Jr., said obligingly. "Here's some advice: be careful."

Lenny snorted. "I am being careful."

Senior Younger, Jr., laid his hand on Lenny's forearm. "Good. Now be ten times more careful than that." Lenny looked for a smile on his face, but there was none.

Chapter Nineteen

President Honeycutt sat in the Oval Office with his two trusted advisors. His two trusted advisors enjoyed sitting in the Oval Office; more so, in fact, than President Honeycutt did. President Honeycutt enjoyed being president, of course, but it was a pleasure he felt most keenly when contrasted with the mundane nature of the things the president actually did. President Honeycutt would brush his teeth fastidiously when he woke up every morning and gaze into the mirror contemplating the fact that he was not just any middle-aged and unattractive man brushing his teeth, but the President of the United States, dutifully dispatching the precursors of tartar and plaque from the First Bicuspids. Sometimes he would remove the toothbrush from his mouth and contemplate his countenance from within his presidential jammies, as if he were an oil painting brought to life, his image augmented by the small stream of foaming greenish toothpaste dribbling from the corner of his sternly set mouth. Life for President Honeycutt became the dialectic experience of simultaneously being and observing. He had lived a balanced life, but once he stepped into the Oval Office it all changed, for at the peak, the landscape is transformed. At the peak, there is no more up, no more terrain, no more land. Beyond the peak there is only the infinite blue expanse of sky. And so President Honeycutt trained his eyes on the only thing that he could see at the summit—himself.

His trusted advisors, however, looked up and saw the president, and in the reflection of his glassy eyes they saw themselves as magnificent puppeteers. They awoke in the morning and brushed their teeth and got out of their jammies and ate their breakfast with undiluted enthusiasm so that they could be done with these tasks and make their way to the Oval Office, where the great decisions that excited them so tremendously awaited. They had started as hangers-on of the most common type, toadies who tended to the affairs of Governor Herbert Honeycutt, when lightning struck and Wade Hoak chose him as his running mate.

Vice President Honeycutt had been a businesslike and serviceable vice president, but when President Hoak gave to him the reins of power he became the reclusive and self-absorbed president he now was. He spent most of his days in the Oval Office where his two trusted advisors briefed him on the nation's business and international developments, tides and currents on Capitol Hill, news from the departments and agencies, and what was on television, a medium upon which President Honeycutt became progressively more fixated. As his presidency continued, he came to watch television at every opportunity, each time any newsworthy event came galloping across the lens. He came to like watching it more than being on it, to enjoy monitoring events more than making them. He trudged through his daily activities in the hope that one of his aides would tell him that there was a matter of pressing importance on the television. He would then have the excuse to turn away from the events confronting him and turn toward the television's electronic solace.

He was in the midst of a briefing by his national security advisor when his two aides entered the Oval Office, excitedly informing him that Col. Cody Clark was on television at that very moment, holding a live news conference. President Honeycutt nodded solemnly and advised the national security advisor to return to his office and wait there until he was summoned again. He then turned on his television to see Col. Cody Clark, together with Dickie Vanderhaltz, facing an eager crowd of reporters from behind a lectern that bore a sign promoting both their candidacies.

Col. Cody Clark began to speak in his characteristically composed cadence. *"Dr. Vanderhaltz and I have come together today to inaugurate a new initiative that will capture the imaginations of all Americans as surely as has Dr. Vanderhaltz's universal daylight saving time proposal, which I earnestly support. Our proposal, which we call the Life before Birth Trust and Estate Plan, would extend the right of financial life to those individuals who have not yet been born. Specifically, our proposal would allow individuals to begin trust accounts and other relevant estate provisions applicable to minors for their unborn children, beginning at conception. We feel that this amendment would redress the widespread economic discrimination against those children who, through no fault of their own, have yet to be born. I need not tell this audience that the morally bankrupt dichotomy between the unborn and born child creates horrifying incentives to shorten terms of gestation when they come into conflict with current tax laws. Clearly, unless we are willing to endure a series of human tragedies, we must redress this grievous wrong. I call on President Honeycutt and the Democratic candidate for president, Senator Don Green, to join me in a tripartisan effort to make this proposal a law immediately."*

Dickie rose and stood next to Col. Cody Clark. He wore a serious, if not grim, expression that Miriam had helped him develop in front of a mirror. *"Any questions?"* he asked.

"I've got a question," President Honeycutt exclaimed. "What the hell is going on here?"

"It sounds as if Clark wants to extend property rights to the unborn," said the first trusted advisor.

"I know what it sounds like," President Honeycutt said, exasperated. "What are we supposed to do about it?"

"Do about it? Why, nothing," the second trusted advisor smirked. "Let him go out and hang himself with this."

"I'm not so sure," President Honeycutt said. "Maybe he's on to something. Maybe I should respond."

"Oh, no," dismissed the first trusted advisor. "It wouldn't be presidential."

"What should I do then?" President Honeycutt asked.

"Stay right here and be the president, of course," the first trusted advisor explained, as the second trusted advisor nodded in agreement.

"Right here?"

"Absolutely."

President Honeycutt contemplated his trusted advisors' advice. "All right, then," he said tentatively, turning back toward the television.

"Trust us, Mr. President," the first trusted advisor said. "You've got nothing to worry about."

In the weeks and then months following Congressman Wheezle's accident, Lenny's life became more and more centered on the campaign in Walcott Falls, and his days became an endless and repetitive stream of events to which he was chaperoned by Buddy Youngblood. He recited Buddy's carefully constructed speeches to carefully chosen groups of people, he answered questions with carefully prepared answers, and he shook hands with whomever was put in front of him. He carried with him index cards wherever he went, with lists of catch phrases to use when he "made a few remarks." *I'm pleased to bring you a message from our town's First Citizen, Congressman Ezra T. Wheezle, who sends you his regards and asks for your support from his hospital bed in Washington, D.C.*

"Sit down," Buddy said to him one night, back at the hotel. "I've got very good news. Don Green is coming to Walcott Falls a week before the election and you're going to speak at his rally. You're going to get national coverage."

"I'm going to what?"

"Speak at Don Green's rally here in Walcott Falls," Buddy repeated. He looked at Lenny's expression as it evolved in response to this news. "What's the problem? You don't think that I'd put you in over your head, do you? Don't worry. You'll be able to tell your grandchildren that you spoke at a rally for the President of the United States!"

Lenny was silent.

"Well, what do you think?"

"Buddy, I'm not sure," he said, getting up from his chair.

"Lenny, we're in a war, we all have to do everything we can between now and November 5 to win this thing. Ezra's plus-minus spread is growing, and now Don Green needs you to introduce him here in your hometown. We're so close, Lenny. We have to keep going."

Lenny nodded and relented. But for perhaps the first time, he really and truly wished that Congressman Wheezle was not in a coma.

The television screen was filled with the face of a young woman with a mournful expression. She looked at the camera and began to speak.

"Warren said that if our baby was born before New Year's Eve, we could give him the legal limit in gifts, and retroactively assign him a portfolio of our equities that we hadn't held long enough to realize capital gains, and by doing so credit all of the taxable income to Junior. I was foolish, and I agreed. Soon, he had me walking the floor at all hours of the night, and sleeping with my legs down and my head up. On Christmas he gave me a jump rope and said that the amount we stood to make by having the baby that week was over a hundred times what we would pay the hospital for the delivery. 'Where else can you find that kind of return on investment?' Warren asked.

"So I did it.

"And I lost my child."

Tears began to well in her eyes as the camera pulled back and a narrator's voice was heard.

"Don't let the capricious distinction between the born and the unborn continue to endanger both our children and our nation's competitiveness. Vote for Col. Cody Clark, the Salvation and Solvency candidate for President of the

United States. And in Florida, vote for Dr. Dickie Vanderhaltz for United States senator."

President Honeycutt furiously pressed a button on his remote control unit, turning the television screen in the Oval Office to black. "Did you see that?" he demanded of his two trusted advisors. "This nonsense is sweeping the country as surely as daylight saving time did! Do you know what the newspapers are full of? Tax babies! Stories about tax babies, babies born to beat the tax laws!" His face flushed with anger. "Am I in the paper? Am I on TV?" he asked with dripping sarcasm. "No. I'm only the President of the United States. But Col. Cody Clark is on TV because he wants to save the poor babies from the tax system. And Don Green, the little twerp, is on TV because he's America's Friend. Whose friend am I? The clowns who want the equipment-that-doesn't-work tax credit?"

"What about President Hoak?" asked the second trusted advisor.

"Wade won't even return my phone calls anymore!" President Honeycutt snapped. He opened the center drawer of the presidential desk and extracted a slip of paper ripped from a legal pad. "See this? This is his phone number in Aruba. I've called twice a week for the past two weeks. I don't know where Wade is! What the hell am I going to do?"

"Don't worry," the first trusted advisor said with a blasé tone. "It's all taken care of."

"All taken care of?" President Honeycutt repeated incredulously. "We've been slipping since Labor Day. This is a three-way race and it's only three weeks away! Our campaign isn't going anywhere!"

The first trusted advisor laughed in an attempt to convince President Honeycutt that his campaign was progressing nicely and that he, the first trusted advisor, had it all in hand. "Mr. President," he said casually, "there's nothing to be concerned about. We've got a hundred million dollars and we're going to saturate the airwaves from now until election day. Every poll shows us in the lead. The fact is, we're a stone-cold lock."

"That's absolutely right," said the second trusted advisor. "Nothing's going to stop us. This tax baby thing has no staying power. Show me one tax baby! We'll demand that he come up with solid evidence. You'll see. He'll fold like a house of cards. We've got the fix on Don Green and we can handle Col. Cody Clark as well. It's all taken care of."

President Honeycutt looked up with new hope. "Do we have something on Don Green? What do we have on Don Green?"

"Whatever you'd like. Just tell us. Do you want him to take drugs? We have a drug rumor ready to go whenever we need it."

"What drug does Don Green take?"

"What drug would you like him to take? Cocaine? Marijuana? Or maybe pills. There's something so desperate about pills. Pills would really be the kiss of death."

"But does he actually do such things?"

"I've never seen proof that he didn't," the first trusted advisor said, turning to the second trusted advisor to make sure that he had no such proof either. "Has he ever taken a test? You could offer to take a test. You haven't taken any drugs recently, have you?"

"Of course not!"

"Besides, it's not really Don Green that worries us so much as does Col. Cody Clark."

"I told you!" President Honeycutt sputtered. "Him and his damn tax babies and his daylight saving time. All because of that little pipsqueak down in Florida, what's his name, the one who's causing all that trouble in the Senate race."

"Vanderhaltz? Forget Vanderhaltz," the first aide said. "He's completely harmless, meaningless. The governor is behind Medwin Rojas, and we've got a fellow of ours down there working on his campaign. Hugh Brock. He was the staff director for Luther Moss, a real pro. He'll handle everything. And don't worry about Clark. We can handle Clark."

"How?"

"An illegitimate child. That ought to cut him up pretty fiercely with his Holy Roller friends."

"But what evidence is there he ever had an illegitimate child?"

"That's not our problem," said the second trusted advisor. "Besides, what if he did have an illegitimate child? It would be our responsibility to alert the American public."

"Even better," the first trusted advisor improvised. "What if he had a tax baby himself? How would that go over?"

"Yes!" the second trusted advisor agreed. "An illegitimate tax baby." He made a few notes on his pad. "I like it."

"Me, too," the first trusted advisor concurred. "I think we should get on it right away." He looked up at President Honeycutt. "You see? There's nothing to worry about. We're going to take care of everything."

"Are you sure?"

"We guarantee it."

President Honeycutt exhaled as he fell back in the First Chair, and a feeling of relief overcame him. Being president was tough work, and it was a never-ending source of pleasure to be able to rise to the occasion at moments like these.

Chapter Twenty

Lenny had grown used to making speeches—it wasn't too hard with Buddy's constant coaching—but he found himself uncomfortable and nervous about introducing Don Green. It was different from the endless series of small community group meetings, coffees, retirement home drop-ins and other small events to which Buddy directed him, where he talked about Ezra Wheezle. And the difference was more than the big hall, the large crowd, and the television cameras that would be aimed at him. It was the glossy impersonality of it all.

Buddy had set up a service kitchen adjacent to the ballroom as his operations center for the rally. Lenny was sitting by an unused steam table and Buddy joined him for a last few minutes of coaching. "Are we ready?" he asked him with an encouraging smile.

"How can I introduce the guy?" Lenny said to Buddy. "I don't even know him."

"His wife *knows* him, Lenny," Buddy responded. "You're just saying a few things about him."

Buddy was right, Lenny admitted. Knowing him and introducing him were two different things. Nobody had to know anybody. They really only had to be able to recognize each other.

They were all plug-ins—Wheezle, Don Green, and now, himself. Each existed to glad-hand and congratulate each other on simply being who they were. The appearance was everything.

"I guess so," Lenny conceded.

"Now, do you know your points? Let me hear 'em."

Lenny took a last peek at his index cards, breathed deeply, and began to tick off his main points. "Glad to be here and thanks," he began. "I've got a message from Walcott Falls's First Citizen, Congressman Ezra T. Wheezle."

"Right. First Citizen. That's very important. It tests well. Focus groups love it. And it stresses the familiarity theme."

Lenny nodded. "Right. First Citizen, I got it. Then, Wheezle asks for your support from his hospital bed in Washington. Then I tell them, I read the mail that people like you send to him, and I know you're well served by Congressman Wheezle—"

"Hammer that," Buddy coached. "That's the convenience thing."

"Right. I got it."

"Beautiful," Buddy said, approving his own work. "And the finish?"

"He's sick right now, but he's coming back, and so forth."

"No, no, no. *He's . . . coming . . . back*. Big time. Drama. It lets us get past the coma thing and hits the dependability point. Then go to Don Green for the big close, got it?"

"I got it," Lenny said yet again. Buddy gave him a lighthearted punch in the shoulder and ambled to another part of the room. *He's . . . coming . . . back*. Right. Lenny shook his head. Maybe if he were Jesus.

He put the cards down and looked around the room. A few local candidates—for the City Council and the State Senate— were clumped around a reporter in another corner. A group of schedulers talked to unseen people on cell phones. And scattered around the room and stationed at all the doors were men in blue suits and inconspicuous ties, Secret Service men, each wearing a single-breasted suit from which a gun could be quickly extracted, a button cuff shirt that was amenable to being wired for a microphone, oxford shoes designed to run in, and a small coiled wire running directly to the right ear.

Suddenly the doors to the kitchen opened and a new phalanx of Secret Service men entered, followed in a moment by Don Green, America's Friend. He was taller than Lenny had thought, and he looked slightly older than he did on television. He had a full head of wavy hair that had been brushed haphazardly into a part that was uninterested in staying put. He looked fit and was remarkably slim, with broad shoulders, narrow hips, and a wide, flat chest.

But Lenny was most taken by his smile. It was a wide, happy smile, a smile that revealed strong white teeth and the healthy pink gums of a child. It forced the corners of his mouth up like tiny arrowheads. It brought his cheeks, eyes, and forehead closer together and unified them into one artistic whole. It was as if he had shopped for smiles and had tried many on before he had found the one that suited him best.

The smile moved into the growing crowd in the service kitchen, taking the body with it, and calling into service the hands to shake and the head to nod and the eyes to shine while fingers pointed to a friend not in arm's reach. The swath that the smile cut from the entrance to the far end of the kitchen passed by Buddy and Lenny. The smile lit up further as it approached them.

"Buddy! Good to see you," Don Green said, extending his hand.

"Hello, Senator. How are you doing?"

"We've got 'em on the run. Honeycutt's so busy with Clark and his crazies that he can't get an arm free to go after us."

"He's in the sling, all right," Buddy agreed.

"What about Ezra?" Don Green asked, his smile suddenly incorporating itself into a look of concern. "Is he okay?"

"Well, that's hard to say," Buddy hedged.

"I see," Green said, understanding the news that was being delivered. "What about his numbers?"

"Oh, they're damn good," Buddy responded, this time more enthusiastically. "We're moving up—we seem to add a few points every day. In fact, we're running a few points ahead of you."

"Well, that doesn't surprise me. You've got the only candidate in this election who's guaranteed not to say anything stupid."

Buddy laughed politely at the remark, taking its cold-blooded essence in expedient stride. "Say, I want you to meet the fellow who's going to introduce you tonight. Don Green, this is Lenny Keeler," he said, propelling Lenny toward him. "Lenny, this is Don Green."

"Hello," the candidate said. "How are you doing this evening?"

"I'm fine," Lenny said, surprised to be asked.

Don Green inspected him for a moment and then beamed down at him. "Do a good job out there, okay?" he said, rubbing his palms together. "Now, shouldn't we get going? I've got a fund-raiser after this dinner and then I have to drive to New York City with a reporter from the *Wall Street Journal* at ten-thirty."

"Okay," Buddy said, as the sound of "Happy Days Are Here Again" floated through the kitchen doors. "It's showtime." His eyes flicked at Lenny. "Go get 'em, kid."

Lenny tried to catch his breath and compose himself, but he was pushed along behind Don Green in the group of local politicians, and found himself walking into the ballroom, where a thousand people stood as one, applauding enthusiastically as the members of the procession found their seats on the stage. Don Green stood at his place between two lesser candidates and waved to the crowd for a moment before sitting. Lenny took a seat further down on the other side of the lectern. He was caught in a quasi celebrity's identity crisis, not knowing whether he was being applauded or if he should join in the applause.

A dinner had already been placed in front of him, but he did not eat. His mind ran over the outline of his remarks as he picked at his plate, oblivious to the local officials sitting on either side of him, each taking a turn saying a few words at the lectern. His thinking was interrupted by the sound of applause and a voice saying, "I want to introduce you to a remarkable young man," his cue. By the time he heard his name he was already starting toward the lectern to the sound of more applause.

He looked out at the room from the lectern. Buddy leaned against a wall, surveying the scene as would a plant foreman. Don Green was turned his way, clapping, as were the dozen or so others on the stage, and the roomful of people who had paid to come see America's Friend looked his way expectantly. All eyes were on him.

Lenny smiled and put his index cards down in front of him. The applause died down and he began to speak.

"First, let me thank you for welcoming me back to Walcott Falls," he began, repeating the sequence Buddy had laid out for him. "It's a pleasure to be back here in my hometown."

There was more applause. Lenny was surprised to find it filled him with a sudden sense of mastery. He breathed it in while he allowed the crowd a moment to quiet down. "But I'm most personally glad to be here tonight because I get to bring you a message from Walcott Falls's First Citizen, Congressman Ezra T. Wheezle, who sends you his regards and asks for your support from his hospital bed in Washington, D.C."

There was applause again, just as Buddy told him there would be. "I work for Congressman Wheezle in Washington," he resumed. "I keep Congressman Wheezle informed about issues, and I read the mail that you send him. My job is to help him represent you, and I think our town is well served by Congressman Wheezle. He's sick right now, but with our hopes and prayers, *he's . . . coming . . . back* to serve us again the way he has for the past thirty-four years."

They were eating it up, applauding, smiling, and nodding.

"And, finally, I'm pleased to introduce to you the next President of the United States, our party's candidate, Senator Don Green, the man we look to for leadership that will carry us into the future, the man who will truly be . . . America's Friend."

The crowd, which had paid five hundred dollars apiece for the chance to applaud the candidate of their choice, was not going to miss their opportunity. They joyously brought their hands together at the mention of his name, shouting their approval with gusto. Lenny stepped back from the lectern and looked up and down the dais. It was going fine, and they were all smiling now; even Buddy was smiling as he leaned back against the wall.

And it was then that the strangest thing he could have imagined occurred to him. *He liked being up there.* He liked the raw juice of crowd response, the cacophony of banging palms, the silent sentry of the television cameras, the emotional rush of support and agreement, and the slight whiff of adoration that came with it. He was supposed to turn the podium over to Don Green, but he found himself unwilling to do so. No, he hadn't had his say yet. He looked down at Buddy's cards and decided that this was his chance to lay to rest his unsettled feelings, to say what he thought about what he'd seen in Washington and on the campaign trail—to give the audience a taste, not of Buddy Youngblood and focus groups and media training, but of Lenny Keeler, the feeling of being twenty-eight years old and from Walcott Falls, Pennsylvania.

He looked out at the crowd and began to speak again.

"*America's Friend*," he repeated. "Well, he'd better be America's Friend, because America needs a friend. My generation needs a friend, because my generation is scared." He nodded a jerky nod, feeling the truth in his own words. "I know that I'm scared. I'm scared that I'm going to work all my life and that one day when I need help there won't be any help there for me," he said, gaining momentum. "I'm scared because all I've seen in life is people trying to get theirs, and I'm scared that there isn't enough to go around. I'm scared that the world I'm being offered is a long chain of buck passing that wants me to continue it, and all the greed and the fear and the indifference is going to pull it apart.

"America needs a friend all right," he said quietly. "The kind of friend who can say '*You've had enough*' instead of '*Take all you want.*' The kind of friend who dares to say '*What about others?*' instead of '*How about me?*' That's the kind of friend America needs. We'll see what kind of friend it gets."

He stopped to catch his breath and realized that the faces that had been smiling now looked up stunned, and the hands that busily applauded were now held still. The change was conspicuous, but he felt a sense of satisfaction. He had put aside the elegantly crafted and painstakingly manipulated message and inserted in its place real feelings. He turned and sat down, leaving the podium vacant for an awkward minute.

Don Green slowly rose from his seat and stepped to the lectern. The ballroom facing him was silent, still taken aback by Lenny's speech. Don Green looked out at them with his jaw set and his eyes open wide with purpose. With a look of confidence and inspiration, he began to speak, "I listened very carefully to what Lenny Keeler had to say just now," he said quietly, "and I'm glad that he said it. He said what young people today are feeling. There's no hiding it. He's telling us what the legacy of the Hoak-Honeycutt administration is going to be—a generation of Americans who believe that their country stands for helping yourself but not your neighbor. That's what he was saying," he said to a roomful of people who had heard Lenny just as plainly as he had. His voice suddenly rose in emphasis. "And I believe, just as Lenny Keeler believes, that the question of whether or not our young people will have faith in America is the *number one issue in this campaign!*"

The audience burst into a fresh wave of applause, relieved to see that Lenny's improvisation was part of the master plan of a piece with Don Green's vision. It was all going to be all right. "And, just like you, I want to make sure that we show our young people that ours is a country that has vastly more to offer than cynicism, hard-heartedness, and greed. That's why I'm here. Because Lenny Keeler is right. Because America needs a friend, a friend with leadership and vision. And on November 5, when America goes to the voting booth, I hope that it will make that friend. And with your help, I know it will," he said, with an enormous finality that plucked the audience from its seat into a sea of cheers.

Don Green stood there and submitted himself to the crowd's devotion for a suitable amount of time, then walked off the stage. Lenny followed at a distance. They walked through the kitchen doors and into a swirl of campaign aides, logistics managers, photographers, advance people, and the other bodies that fill every room during a campaign.

Buddy followed Lenny through the kitchen, weaving among the serving tables and ovens. "Lenny, what the hell were you doing out there? This guy's going to be President of the United States. You don't get cute with him."

Before he could say more, or Lenny could respond, they were interrupted by Don Green. He shook Lenny's hand enthusiastically. "That was a tremendous little talk."

"It was?"

"Absolutely. I'm going to use some of it. It's a great vehicle for reaching younger voters. You don't mind, do you?"

"No," Lenny said, shaking his head slowly, "not at all."

"Great," and turned to Buddy. "Thanks, Buddy, that was great work." He patted Buddy on the back and turned away, and was swept, along with his advance people and schedulers and Secret Service men and photographers, out of the room in a whoosh that, for an instant, left a vacuum behind.

Standing next to Buddy, Lenny watched the kitchen doors swing back and forth until they stopped. He had said what he thought, and Don Green had seized it in midair and effortlessly redirected it to his own purposes. There was no belief, no conviction, no heartfelt truth that could not be turned into a message for public consumption, a group-tested banner, a headline, a slogan. *He's a Congressman . . . So You Don't Have to Be.* The system had taken his best shot and turned it into product. He looked at Buddy and told him what he should have long before now.

"Buddy, I quit."

And with that he turned and walked out through the doors and was gone.

Chapter Twenty-one

Dickie's Democratic opponent was a man named Gordon Burke. He was a good-looking, athletic man of fifty who had devoted his life to public service. He had won a Rhodes scholarship and returned to attend Harvard Law School. When he graduated, he eschewed the offers of corporate and Wall Street law firms to become a foot patrolman in his hometown, Jacksonville, instead. He quickly advanced through the police department to become its chief, where he gained national attention for his sensitive and effective approaches to the problems of drugs, domestic violence, and police-community relations. He was then elected mayor, and his program for downtown revitalization and local economic development was acclaimed by urbanologists across the nation. He was articulate and possessed a kindness of spirit that was obvious to anyone who met him. Fortunately, thought Miriam, he was black, and therefore stood no chance of getting over 30 percent of the vote.

Miriam's instinct for the campaign trail was second to none. She knew that if you played, you played to win, and a winning strategy for Dickie's Senate campaign involved going after Medwin Rojas as hard as they could, since Dickie's votes would only be pried from Medwin's Republican ranks. And so they hammered him with universal daylight saving time and then with the property rights of the unborn. The Republican nominee, of course, had the advantages of incumbency and his alignment with President Honeycutt, but the harder Dickie pushed and the greater Col. Cody Clark's taste for campaigning grew, the less formidable these assets became. Dickie was rising steadily in the polls, but not by enough. With two weeks left he crossed the 20 percent line, sufficient for a run on Gordon Burke for second place, but still not enough to win.

Miriam organized Dickie's campaign to emphasize his few advantages. She used the Daylighteers to create word of mouth that let him go from neighborhood to neighborhood to meet the electorate in comfortable and personal surroundings. She hitched Dickie's advertising to Col. Cody Clark's, just as his finances were multiplied by their arrangement with him. And she never let Dickie square off toe to toe with anybody of average intelligence or better. They would snipe at Rojas and wait for the break that would have to come if they were to win. Miracles would do no good, she reasoned, unless you were prepared for them.

With one week left, Dickie and Miriam returned to their hotel in Miami after an evening of appearances. Dickie had already turned in and Miriam was going over schedules when the phone rang. She picked it up without taking her eyes from the page.

"Hello?" she asked.

"Hello, Miriam? It's Hugh. Hugh Brock."

She looked up, puzzled. "Why are you calling?"

"I'm managing Medwin's campaign, Miriam. Why is it surprising that I call?"

"Because you haven't called so far, Hugh," she said coldly. "What is it?"

"Do you have a few minutes?"

"Don't you think it's a little late?"

"I'm in a bar three blocks away, a place called Domino's on

Hassey Street. There are booths in the back. I'll be in the third one."

Miriam grew puzzled. "Why so secretive?"

"I have my reasons," Hugh said. "Will you come?"

She was too curious not to. "Okay. I'll be there in ten minutes," she said, and set out into the night streets. Domino's was a small affair with a gaudy neon front, frequented by the people who worked in the nearby hotels. A few of them turned to watch Miriam as she entered, but she stepped quickly past them on her way to the back.

Miriam found Hugh and dropped into the booth. He was wearing a rumpled seersucker suit and his tie was undone. A waitress came by and took her drink order. "Okay, what is it?" Miriam said.

Hugh's face soured. "How about, Hello?"

"I said hello on the phone," she snapped. "What do you want?"

"You don't like me very much, do you?"

The waitress returned and placed a bourbon and soda before her. "Back on the Science Committee you were an officious asshole with no sensitivity for anybody who worked for you. What do you think?"

"Didn't I give you your big chance with the equipment-that-doesn't-work tax credit? And didn't I give you a job in the first place?"

"And paid me $20,000 a year," she answered. "Look, Hugh. I'm running a Senate campaign now, with a budget of a million dollars a month. You had me clipping newspaper articles." She rolled her eyes. "How I wish I'd been there when Moss canned you. I would have enjoyed that no end."

Hugh's anger flared at the memory. "I bet you'd have liked that. I was humiliated by the little son of a bitch," he said.

"Who? Moss?"

"Moss? Hell, no! I'm talking about Vanderhaltz. Was I ever taken in by that weasel. He shows up, cons me into giving him daylight saving time, then plays naive while he puts together his own political operation." He shook his head bitterly. "It was a textbook operation, too. Particularly the way he brought his buddy Schang into it." He threw back a mouthful of gin. "Vanderhaltz," he said, repeating his mantra of frustration and resentment. "Well, he's getting what he must have planned all along, this Senate race. But he doesn't have a chance, Miriam. You know that."

Miriam marveled that somebody who was capable of mistaking Dickie for a manipulative, let alone cunning, individual could be entrusted with as responsible a position as Hugh's. He was still right about Dickie's chances though, but she wasn't going to give him the satisfaction of agreeing with him. "Don't be so sure, Hugh," she said coolly. "It's not over yet."

"Oh, come on, Miriam. Medwin has this thing wrapped."

She folded her hands around her glass. "Then why am I here?"

Hugh leaned forward. "Because I want to clean Dickie's clock. I want to ruin him. I want him to be humiliated."

"And you're telling me this because . . . "

Hugh smiled. "I want you to work for us."

"Me? For you? For Rojas?"

"Exactly. I want you to jump. Just picture it," he said wistfully, his hands sweeping across an imagined banner headline. " 'Campaign Manager Jumps Ship During Final Week!' It would finish him off good." He appraised her reaction. "What do you say?"

"Forget it!"

"Let's face facts. Medwin is going to the Senate. I'm offering you a chance to go with him. I'm going to run his new office, and there's a job for you." He lowered his voice confidentially. "How'd you like to be legislative director?" he asked. "We can agree to it right now."

"Legislative director?" she repeated. He nodded emphatically. She gazed down at the tabletop. "Just to screw Dickie?"

There was a time when she would have traded the world for

it. But that time was gone. She looked at Hugh and thought of her life when she knew him. It was only months ago, but it might have been aeons, and she could never go back.

And she wouldn't turn away from Dickie now. It was time to face the facts: she was falling in love with him. Or perhaps she was only telling herself that Dickie was the object of her love as opposed to the vehicle of her ambition. Would she be in love with him had they not somehow blundered their way to where they were today? No, probably not. Would she love him the day after he lost his election? She preferred not to answer. But they *were* where they were, and he hadn't lost the election, yet. And if she allowed herself a little emotional slack, if she helped the feeling along by allowing Dickie's meteoric rise to fill its sails, was that a crime? After all, if Dickie won his election, there was a chance that she would be in love forever. And if he didn't . . . well, she had yet to feel this way about anybody else. "Get lost, Hugh. I wouldn't sell out Dickie for a dozen of you."

"Fine," Hugh said. "Go ahead back to Dickie. We're going to kick his ass."

She would have answered him, fought back, but at that instant a blinding flash of light went off at the side of the table. As her vision returned, Miriam managed to discern the presence of Charley Robinson, a political columnist for the *Miami Herald*.

"Sorry about the flash, kids," he said with a chuckle. Miriam and Hugh squinted at him standing at their table, a small camera in his hand. "The problem with these clandestine meetings is that you can't have them at places where the working press drinks. Now who's going to tell me why you're having a secret meeting in the middle of the night?"

"I will," said Miriam, her face suddenly glowing as she saw her opportunity. "Hugh asked me to meet him because he wants to jump ship and join the Vanderhaltz campaign."

"I what?" Hugh exclaimed. "What are—"

"Come on, Hugh. If you want to come over to us, then you're going to have to announce it sometime."

Charley Robinson shook his head. "Really, Miriam. Do you expect me to believe that Hugh would cross over to Dickie's campaign?"

"Charley, why else would we be hiding here? Why wouldn't we be in the bar back at the hotel? Or in Hugh's suite, or mine? Tell him, Hugh," she said smugly.

The columnist scratched his head in confusion. "Well, I admit you've got a point there. Hugh, why are you hiding out here?"

Hugh was scarcely able to contain himself. "Charley, the real story is that I asked Miriam to meet me here so I could ask her to leave the Vanderhaltz campaign and come over to us."

Miriam laughed derisively. "Come on, Hugh. Who's going to believe a story like that? Not a word of it makes sense. Medwin is supposed to be way ahead of Dickie in the polls. You do think you're way ahead of us, don't you, Hugh?"

"Of course, we are," he said angrily.

"See? Why on earth would Hugh bother to bring me over to Medwin's campaign when he's way ahead with a week to go?"

The columnist looked more confused as each word flew by him. "Good question, Miriam. How about it, Hugh?"

"Because—" Hugh started, but cut himself short. It would serve no one, and only embarrass himself, to reveal the depths and origins of his animosity toward Dickie. "It's . . . it's personal, Charley. I can't go into it."

"There!" Miriam said triumphantly. "You see?"

The columnist made some quick notes on a pad. "But why would Hugh want to bolt Medwin's campaign?"

"Who knows?" Miriam shrugged. "Maybe he's going to get dumped the way he was dumped by Luther."

"Were you dumped by Luther?" the columnist asked, stunned.

"No, I wasn't dumped by Luther. We simply—"

"Oh, bullshit, Hugh. Moss dumped you like a truckful of dirt. Charley, go ask Art Mack whether or not Hugh got canned." The columnist jotted a reminder to do exactly that. "Besides," Miriam added, "what kind of a lead are you showing? Our own data says we're within six points."

"Six points!" Hugh blurted.

"Is that a denial?" the columnist asked.

"Of course it's a denial," Hugh said, exasperated. "We're twenty points ahead and I have no interest in joining the Vanderhaltz campaign. Not a word of it is true!"

"Not a word?" Miriam asked. "Charley, let's go down to the Lee Avenue police station. We'll both take polygraph tests right now. Let's ask Hugh if he got sacked by Moss. Let's ask him if he called me to meet him here. We'll see who's lying. Hugh can't even come up with a good story about why we're here!"

The columnist looked at his watch. "Look, it's almost one in the morning. I can still make the final edition of tomorrow morning's paper. Hugh, I'm going to have to go to press."

"But you can't!" Hugh pleaded.

"Unless you can tell me why you're here, all I can do is print your denial."

"But it's not true!"

"So you are denying it?"

"Of course I'm denying it," Hugh shouted. He whirled toward Miriam. "How could you do this to me?"

"Calm down, Hugh," the columnist said. "If you want to explain why you asked Miriam to come see you in an out-of-the-way place in the middle of the night, you have my number." And with that he turned and walked away.

When the door had closed behind him, Miriam let out a laugh. Hugh looked up at her, seething. She stood and collected her purse from the table. "Imagine tomorrow's paper, Hugh. 'Campaign Manager Jumps Ship During Final Week!'" She smiled broadly. She had turned the election around.

President Honeycutt was discussing the economy with the secretary of the treasury when his two trusted advisors entered to inform him of an unanticipated need to watch television. He put his fingers to his chin and with a somber expression dismissed the secretary of the treasury. "What's going on?" he asked his trusted advisors as he triggered the television with his remote control.

"Clark is having a press conference," the first trusted advisor said. "We hear it's about the tax baby thing."

"What tax baby thing?"

"Remember? Our allegation that he's fathered an illegitimate tax baby. It was in the *Washington Times*."

President Honeycutt nodded. "Yes, yes. I remember that. Is something wrong?"

The first trusted advisor laughed. "Wrong? Hell, what could be wrong? We've got Clark preoccupied with the allegation that he's fathered an illegitimate tax baby. What could be better?"

The image of Col. Cody Clark filled the screen. "Good afternoon," Col. Cody Clark began. "I'm here to make the following statement. I am deeply disturbed by the assertion made recently by the President Honeycutt campaign and the Republican National Committee that I fathered an illegitimate child, specifically an illegitimate tax baby. This assertion is patently absurd and has no basis in truth. The fact is that no such child exists or ever existed, either after or before birth.

"In order to expunge this pernicious rumor from the public record, and at great personal cost to myself, I have invited my personal physician to this press conference to discuss with you the most intimate details of my medical history. I regret having to do this, but I insist that the record be cleared."

The first trusted advisor's head reared back in laughter. "He's going to put his doctor on television! Can you get over this?" He cackled uproariously. "This is priceless." His laughter was contagious—even President Honeycutt joined in.

The doctor took the podium, adjusted his eyeglasses, and looked down at his notes. Moments later, President Honeycutt wasn't laughing anymore.

*   *   *

Lenny walked into the office and sat at his desk. It was late—he
had driven all night after the Green campaign rally and it was already midnight when he reached Washington. There was nobody
in the building save the Capitol police and no sound other than
the clicking of their shoes in the halls and the buzzing of the
overhead lights when he turned them on. He began to rummage
through the drawers of his desk, getting some personal things
and a few position papers he'd taken some pride in. There wasn't
much, really, he thought, to show he'd ever been here. Just as well.
He'd clear his desk, leave a note, close down his apartment, go
back to Walcott Falls, find a job, and start a life.

He went over to the supply cabinet and pulled open the
drawer that held interoffice envelopes. He took three of them
back to his desk and put some of his papers into the first. He
started wrapping the string around the two fasteners on the back
of the envelope when he noticed his own handwriting in one of
the address spaces. It said:

Social Security Liaison
449 Russell SOB

He remembered sending some constituent mail to that office
a few months before. From there the envelope had found its cir-
cuitous way back to the House Office Buildings. It had first been
sent to a congressman in the Longworth Office Building, then
to a union's office downtown. From there it had found its way
back to him. These envelopes tell stories, he thought, tracing
tales as they moved through official Washington, from office to
office. He looked down to the last names on the envelope, wondering who had sent it back to Congressman Wheezle's office.
There was only an address:

1688 K St., NW, Suite 560

No matter, he thought, and tossed it onto his desk and
opened the second envelope. He put his address book and his

House and Senate phone books into it and tied the back, glancing at the addresses as he did. He stopped again when he saw at the bottom the same address, without a name: 1688 K St., NW, Suite 560. He was familiar with most of the offices with which Congressman Wheezle's office traded correspondence, but this address rang no bells. Curious now, he picked up the third envelope and looked at the last address. The same. He walked back to the drawer and pulled out a handful of envelopes. Of them, there were immediately five more. He pulled out another handful. It kept coming up—1688 K St., NW, Suite 560—until, finally, one had a name listed above the address: N.C.N.E.D.

It was familiar, but from where? N.C.N.E.D. N was for National, he thought. C was Committee, or Coalition, or Congress. Maybe Christian, but probably not. The National Committee on, or for, Something. He grabbed a phone book and started to go through the NC listings. There were pages of them—National Caucuses, Councils, Congresses, Committees, Conferences—and then he came upon it. National Coalition for New Economic Direction. 1688 K St., NW.

National Coalition for New Economic Direction. It was the Republican political action committee that was out to defeat Congressman Younger in order to pass the equipment-that-doesn't-work tax credit. He sat back and thought. The National Coalition for New Economic Direction had been regularly sending materials to a Democratic congressman's office. But why? To whom? Perhaps it was completely innocuous. All of these groups had mail sweeps of the members of the Economic Affairs Committee, Republican and Democrat, and often the entire House. But even so, why so many envelopes by messenger? Why not just the usual mail, or fax? And if the N.C.N.E.D. was regularly sending something to somebody in Congressman Wheezle's office, then was somebody in Congressman Wheezle's office regularly sending something back?

He dumped an armful of envelopes on the floor and began to read every address. There were three that had been sent from

Congressman Wheezle's office to 1688 K St., NW, Suite 560. The third, he noticed, had the word FORWARD rubber-stamped over the K Street address. The next address was:

Cascade Air Courier

National Airport

He reached for the phone book again and flipped through the advertising pages for couriers. In a small boxed ad he found *Cascade Air Courier. Cascade Airlines. Same day service to Idaho, Montana, and Wyoming.* He looked back through the three N.C.N.E.D. addresses on the three envelopes.

The handwriting was the same on each. It was Jeff's.

He got up and walked into Jeff's office and opened the center drawer of his desk. He was in luck. Amid the pencils, notes, business cards, loose change, and Post-it notes lay a file key. He opened Jeff's filing cabinet and started at the bottom drawer.

He found it quickly, a file with about an inch of correspondence on N.C.N.E.D. letterhead paper. He read the first letter.

Dear Jeff,

I want to thank you for the most recent position papers you wrote on the equipment-that-doesn't-work tax credit. The material about insourcing of foreign components and the trade deficit has been quite helpful in our Idaho fund-raising.

Thanks again. I'll keep you posted.

A look of dismay overcame him. It was what Jeff had him write when they switched positions on the equipment-that-doesn't-work tax credit. Jeff had been sending the documents Lenny wrote through the National Coalition for New Economic Direction, to Idaho, where they were being turned into speeches, pamphlets, and fund-raising materials for Congressman Younger's opponent.

Had Wheezle been involved, too? He had to have known. This had to be his operation from the word go. He certainly wanted Senior Younger, Jr.'s, chairmanship badly enough. And Jeff didn't have the initiative to go out and do this on his own. Wheezle was trying to devour his chairman and betray his party, and The Speaker, in the process.

Lenny took the folder out to the Xerox machine and switched it on. He looked at the clock. It would be about ten o'clock in Idaho. He could still call. He was done with politics, but he owed the old man that much.

Chapter Twenty-two

Senior Younger, Jr.'s, wheelchair was parked in front of a mirror backstage at the theater where his campaign's final debate was about to take place. A makeup man worked the old man's face with powder and eyeshadow. Senior Younger, Jr.'s, campaign manager sat next to him, nervously tapping his shoes on the floor as the candidate prepared for the greatest challenge of his political career by snoring, loudly. A campaign volunteer stuck his head in the door.

"There's a phone call from Washington for Senior," he said.

The campaign manager nodded and picked up the phone. "Yes?" he asked.

"This is Lenny Keeler. I'm a friend of —"

"I know who you are," the campaign manager said, cutting him off. "Senior threatens to fire me and give you my job at least twice a day. Apparently, you're the only person left in politics he still trusts. And frankly, the way this campaign is going, you can have my job."

"Is it that bad?" Lenny asked.

"We're twenty points down with a few days left to go. Senior keeps on talking about his secret plan, but I haven't a clue as to what it is. Nor, I think, does Senior."

"Maybe I can help. Can I talk to him?"

"Hold on a minute." The campaign manager shook Congressman Younger's shoulder. "Senior, Senior," he said softly.

"What the hell is it?" Senior Younger, Jr., barked as he woke. "Is it time for the damn debate yet?" He lashed at the campaign manager's shins with his cane. "Let me sleep!"

"Senior," the campaign manager said, voice rising. "Lenny Keeler's on the phone."

Senior Younger, Jr., stopped protesting and took the phone. "Lenny, my boy! I'm so glad to hear from you! My people here don't know the first thing about politics! You just watch me out there tonight, son, I'll be on C-SPAN. I'll show them a thing or two!"

"Listen, Congressman Younger," Lenny said earnestly. "I found some files in my office. Congressman Wheezle's office director has been sending material to the National Coalition for New Economic Direction. They've been using it to campaign against you. Wheezle has been helping the National Coalition defeat you!"

"He has, eh?" Congressman Younger smiled, shaking his head in admiration. "Who'd have thought he had it in him?"

"You're not mad?"

"Hell, no. I'm more impressed that he's finally gotten tired of waiting for me to die," he answered with a laugh.

"But what about those files? Aren't you going to do something about this?"

"Well, I suppose Wheezle has to be slapped if he ever wakes up, but not because I'm mad. After all, I'm going to win the election."

"You are?"

"Of course I am," Congressman Younger said. "I finally have my secret plan."

"What plan?" Lenny said, beseechingly. "What can you possibly do? You're down by twenty points with one week left! You're going to lose this election, Congressman Younger, and they're going to put you in a home!"

"Twenty points? In a week? You can get fifty points in a day if you play it right. Franklin D. Roosevelt got a fifty-point swing on the war issue in one day."

"But that was Pearl Harbor, Congressman. The country was attacked by Japan!"

"You can criticize the method all you want, but you can't argue with the result." He turned to his campaign manager. "Marvin, aren't we ready yet?" he asked impatiently. "Is my brown suitcase out by the stage?"

"Everything's the way you wanted it, Senior."

"Good," Congressman Younger said, returning his attention to Lenny on the phone. "Now you just run along and turn on your television, because I'm going to kick this fellow's fanny. And Lenny?" he said, his voice softening. "Thank you for calling. You were kind to try and help an old man like me." Lenny was about to answer when he heard the receiver click.

The campaign manager wheeled Senior Younger, Jr., out of the makeup room and onto the stage. In a moment the debate began.

Senior Younger, Jr.'s, opponent set an aggressive tone at the outset and carried on relentlessly, besieging Congressman Younger with questions on the details of government programs, local economic conditions, and his legislative record, rapidly moving from one question to the next before Senior Younger, Jr., could answer. It was a plan obviously designed to fluster the older man, and it did. Senior Younger, Jr., squirmed under the pressure.

When Senior Younger, Jr., depicted his positions in simple terms, his opponent derided him for failing to understand the complexities of modern issues. When he acknowledged the complexity of an issue, he found himself assailed for equivocating. These exchanges left Senior Younger, Jr., shaking his head and looking his years, which were seventy in excess of his opponent's. Lenny watched him unhappily on the television. If Congressman Younger hadn't been twenty points down in the polls before the debate, he would be now.

As the debate neared its end, the candidates were invited to present a concluding statement. The opponent went first. He took a gentle, patronizing tone, commending Senior Younger, Jr., for his decades of service and expressing the gratitude that Idahoans everywhere would always feel for him. He then went on to say that it would be irresponsible to entrust decisions about the nation's defense to a man of 114, just as it would be foolish to let such a man define the nation's future.

The audience responded with enthusiasm and support. "And now," the moderator said, "we will have a final statement by Congressman Senior Younger, Jr."

Senior Younger, Jr., looked old and battered as he slowly wheeled his wheelchair to the center of the stage. The audience looked up at him, waiting for some sign of life. He looked back at them with serene indifference.

"I was five years old," he began, sounding scratchy and muted at first, "when my grandfather, Cicero Younger, whose son, my father, Senior Younger, Sr., was Idaho's first congressman," he said, "took me for a camping trip up in the mountains near Bonners County, almost at the Canadian border. It was 1890. It was Indian country then. You could walk or paddle for days on end and if you saw any people at all it was only because they wanted you to see them.

"That summer we went up to Priest Lake with John Marshall Bonners himself, our first governor." His voice gained the smallest increment of strength. "It was almost sundown when we got there. When we made camp I lay on my back and looked at the night sky. It was big and wide and it was black, but it was bright, too, the way the night sky filled with stars can be. I lay there before I fell asleep, listening to my grandfather and John Marshall Bonners discuss how beautiful the country was and how they hoped that it wouldn't change, not even, they said, now that Idaho had become a state."

He curled forward in a cough and then straightened himself with great effort. "I wish that I could remember more of what my grandfather and John Marshall Bonners said that night. I know they talked about their vision of what our state and our land could become, but I don't remember much else. I was entrusted with a great secret that night, but as I grew, I forgot it. It was the secret that is forgotten in every generation, the secret that our lives make us relearn only so that it can be retold to other little boys and then forgotten again." He shook his head, lost in the memory. "Instead," he sighed, "I remember that I lay there and thought that everything fit under the sky, and that the world made sense to me.

"I console myself to think that, although I cannot recall everything my grandfather and John Marshall Bonners said about the future for which they had worked all their lives, I learned respect that night for the vastness of the sky.

"But the sky's not so big anymore, is it?" he asked, growing more animated. "It doesn't seem big enough to hold everything under it, the way it once did. Things come loose under the sky because the world is too crowded, and so we lose the things we believe in and the things we love. There's no room for them. The sky can't cover them anymore, and they slip away." The audience shifted uneasily as Senior Younger, Jr., paused to survey their faces. "After a while, you don't know what to believe or what to feel or where your roots are. Young people come along, young people like this man here," he said, jerking his cane toward his opponent, "and they tell you that they know what you should believe. Horseflop!" he snorted with unrestrained contempt.

"Now don't get me wrong. I've got nothing against young people. Everybody has to be young once just to get it out of their system. But some of you are so young that you never lived in a world where the sky was big enough to hold everything underneath it. But I did once, and I can tell you the difference."

The audience listened, some touched, some bewildered, and some saddened by the sight of the old man, by the old man's memories, and by the thought that they would never have such memories for themselves. Senior Younger, Jr., suddenly rose from his wheelchair. "Didn't think I could do it, did you?" he demanded with a bellow that astonished the gasping crowd. "You think I'm worthless because I'm 114. Well, I'm old, all right. And my patience is limited, and fools like this fellow here bore me very, very quickly.

"I'm probably the oldest man you ever saw. But all that means is that I remember more than any of you." He turned and signaled to somebody offstage. A man walked out from the wings bearing a brown suitcase. Senior Younger, Jr., sat down in his wheelchair and the man put the suitcase in his lap. Senior's aged and fragile hands reached in and reemerged holding a guitar with a large round sound hole and a small body and neck.

"This guitar belonged to my grandfather, Cicero Younger. He bought it in Kansas City, Missouri, in 1854. He played it for me and John Marshall Bonners that night at Priest Lake, as I lay in my sleeping roll and looked up into the blackness of the night sky. I'm going to play for you what he played for me that night." And with that his spiny fingers placed themselves on the strings and he began to pluck out a G chord. The audience was hushed. Senior Younger, Jr.'s, opponent fidgeted uncomfortably, hoping to make eye contact with the moderator. But the moderator, like everyone else, was staring at the old man. Congressman Younger then let loose a coarse, flat singing voice.

> *"Oh give me a home*
> *Where the buffalo roam*
> *And the deer and the antelope play*
> *Where seldom is heard*
> *A discouraging word*
> *And the skies are not cloudy all day*
>   *Home, home on the range*

> *Where the deer and the antelope play*
> *Where seldom is heard*
> *A discouraging word*
> *And the skies are not cloudy all day*

> "*How often at night*
> *When the heavens are bright*
> *With the light of the glittering stars*
> *I stood there amazed*
> *And I asked as I gazed*
> '*Does their glory exceed that of ours?*'"

His fingers played a series of bridge chords to the chorus, sliding up the neck with an unexpected gracefulness, and the crowd, taken by the old man and his song, could not help but sing along in plaintive unison, as if by singing with him they could see the America that Senior Younger, Jr., saw. Their voices rose together.

> "*Home, home on the range*
> *Where the deer and the antelope play*
> *Where seldom is heard*
> *A discouraging word*
> *And the skies are not cloudy all day*"

He played the bridge chords again and they all repeated the chorus again, and then he played it a third and final time, more people joining in with each repetition. The moderator considered asserting himself but he could not interrupt the song's haunting beauty. Senior Younger, Jr.'s, opponent tried to look detached, but for him, too, the song brought back memories of a child who could look up and see the sky and not the need for new weapons in space. Everybody slowly stood, as if in church, as they sang along. And when they stopped singing, it was only because Senior Younger, Jr.'s, brittle hands could play no more; had they the chance, they would perhaps have stood there forever—some smiling, some weeping, some with their hands resting lightly on their children's shoulders, some tightly gripping the hands of the one they loved—singing the same simple melody all night long. There was a moment of pristine silence when Senior finished, and then a thunderous wave of deep, cathartic cheering rose out of the audience. Senior did not smile, but instead sat calmly in his wheelchair with his hands folded in his lap. Lenny watched him on the screen, with tears in his eyes, partly out of love for Senior Younger, Jr., partly because he had seen, for just a moment, what Senior had once seen, partly because he now knew that Congressman Wheezle's morally bereft scheme had failed, but mostly because the 114-year-old son of a bitch had just stolen back the election and kept himself out of a home with the most outlandish political stunt that Lenny had ever heard of.

Chapter Twenty-three

In Lenny's absence, Buddy Youngblood had saturated the local airwaves with ads cobbled together, under the guidance of Fabian Hostetler's theory of perceptual mechanics, out of footage shot in Congressman Wheezle's precoma days. In a small house on a quiet street in Walcott Falls, the man with the bushy mustache who had encountered Congressman Wheezle and Buddy's film crew on his way to work at Wyatt Industries—who had taken the congressman to task on the issues of day care, drug treatment, and education, receiving nothing but sidestepping, double-talk, and evasion in return—sat on a couch with his wife and his mother-in-law in a cramped living room, watching a made-for-TV movie. The movie gave way after a few minutes to commercials; first for laundry soap, then for motor oil, and then for Congressman Wheezle.

On the television screen, Ezra Wheezle was running up the East Steps of the Capitol on a sunshiny morning.

"You get up early in the morning to fight for yourself and your family. Ezra Wheezle gets up early in the morning and fights for you. You're fighting to keep your job. Ezra Wheezle is fighting to help you keep it. You're fighting to keep your taxes down. Ezra Wheezle is fighting to keep them down, too.

"If you were in Congress, would you fight for anything different? Ezra

Wheezle doesn't think so, and that's why Ezra Wheezle's a congressman . . . so you don't have to be!"

"Goddamn!" the man with the bushy mustache shouted. "It's that bastard who was at the plant."

The wife and the mother-in-law nodded and watched Congressman Wheezle mount the steps, unaware of the fate that waited for him when he reached the top. Suddenly, the image shifted to Congressman Wheezle standing at the gate of Wyatt Industries, shaking hands as the morning shift filed past.

"There!" the man said to his wife. "You see?" The narration continued.

"You deserve three things in a congressman. You deserve a congressman who's dependable, who'll be there in Washington representing you, so that you don't have to be. You deserve a congressman who's familiar, who's been a congressman for a long time, someone you've had a chance to get to know. And you deserve a congressman who's convenient, who won't take up too much of your time with complicated issues that he's supposed to understand instead of you. And that's why Ezra Wheezle is your congressman. So you don't have to be. So vote for your congressman, Ezra Wheezle, on November 5."

As the narration went on, the image shifted to the man with the bushy mustache himself, enumerating, in an animated manner, his complaints. But rather than his well-founded and substantial grievances, he heard instead the conviction with which the narrator asserted the candidate's dependability, familiarity, and convenience.

"Hey! That's me!" the man with the bushy mustache cried.

"Howard, that's you!" his wife cried. "Look, Ma, it's Howard!"

"It's me, hon! It's me!" he said again, rising to his feet. "Look!" he commanded, pointing to the set.

His wife jumped up and hopped up and down in place. "Howard's on TV, Ma! Howard's on TV!" She pressed her hands against her chest and beamed.

"I'm on TV!" the man with the bushy mustache cried. "I'm a star!" he exclaimed, pumping his fist in the air with satisfaction. "Shoot," the man said with a smile. "I'm voting for that guy!"

✳   ✳   ✳

The day after the debate, Senior Younger, Jr., made an appearance at a senior citizens center. Television cameras were there to
see him wheel past his wheeled constituency. He had been
speaking for only a moment when he heard a voice from the
back of the room.

"Play the song!" the voice demanded.

"Yes," more voices joined in. "Play the song!"

A guitar was placed in Senior Younger, Jr.'s, lap. He slowly examined it, then positioned it against himself and began to play.

> *"Oh, give me a home*
> *Where the buffalo roam*
> *And the deer and the antelope play*
> *Where seldom is heard*
> *A discouraging word*
> *And the skies are not cloudy all day"*

And so it went, at schools, shopping centers, churches, and
wherever else Senior Younger, Jr., went. "Play the song!" they
cried. And he did.

The tape of Senior Younger, Jr.'s, debate performance began
to circulate. C-SPAN had it, of course, then the networks the
next night, then the pundit talk shows. In a few days, a studio
called. It had taken Senior Younger, Jr.'s, tape and put some basic
instrumentation behind it, the doubled violin and saxophone of
norteño music, a bass and drum, a second guitar, a squeeze box.
The song acquired a lazy, Tex-Mex feel. His campaign manager
gave his approval and the tape of his debate became a video,
played on the pop and country cable video stations once an
hour. He sang it on the *Tonight Show*. He sang it on *Good Morning
America*. He sang it at every stop he made, until his fingers were
too sore and arthritic to play, so he just sang it while somebody
else played it for him.

By election day, it was the number one song in the country.

Wherever you went, there was Senior Younger, Jr.'s, voice, on car radios and boom boxes, in elevators and in department stores, anywhere that music was part of the environment.

Lenny was happy for Senior Younger, Jr., and Senior Younger, Jr., seemed happy for himself—the more the song was played the more of a folk hero he became and the greater grew his lead, until Senior Younger, Jr., was a thirty-point shoo-in in the First Congressional District of Idaho, and his fifty-point turnabout complete.

Chapter Twenty-four

Buddy Youngblood sat in a Walcott Falls hotel room on election night, biting a knuckle nervously, taking calls with precinct totals, and watching the local television news. He checked his watch. It was ten-fifty-five, time for the local stations to announce regional results.

A newscaster appeared on the screen. Buddy rubbed his chin nervously. "And now Pennsylvania Senate and congressional races. In the Senate race, Democratic incumbent Roger Heath has won by a slender margin over his Republican challenger. Again, Roger Heath the victor in the Senate race." Buddy clapped his hands together and before he could do anything else, the newscaster continued. "In congressional races, we have the following . . ."

Miriam, Dickie, and Laslo sat in a crowded suite in downtown Miami. Miriam had the phone cocked on one shoulder and was jotting numbers on a pad trying to listen over the sound of the TV. "Got it," she said, and hung up. "You're winning in Tallahassee and Jacksonville."

"I am?" Dickie asked. "Where does that leave us?"

Miriam looked at her notes. "I'll get a count in a few minutes.

But I figure us for eight to ten points ahead of where the polls had us."

"Why are we doing so well?" Dickie asked.

"Because there are people who wanted to vote for you but didn't want to admit it to a polltaker. And, of course, there are Laslo's people, who, I presume, refuse to answer polltakers' questions."

"You presume right," Laslo said, focused on the television before them.

"And in the Florida Senate race," the newscaster was saying, "we have a very tight three-way race between the two major-party candidates and renegade geology professor Dr. Dickie Vanderhaltz. Still way too close to call. We'll be back to this one all night, I can assure you."

In Walcott Falls, Buddy was on the phone again, as the newscaster continued, " . . . between incumbent Congressman Ezra Wheezle of Walcott Falls and challenger Sam Spinner. Of course, this race has been clouded by the issue of Congressman Wheezle's health. But the votes are in, and we are now prepared to predict that the winner will be incumbent Congressman Ezra T. Wheezle, now elected for his eighteenth term. Congressman Wheezle, victorious."

"Is that what you've got?" Buddy hollered over his phone to a downtown precinct watcher. "How far ahead did we run?" He jotted some numbers down on a scrap of paper and put them in his shirt pocket. "Goddamn, yes!" he muttered, and began to dial a phone number. "We're in, let's roll," he barked, and with that put the phone down, grabbed his suit coat, and stormed out of the room.

The national anchorman cupped a hand to his ear as the news of local races ended. "Ladies and gentlemen," he said, our computers and our staff of expert statistical analysts have arrived at some predictions regarding the presidential election. Let's go back to our Electoral College Scoreboard. Keep in mind that the magic number is 270—a candidate must receive 270 electoral votes to win a majority in the Electoral College and be elected as president. When we last left the board fifteen minutes ago, our computer analysis scored it this way. The states in red," and here the left half of the map and some of the bottom lit up in a bright bleeding scarlet, "have been awarded to Republican President Herbert Honeycutt, for a total of 246 electoral votes. The states in blue," and here most of the upper right corner of the map was illuminated in a kingly blue, "have been awarded to Democrat challenger Senator Don Green—by our count, 242 electoral votes. No electoral votes, I might add, have been awarded to the third party candidacy of Col. Cody Clark of the Salvation and Solvency campaign."

Col. Cody Clark looked up from his dinner table in his hotel suite. "I suppose I'm not going to win, am I?"

"No," his assistant said.

"That's fine," he assured all those within earshot, as he rose and turned off the television. "The Lord has bigger plans for me."

"As it stands now, fifty electoral votes remain to be decided. Let's turn to those states. First, Idaho. Four electoral votes. We're predicting the winner there to be, by a sizable margin, President Honeycutt." The screen went through a series of graphics involving President Honeycutt's visage and the crimsonizing of Idaho within an outline of the national map. "And, while we're on Idaho, we should also announce that Democratic incumbent Senior Younger, Jr., fresh from his number one hit record, has been reelected in a landslide to the House of Representatives for an unprecedented thirty-ninth term, serving in that body since 1920. But Idaho nonetheless remains Republican and goes for President Honeycutt, and that makes the electoral score Honeycutt 250, Green 242.

"Next, Washington state," the news anchor continued, "with eleven electoral votes, going for Senator Don Green by a small margin. Washington state goes for Green. Also going into the Green column—Oregon, with seven electoral votes. And in those Senate races, it looks like Senator Joe Paris of Oregon and Senator Arthur Gibson of Washington, both Republican incumbents, will win reelection, but only by the slimmest of margins. That would add up to fifty-two Republican senators in the next Congress. And Hawaii, with its three electoral votes, also for Green. Now, let's go to our electoral scoreboard," he said as the screen azured the gray shells of Oregon, Washington, and Hawaii. "We see Senator Don Green with two hundred sixty-three electoral votes and President Herbert Honeycutt with two hundred fifty. It's very close.

"Which brings us to Florida, where strange things have been happening all night. Florida has been in the headlines throughout this past year, first with the tragic death of Senator Luther A. Moss, then the rise of the so-called Daylighteers and their Sunshine Initiative, and the unforeseeable third-party Senate candidacy of Daylight guru Dr. Dickie Vanderhaltz, a young professor of geology at a local university, and his affiliation with the national candidacy of Col. Cody Clark. Well, the remarkable story of Florida politics has spilled over its borders tonight.

"Turning first to the Senate election, our analysis indicates that the winner in the Florida Senate contest will be . . . Dr. Dickie Vanderhaltz, the first third-party candidate to win election in the Senate since the early 1970s. In a major upset, the new senator from Florida, Dr. Dickie Vanderhaltz."

In their hotel suite in Miami, Miriam grabbed Dickie and kissed him enthusiastically. He pulled back and looked at her, and for a brief glimmer of a moment he remembered who he had been only a few months before. He remembered what it was like to be scared and lonely, and to have no confidence in what the future might hold. And it occurred to him that this woman had changed his life in a way that he would never have thought possible, and that if he had the sense to latch on to her and the tenacity never to let go, then his life would be as perfect as the one of which he'd dreamt. And as he looked at her, she looked at him, and for a brief moment she remembered who she had been only a few months before. She remembered what it was like to be scared and lonely, and to have no confidence in what the future might hold. And it occurred to her that this man had changed her life in a way that she would never have thought possible, and that if she had the sense to latch on to him and the tenacity never to let go, then her life would be as perfect as the one of which she'd dreamt. Miriam kissed her king, and Dickie his kingmaker.

"And now, in the presidential race," the news anchor continued. "Our computer has consistently found Florida too close to call, but with over 80 percent of the votes in, including almost all of the rural areas in inland and northern Florida, we can predict with certainty that the winner of Florida's twenty-five electoral votes will be . . . Col. Cody Clark, who will receive about 35 percent of the state's popular vote, in contrast to Senator Don Green's 33 percent and President Honeycutt's 32 percent. So, Col. Cody Clark's strategy of allying himself with the Sunshine Initiative, of turning the nightlife culture of Miami Beach and Palm Beach into a political issue, has proven inspired.

"This finishes our electoral vote tally with the following results: Senator Don Green has won 263 electoral votes, President Herbert Honeycutt 250, and Col. Cody Clark 25. President Honeycutt, incidentally, has won more popular votes than Senator Don Green, but that is not relevant tonight. No individual candidate has received 270 electoral votes, a majority of the 538 votes cast in the Electoral College, and without that majority, the selection of a president will fall to the House of Representatives. I turn now to our experts, for an analysis of this situation. Has this ever happened before?"

"Yes it has," said a bespectacled figure at a desk near the anchorman's. "It was 1824, and the candidates that year were four: John Quincy Adams, Andrew Jackson—"

"Jesus Christ," muttered Buddy, as he watched the electoral map behind the commentators add its final piece, a limp verdant electoral appendage dangling off a blue and red eastern seaboard. Col. Cody Clark, twenty-five electoral votes. "Does anybody realize what this means?"

"This means that we could face a Constitutional crisis," President Honeycutt's first trusted aide said in the Oval Office, grimly assessing the situation.

"This means that Daylight Initiative campaigns are going to pop up in all fifty states," Laslo said in a Miami hotel room. "There's no stopping us now."

"It means that a blatant amateur can win a Senate seat without any professional media guidance," Buddy said, in a Walcott Falls ballroom.

"It means that Dickie Vanderhaltz is the ranking officer in the nation's third largest electoral party," Hugh Brock said, barely restraining his invective from a bar somewhere in South Florida.

"It means," said Rollo Plank with a wide smile that made Columbus, Ohio, shine, "that I get to pick the next President of the United States!"

"Well," said Steve Lowry, his point man, not quite so enthusiastically, "it means you're going to have to get 218 Congressmen to agree on one."

Chapter Twenty-five

Dickie woke up in the Presidential Suite of the Tampa Statler. The open curtains revealed a panoramic view of a sun-splashed downtown and the Gulf. A warm breeze played with the ends of Miriam's hair as she lay beside him, facedown and asleep. He reached over and slowly lifted the sheet from her. She shifted a bit and settled with her left knee tucked up beneath her and her ass thrust toward him. The temptation, combined with his exhilaration, was too great. He ran his hand lightly over the smooth curves, then lifted it and swatted her with a satisfying smack.

She shrieked and sprang up on her arms, then rolled over to see him beaming at her, delighted. It took her a second to remember where she was. She glanced at the clock. It was eight A.M.

"Get up," he commanded joyously, as he swung his leg over her and started to hump her playfully.

"Oh sweet Jesus," she cried, pushing him off her. "Not now. We didn't get to bed until four."

He folded his arms across his chest. "But, I'm a United States senator." She did not move and his smile quickly turned into a pout.

She looked up at him with growing satisfaction. He *was* a senator, a senator all her own. "Congratulations," she said softly. She leaned forward and kissed him, then paused to admire her handiwork. He looked into her eyes and reached for her again. "No time for that right now," she said. "You've got to get out a statement for today's cycle." She got out of bed, slipped on a bathrobe, and walked to the laptop computer on the desk by the open window. "Okay," she said. "Anything in particular you want to say?"

"I'm a senator. I can say anything I like."

"Dickie, now that you're a senator, the last thing you can say is anything you like. You just got elected with 35 percent of the vote on a third-party ticket. You'd better watch your step, or you won't be reelected."

"I never thought of that," he said, and rose to pace the hotel room floor. "After all, you could say that 65 percent of the people don't like me, couldn't you?" She nodded and he continued to pace. "We've got to reach those people, don't we? Okay, that's what I intend to do. I want my statement to say that I won't rest until 100 percent of the people of Florida like me! All of 'em," he exclaimed, sweeping his arm in front of himself, imagining broad vistas of supporters.

Miriam watched as he rambled.

"Sit down," she said. "Let me do this." She read aloud as she tapped out the statement. "Early this morning, the people of Florida made me their United States senator. This is the happiest and proudest day of my life. I thank both State Senator Rojas and Mayor Burke for their graciousness after a long and tiring campaign. I appreciate the trust placed in me by my fellow Floridians, and promise to bring to Florida the kind of representation it deserves."

She paused a moment to savor the statement's cryptic conclusion and then picked up the phone to call the press room on the first floor of the hotel.

"Hello? This is Miriam Moskowitz with the Vanderhaltz campaign." She paused and smiled. "Yes, thank you, we're very excited." She crossed her legs and switched the phone to her other ear. "I'm calling because Senator-elect Vanderhaltz has a statement he'd like—" She sat forward suddenly. "Senator Paris? And Senator Gibson? Both of them?" She glanced at Dickie, who stood innocently looking out the window. "No, this is the first we've heard of it. Of course. We'll be down in an hour for a press conference. Thanks." She gently placed the phone down. "Paris and Gibson lost," she said to Dickie.

Dickie nodded. "And?" he asked, recognizing neither the names nor her point.

"Dickie, don't you get it? Paris and Gibson lost their Senate races to Democrats. There are only fifty Republican senators. Only fifty, get it?"

"And?" he asked again.

She whirled from the table, chewing on a fingernail as she explained the arithmetic. "There are fifty Republicans, forty-nine Democrats, and you. The first thing the Senate will do when it convenes in January is elect a majority leader. But neither party has a majority. So what's going to happen when they have the leadership election next January?"

He thought about it as hard as he could. "Well, that depends on how I vote, doesn't it?"

"Exactly!" she squealed as she raced to the window and hugged him excitedly. "It's all up to you!"

"But what difference does it make?"

"Dickie, it makes all the difference. The majority party gets everything: control of the Senate floor, chairmanships, everything. The minority party gets nothing, Dickie. Nada. Zippo."

"But wait," Dickie said, trying to fathom the situation. "What if I voted with the Democratic senators? Then there would be fifty Democratic votes and fifty Republican votes, and there would still be a tie."

"The vice president, as president of the Senate, casts a vote to break the tie."

"But who's the vice president? Nobody won the presidential election."

"It doesn't matter. The House of Representatives is going to elect the next president and vice president, and the House of Representatives is Democratic. Whoever they elect will be voting with the Democrats, Rollo Plank will see to that. So it's really 50–50. No matter how you slice it, yours is the last vote."

Dickie considered his new identity—*the last vote*. "Then how am I supposed to vote?"

Miriam laughed and hugged him again. "Dickie, my darling little man," she cooed, "you are about to be subject to the greatest bidding war that has ever taken place in the history of our republic. People are about to beat a path to your door and they are going to offer you anything your heart desires, all in exchange for one vote. We are going to trade it for the greatest pile of political booty ever amassed."

He nodded as he began to understand the position into which he had blundered. "I've got it," he burst. "Universal daylight saving time! Whichever party supports universal daylight saving time gets my support!"

She looked at him, amused, "Daylight saving time? Forget universal daylight saving time." She laughed. "That was yesterday, Dickie, small potatoes. We're going to load our wagon so full that your reelection will be assured before you take the oath for your first term! Don't you understand? We can have anything!"

He looked at her quizzically. "Anything?"

"Anything!" she triumphed.

His eyes opened like morning flowers. He suddenly understood. "Anything!"

"Yes," she replied, reeling as majestic waves of victory swept over her. Tears crept out of her eyes, down her cheeks, and into her trembling, brimming smile. "Anything."

"Anything!" he roared, and in a joyous instant he knocked her over and onto the unmade bed, casting her down with the strength of a champion, and was on her, filling her with his awesome new power. She laughed dizzily as he took her, thinking of the days ahead, when at the last moment she realized what he was doing and enjoyed a bright, brief flare.

Washington held its breath for weeks awaiting the election's resolution. Rumors circulated daily regarding deals that would soon be struck. Reporters clung to every shred of gossip, escalating innuendo into front-page news, and manufacturing innuendo when there was none to escalate. Most rumors concerned the House of Representatives, but their vote would be moot if Col. Cody Clark bartered away his electoral votes in exchange for some concession from either Senator Don Green or President Honeycutt.

"What are you going to do?" Miriam asked Col. Cody Clark when she, Dickie, and Laslo gathered with him to discuss the situation.

"Why, nothing," he answered with a tone of surprise. "What do you expect me to do?"

"If you directed the electors you won in Florida to vote for either Green or Honeycutt, whoever you picked would have a majority of the Electoral College, and would be president."

"Well, you can forget that," he said. "I wouldn't come near Honeycutt now, after what he said about my unfortunate situation. And I wouldn't have anything to do with a heathen like Green, either."

"But if you joined with Dickie, and we could deliver the White House and the Senate, both, as one package! It would be the greatest deal ever made! You can't just walk away from this," Miriam protested.

"I certainly intend to," Col. Cody Clark said. "I'll just take my check and leave, thanks. I turned fifty million in this election, and I'm grateful to the Lord for the opportunity to make that kind of return while serving the public. Frankly, I don't want to tax the Lord's ability to give."

"Then what are you going to do?" Miriam asked.

"I'm going to pray," Col. Cody Clark said with a smile.

Chapter Twenty-six

We are gathered here today because we have once again been reminded that our ballots are not enough." Loudspeakers carried Col. Cody Clark's voice out to the crowd on the Mall, as he stood in front of the Lincoln Memorial. "We have gathered to ask that one more ballot be counted, the ballot of God. Lord, our polls are still open, and we are here to receive your vote, to ask you for a sign as the House of Representatives meets to make its final decision."

It was cold as hell that afternoon. To the surprise of everybody but Col. Cody Clark, tens of thousands of his supporters appeared to pray on the hastily convened National Pray for Leadership Day. "It's a foolish idea," Laslo had said when Col. Cody Clark announced his intentions. "What do you expect to happen?"

"The Lord will provide us with a sign," Col. Cody Clark replied. "The Lord is like a stock market indicator that does not miss the turning points in the cycle. We will learn who the Lord has chosen to be the next president, make no mistake about that."

Laslo had been withholding his opinions of Col. Cody Clark's religious beliefs out of respect for such outlandishly good ideas as tax babies, but was now forced to express his concern.

"Frankly, Colonel, I think it's a little wrongheaded. In reality, Honeycutt, Green, and you ought to fight it out in the presence of females, like the large males do in the herd. The Founding Fathers certainly missed the boat on that one," he snorted.

But Col. Cody Clark was insistent, and now, his words wafted out on clouds of frosty breath. "Lord," he prayed before the crowd, "this is the hour of our nation's need. In the midst of our mismanagement, Lord, we look to your reorganization. In the midst of our failure, we look to your restructuring. For you are our consultant, Lord, and we are calling you in. Lord, give us your sign, and enlighten us," he said, and as he asked to see the light, a light appeared, not a Mosaic column of fire, but a tiny red dot suddenly flashing at a station nurse's desk on the seventh floor of Walter Reed Memorial Hospital, a call light that had not been used since the patient in room 719A had been admitted three months before. But much as Col. Cody Clark intended, it was the light that showed the way just the same.

The Speaker rocked back in his chair, a tall glass of single-malt Scotch sitting in front of him. "Throughout my career, friends," he smiled broadly, "I have loved the Constitution. It is a remarkable document that has served our nation well." He took a deep drink from his glass and smacked his lips appreciatively. "And my faith has finally been rewarded because, thanks to the Constitution, we are about to pick the next President of the United States."

With The Speaker sat the leaders of the major factions in the Democratic caucus of the House of Representatives, the same factions that had, in fact, been at each other's throats throughout the last term, and had only agreed to Don Green as a compromise candidate under pressure from the other forces in the national Democratic party, forces now absent from the equation. "I've called you guys together—and that includes Edith, of course"—he said as he smiled at the female representative from suburban Cleveland, "because you're all reasonable people. If we can act like reasonable people, then we can pick the next president right here and now."

The pro-labor liberal from Queens raised his hand immediately. "Rollo, I don't see why we have to go through this. After all, don't we have an obligation to Don Green?" He looked around the room for support. "Don is our party's candidate. I voted for him once and I intend to do so again."

The Speaker raised his palms peacefully. "I understand how you feel, Morton, but allow me to make this point. Our Founding Fathers, in their wisdom, foresaw this situation and charged the House of Representatives with the responsibility of selecting the next president. Our Founding Fathers did not obligate us in such a situation for any particular candidate. In fact, my own interpretation of the Constitution is that this body is intended to pick a candidate who would bind our nation together, and if we elect a candidate who has already failed to do so, we would be derelict in our duties. So, from a Constitutional perspective, I favor picking whomever the fuck we like, and anybody who objects can take it up with the Founding Fathers."

"But what precedent might we point to for this type of thing?" asked the minority congressman from Chicago.

"A good question, Reggie," The Speaker replied. "In 1824 the Electoral College failed to produce a majority and the election was turned over to the House of Representatives, which elected John Quincy Adams, who didn't have a majority of the popular vote. So there is a clear historical precedent for doing whatever we think is best for the country."

"But if we don't choose Don Green, how can we explain selecting an individual who hasn't received a single vote in a popular election?" asked the congressman from South Carolina, who supported the merchant marine and protection for the textile industry.

"I don't look at it that way, George," The Speaker intoned. "I think that the voters have already repudiated Don Green, and President Honeycutt for that matter. So how can we legitimately claim to be transacting faithfully our responsibilities by choosing him?"

The Speaker's audience appreciated his impeccable logic. Selecting Don Green, their party's candidate, would clearly be viewed as an act of political henchmanry that would be condemned by the people now and history later. "Fine," said The Speaker, taking their silence as consent. "The only remaining issue is who we're going to pick."

At once, several members began to speak. Names collided in the air. "Now wait," The Speaker said. "We need to begin defining the characteristics of the person on whom we'd want to bestow this office. So I'd like each of you to give me one requirement for the person we choose, one condition that has to be met. Then we'll see if we can come up with anybody who would satisfy them. And just to make things easier, I'm going to go first. Whoever we choose to be president has to be willing to work in very close cooperation with the House leadership."

"Come on, Rollo," the neoliberal from New Mexico snapped. "All you're saying is that he has to be a good friend of yours."

"What's wrong with him being a good friend of Rollo's?" asked the farm state congressman, who had done well by being one.

"Wait a minute," the female representative from suburban Cleveland said. "Who said it was going to be a he?"

"Now everybody hold on!" The Speaker shouted. "All I said was that I insist on willingness to work with the House leadership. After all, what's the point of picking a president if he's not going to let us help him run the country?"

Everyone saw The Speaker's point. If it came down to a choice between a president who was sympathetic to their water projects, defense bases, urban transport systems, and local development grants, and one who was not, then it was no choice at all. "I'll ask Frank to go next," The Speaker said.

The farm state congressman sat forward in his chair and rubbed his palms together. "Rollo," he began, "the family farmer is hurting out there, and he's going down. We can't let that happen. The next president is going to have to support our farm bill."

"Oh, please," said the neoliberal from New Mexico, a mining state. "A free ride for soy beans. Maybe some of us would like a free ride for copper and zinc, too!"

"Maybe some of us might like to try eating copper and zinc," the farm state congressman shot back.

"Now hold on!" The Speaker bellowed. "Frank has every right to ask for support of the committee farm bill. George, you're next."

The congressman from South Carolina drew in his breath. "Rollo, I'm a little more concerned about what happened to Luther Moss's Senate seat."

"How's that?" The Speaker asked.

"Well, out of nowhere comes this fellow Vanderhaltz, the geology professor, and he wins on the universal daylight saving time issue. I'm worried that the Republicans are going to grab ahold of this thing and run with it. It might work well in the South."

"I understand your concern," The Speaker agreed.

"So I insist that the president agree not to oppose universal daylight saving time when it comes up on the legislative calendar next year."

"But how can you—" the pro-labor liberal began, before The Speaker cut him off.

"That's what he wants. We don't need to get into a debate over the relative merits of each other's political needs. We're simply trying to understand each other. Now, Edith is next."

The female representative from suburban Cleveland cleared her throat. "I want a minimum wage for home work."

The Texas congressman's eyes widened. "This again?"

"Home work is work."

"Hold on," The Speaker said. "Is that what you *have to have*, Edith? Are you being fair here?"

"All right," she conceded. "I'll settle for a president who hasn't committed himself against it."

"But virtually every major figure has committed against it," the neoliberal from New Mexico complained. "Rollo," he pleaded, "do we really have to—"

"Yes, we do," The Speaker said. "Next."

"I could ask for a black vice president," the minority congressman said with a broad smile, as he looked slowly around the room.

"Be serious," the majority leader said.

"Why not? All of you want a white vice president." The minority congressman said. "But I'd be willing to settle for . . . ," he paused as he thought for a moment, " . . . five Cabinet appointments, including State and Justice, and the next two Supreme Court seats." He paused, then improvised. "And a national holiday for Bird and Trane."

"Who the hell are they?" the congressman from East Texas asked.

"Done!" said The Speaker.

The neoliberal leaned forward. "I find it incredible that in all of this discussion I haven't heard a word about renovating, renaissance, renewal, rebuilding, repairing, or re-anything. Where have all of you been?"

The Speaker answered. "Get to the point."

"All right," the neoliberal said with disdain. "The president has to commit to a Rebuilding America program, the cornerstone of which is the equipment-that-doesn't-work tax credit."

"For Pete's sake," moaned the pro-labor liberal from Queens. "Don't you guys ever give up?"

"Tax credit it is," The Speaker noted and pointed to the congressman from East Texas. "A.H., you're next."

The congressman from East Texas smiled modestly. "Boys," he said, "where I come from in East Texas, we only want two things—expensing of intangible drilling costs and percentage depletion of oil reserves."

"Okay, it's on the list. That leaves Morton," The Speaker said, turning to the pro-labor liberal from Queens. "What'll it be, Mort?"

The pro-labor liberal from Queens cleared his throat. "Rollo, I'm worried about what our party stands for. Its ideals and its future. We've got to stand up to these Fundamentalists, like Colonel Cody Clark. We've got to take them head-on, Rollo."

The minority congressman from Chicago, the female representative from suburban Cleveland, and the neoliberal from New Mexico all agreed.

The pro-labor liberal nodded to acknowledge their support. "Well, if we're going to stick it to these guys, I can think of no better place to start than with this daylight saving time nonsense."

"So what are you asking for?" The Speaker asked.

"The president has to commit himself against the universal daylight saving time initiative."

"Now, wait a minute," the congressman from East Texas sputtered, along with the congressman from South Carolina. "You've got to deal with reality."

"The reality is that these Daylight types are nuts."

The congressman from East Texas turned to The Speaker and spoke bitterly. "Well, I hope you're happy now, Rollo. Morton is ready to give up our seats in the South just to keep his hands clean and his heart pure."

"It's better than turning into the other party," said the minority congressman.

"Oh, that's just fine," said the congressman from South Carolina. "What about bartering your vote for racial appointments? I thought we were a national party."

"We were a national party until you injected this regional thing," the congressman from a farm state said.

"That's rich," sneered the Texas congressman. "When did you have any concerns that went beyond the pasture fence?"

"That's enough!" bellowed The Speaker.

The neoliberal shook his head. "Rollo, we all know you've got the best of intentions. But I don't see how we're going to get through this. We've got to find somebody who is prepared to support tax breaks for oil and gas producers, farm income supports, and the equipment-that-doesn't-work tax credit, who's willing to make Reggie's appointments, who's close to you, and who's neither opposed to nor in favor of universal daylight saving time."

The Speaker could not help but get the point, and he began to speak defensively. "I know it's a tough list, but if we spent a little time on it, and tried to be reasonable . . . "

"Rollo, these are the issues that divided us in the last election," the farm state congressman said. "They've always divided us. The only way we could all agree on someone is if they had no opinions at all."

The congressman from East Texas rose and faced The Speaker. "Damn it, Rollo, he's right. We're not going to get anywhere unless someone walks through *that door* who slept through the last election."

He had barely finished his sentence when the very same door to The Speaker's office produced the sound of a knock. The Speaker, like everybody else, was momentarily taken aback, but quickly said, "Come in!" There was silence in the room as the door swung open to reveal their answer—a thin, pale man standing with arms open wide, a beaming smile on his face.

"Rollo!" Ezra Wheezle said. "I'm alive!"

Chapter Twenty-seven

The Watergate Apartments, Miriam told Dickie, were the only place to live now that he was a senator, and the only place that she would live now that she was living with a senator. It was almost Christmas, and Miriam now knew the full meaning of giving in the Christmas season. It meant that, as she had predicted, the two parties were going to give her anything she wanted. They began by intimating that Dickie's philosophical outlook was naturally allied with theirs. But once Miriam assured them—in Laslo's absence—that Dickie didn't have a philosophical outlook, they all got down to brass tacks and started making a list.

They had been to Capitol Hill to pursue these discussions that morning and had not been back for more than five minutes when Laslo, who had lately been busy arranging Daylight initiatives in forty-nine states, arrived.

Miriam let him in and he followed her back into the apartment.

"I've been doing a good deal of thinking about our position," he said, "and I think I've got it figured out."

Miriam sat down on the couch next to Dickie and put her feet up. "Laslo, what are you talking about?"

Laslo sensed her disdain, but continued. "We announce our position publicly, out in the open. That's the key. We announce that we're going to vote for whichever of the two parties supports the provisions of the Principled Naturalist Omnibus Salvation Act. It's like a public auction of our vote."

"Laslo," Miriam interrupted wearily.

"See? The two parties will have to compete for our support. The highest bidder wins," he said with satisfaction, "and they can't back out."

Miriam pushed the hair off her forehead and gestured toward a chair. "Laslo, sit down."

Laslo stalked the chair and deftly lowered himself into it. "We'll ask for letters of commitment from their entire memberships, every Republican or Democrat. That guarantees us unanimous support for some provisions of the act, see?"

"Laslo—" Miriam interrupted again.

He raised a silencing hand. "And then we can—"

"Laslo, shut up!" she shouted, startling Dickie, and finally getting Laslo's attention. "Laslo, what I'm trying to say is, we've already had our meeting with the majority leader. We saw him in his office this morning."

Laslo stared at her coldly. "Shouldn't I have been there?"

"Dickie's a senator, Laslo. He can run his own show."

"A senator!" Laslo spat. "He's barely capable of living in the woods!"

"Laslo," Miriam broke in, "the majority leader has agreed to give him Moss's seniority, Moss's chairmanship of the Science and Engineering Committee, and all of Moss's standing. Dickie is going to be untouchable, and when he's reelected with something like 70 percent of the vote six years from now he's going to be touted as a national candidate pretty quickly. President Dickie Vanderhaltz, Laslo. That's what we're after."

"We? Who is we?"

"Dickie and I. His fiancée," she added.

Laslo folded his arms and smiled his smallest, hardest smile. "I should have known."

"We didn't forget you, you know," Dickie offered. "We got some concessions on the Daylight issue."

"Like what?"

"We're going to have a study commission," Miriam reported. "And the majority leader has agreed to support an experimental two-year arrangement. It's all going to be announced in a press conference next week."

Laslo glared at the two of them. "You think that's payback for everything I've done?" he said, his anger mounting. "I made you, Dickie. If you think you can dump me now, you're going to be very sorry."

"Laslo, be reasonable," Miriam said.

"Reasonable! Why should I be reasonable?" he said, with barely restrained rage. He had underestimated the little minx again. "You'll pay for this treachery!" And he flew out the door and down the hall, tossing threats over his shoulder all the way.

Senior Younger, Jr., was eating alone in the Members Dining Room in the Rayburn House Office Building when Bart Boyer, his neo-liberal colleague from New Mexico, approached his table. "Can I speak to you for a moment, Senior?" he asked solicitously.

"I don't see why not," Senior Younger, Jr., said, looking up from his vegetable soup.

The neoliberal took a seat opposite Senior Younger, Jr. "First, I want to congratulate you on your victory, Senior."

"Sure you do, Bart," Senior Younger, Jr., said. "When I was down twenty points in the polls, did I hear from you? Did I get a bit of help from the Congressional Campaign Committee? Not a cent."

"Please, Senior. You know how these things are. You looked too far gone to spend money on. Besides, you did just fine without our help, didn't you?"

"With less help than you think," he said, thinking of Congressman Wheezle.

"And congratulations on the record," Boyer said, breezily changing the subject. "How many have you sold? A million?"

"Something like that," Senior Younger, Jr., said. "It's still number one on the country charts."

Boyer reached into his briefcase and pulled out a copy of Senior's CD. "My kids are real fans. Asked me to get your autograph, if that's okay," he said. He looked up embarrassedly and extended the box and an autograph marker toward Senior Younger, Jr.

Senior Younger, Jr., quickly scrawled his name. "Now, is that what you wanted?"

"Well, no, Senior. I have something much more important to discuss." As he put the CD back in his briefcase, he glanced around to make sure no one was close enough to hear. "Rollo Plank recently had a group of us in to discuss the presidential election. He thinks that if a broad-based group of House Democrats could get together and agree on a candidate, then we would be in a good position to sell that candidate to the Democratic caucus and, well, sort of have a president of our own."

Senior Younger, Jr., listened noncommittally. "What about Don Green?"

"Rollo's feeling is that Don's already lost the election. Don's a proven loser. Besides, there's never been much in the way of warm feeling between Rollo and Don."

Senior Younger, Jr., maintained a skeptical expression. "And were you able to agree on somebody?"

Bart Boyer nodded.

"I see," Senior said, wiping his mouth with a napkin. "And who is the next President of the United States going to be?"

Bart Boyer took a deep breath. "Ezra Wheezle."

Senior Younger, Jr., dropped his spoon. He stared at Boyer for a minute before picking it up. "Ezra Wheezle's alive?"

"He's not in a coma anymore, Senior. He woke up. Yesterday."

Senior took it in, and then asked, "Why him?"

The neoliberal congressman drew another deep breath and out came the whole story, how the alternative at this point was a pro-

longed battle within the caucus that would be waged in the newspapers and on television, discrediting their party for a generation.
Admittedly, Bart Boyer admitted, Senior Younger, Jr., might not be
as concerned with the prospects for the party over that time frame,
but he should still be willing to go along with The Speaker's program, if only out of loyalty.

Senior Younger, Jr., felt little loyalty to anything, let alone the
party, but as the words flew by, he calculated. He smiled. "Bart, I'll
be happy to go along, for the good of the party. If we'd be best
served by making Ezra the next president, then I will do everything
I can to make sure that the next president he will be. And I can assure you," he added, "that I will deliver my support to him personally at the earliest possible moment."

The first thought that Ezra Wheezle had when he awoke from the
hazy netherworld of his coma was that he had probably been asleep
for a very long time. The second was that he wondered how his
campaign was progressing. The third was that he wondered where
he was and the fourth was that the awesome pain in his chest and
head, the last thing he could remember, was gone. The fifth thing
he thought was that he was in a hospital room and the sixth was
that, if he was in a hospital room, then there would be a panel built
into the bed rail with a button on it, above which was a simplified
picture of a nurse. He slowly lifted his hand and pushed it. A few
moments later a nurse strode into his room. Congressman Wheezle raised his hand slightly and emitted a low, guttural noise, the
most he could manage, at which point the woman jumped back a
good six feet, clutched her hand to her breast, and shrieked, "Jesus
Christ! He's awake!" which led Congressman Wheezle to suspect
that what had happened to him and the consequences for his campaign were probably even worse than he had at first imagined.

A parade of people suddenly appeared before Congressman
Wheezle, each looking into his eyes with a penlight and a mixture
of fear and amazement. First came a resident, then an older doctor, and finally a middle-aged man who identified himself as the

chief of medicine. The chief of medicine excused all the others from the room and sat down by Congressman Wheezle's bedside and told him the story. He had been in a coma since before Labor Day, news of his illness was basically a secret, his custodial care was being directed by a Mr. Steven Lowry and, on the day following the presidential election (which, incidentally, did not produce a president), Mr. Lowry had relayed orders from The Speaker that Congressman Wheezle's life-support system be turned off. Were it not for standard hospital procedure of reviewing such cases for a six-week period, it would have been.

Congressman Wheezle was pleased to hear that The Speaker had decided to take him off life support after election day, because it meant that The Speaker had reason to keep him *on* life support *until* election day, which meant that whether he was alive or dead had something to do with the election. He gathered his courage and looked the chief of medicine squarely in the eye. "Tell me, Doctor," he asked, "am I still a congressman?"

The chief of medicine searched his memory and answered. "I think so."

It was all Congressman Wheezle needed to hear. He got up out of bed, found his clothing in the closet, and started to dress.

"You're not thinking of leaving, are you?"

Congressman Wheezle was knotting his tie in a mirror. "Why not?"

"Well, you've been unconscious for about three months. Frankly, it's a miracle that you're awake, let alone walking. There are a host of questions concerning your recovery. You should stay in bed where we can examine you."

"Nonsense," replied Congressman Wheezle. "I feel just fine." He slipped an arm into his coat. "I'll come back in a day or two and we can go through the whole battery of tests. Right now, I've got business to take care of."

Shortly thereafter he would find out that he was going to be the next President of the United States.

Congressman Wheezle was pleased to become President of the

United States. He had never had a burning ambition to be president, had, in fact, never harbored an ambition other than Senior Younger, Jr.'s, chairmanship, but he was happy to become the president because it was a favor that that The Speaker needed, and Congressman Wheezle was always pleased to do whatever his friend The Speaker needed to have done. He certainly bore Rollo no animosity for ordering his life support turned off—after all, his death would have forced a special election in February, when voter turnout would be low and his seat easiest to defend, which struck Congressman Wheezle as good political strategy, even if it meant his dying.

From the moment he swung open the door to The Speaker's office, he saw the presidency as a duty owed to party and colleagues. He sat down among The Speaker's informal gathering and answered its questions methodically. Yes, he had never opposed universal daylight saving time. No, he had never favored universal daylight saving time. Yes, he favored an open mind toward minimum wage for home work, 115 percent of price parity for farmers, water projects for Californians, appointments of black candidates to the Cabinet and Supreme Court, and the equipment-that-doesn't-work tax credit. Would he be willing to run the country in the name of the House of Representatives?

"Sure," he replied agreeably. "Whatever you guys want."

If there was a moment's hesitation on anybody's part, The Speaker squelched it as he rose from his desk and thrust his massive paw toward Congressman Wheezle.

"Congratulations, Ezra!" he boomed. "You're going to be the next President of the United States!"

In the space of a few days The Speaker's band made their way through the House Democratic Caucus, and the hard-core group that supported Congressman Wheezle started to expand. The news media quickly picked up the rumor that a deal had been struck, informal counts showed 150 hard votes for Congressman Wheezle, and a bandwagon started to form, all orchestrated by The Speaker. He promoted Congressman Wheezle as the candidate of national

unity, a middle-of-the-road president whose interests were custodial rather than partisan, selected to salve the wounds created by an
election gone haywire. The alternative to Congressman Wheezle,
he repeatedly pointed out, was a struggle that would leave the nation without a leader. The Speaker also had the sense to keep Congressman Wheezle quiet and low-key, providing selected media
representatives access on a limited basis, feeding them such polling
results as the fact that only 2 percent of the population objected to
Congressman Wheezle or had negative impressions of him, while
moving quickly past the fact that only 3 percent of the population
had ever heard of him at all.

With this organization behind him, the probability of Congressman Wheezle's elevation grew. People came to call. Lobbyists
backdated get-well cards and sent them to the hospital in the hope
that Congressman Wheezle would believe they were lost in the
mail. Representatives of other governments presented themselves
and discreetly mentioned their willingness to locate new investment
facilities in the Walcott Falls area if that was desired.

Congressman Wheezle, in the euphoria of his resurrected circumstances, had forgotten about his arrangement with the National Coalition for New Economic Direction until he looked at
his schedule and saw Congressman Younger's name on it. Congressman Wheezle froze in his tracks as it all came back to him and
he realized there was nothing he could do. He certainly couldn't go
to The Speaker and explain that he had worked to unseat a Democratic chairman. He would earn The Speaker's eternal wrath
and, therefore, cost himself the presidency, an office he was coming to believe he would enjoy. He could only hope that Senior
Younger, Jr., was still ignorant of the matter, and was calling to express the predictable sentiments regarding Congressman Wheezle's
forthcoming promotion.

But that was obviously not the case. As Congressman Wheezle
offered a polite greeting, Senior Younger, Jr., impatiently tapped
the floor with his cane. "Come on, Ezra. You know why I'm here,"
he snapped.

Congressman Wheezle gave a tight smile. "Well, I presumed you wanted to wish me well, as I do you, given both of our recent good fortunes." His faith in this story grew as he told it. "This song of yours is sweeping the country," he said.

"Shut up, Ezra. I'm here because I've got you by the balls," he said, swinging his cane sharply across Congressman Wheezle's shin.

"Damn it, Senior!" Congressman Wheezle said, rubbing his leg. "How the hell do you figure that?"

"Because I have all the correspondence between your office and the National Coalition for New Economic Direction."

"What do you mean, Senior? I've never even signed a letter to the National Coalition for New Economic Direction."

"Stop it, Ezra," Senior Younger, Jr., ordered as he rapped Ezra's other leg with his cane. "Do you think you'll get away with it because you had somebody else sign them?"

It was worth a try, Congressman Wheezle thought. "Well, maybe you have something that somebody in my office wrote, but what does that have to do with me?"

"We can ask Rollo if that's how he sees it."

Congressman Wheezle bit his lip. He was out of options. "Look, Senior," he said, engineering a quick confession. "I'm sorry you found out about this, not because I'm embarrassed, which I am, but because this might give you the wrong impression of what I really think of you." He continued as Senior Younger, Jr., watched impassively. "I have great personal respect for you. I just never expected you to live to 114."

"One hundred fifteen now."

"Whatever," Congressman Wheezle said impatiently, having nothing else left to say.

"I accept your apology," Senior Younger, Jr., said. "But that doesn't mean you're not going to pay for it."

"What do you have in mind?"

Senior Younger, Jr., rubbed his palms on his thighs. "Damn, Ezra," he said with a look of frustration. "I'm not exactly sure. I've got the President of the United States right where I want him and I don't know what the hell to do with him."

"Be reasonable, Senior."

"Stop worrying, Ezra. I'm too old to want anything important." Senior Younger, Jr., looked up decisively. "All right, then. This is it. Who's running for your seat in the Pennsylvania Fourth?"

"You don't know him. He's the mayor back in Walcott Falls, and he's going to make a great candidate."

"No," said Senior Younger, Jr. "He's going to make a great mayor, because he's not going to run for your seat. Lenny Keeler is."

Congressman Wheezle's eyes widened. "What are you talking about? How do you know Lenny Keeler?"

"Oh, we've bumped into each other and I think he'd be a great congressman. It would be interesting to see what he does."

Congressman Wheezle blanched. "Oh, Senior, I think we'd be making a terrible mistake," he said.

"I think you've already made a terrible mistake," Senior Younger, Jr., snapped.

"Please, Senior," Congressman Wheezle pleaded. "I have local obligations."

"Look on the bright side, Ezra. You're going to be the president. You're relieved of your local obligations."

"But why can't you ask for something like a grant, or some kind of public works thing?"

"I don't need that sort of thing anymore, Ezra. What I do need is—a friend."

Congressman Wheezle took Senior Younger, Jr.'s, hand in his own and leaned forward. "I'll be your friend, Senior," he said earnestly.

Senior Younger, Jr., whipped his cane across Congressman Wheezle's shin. "You're going to make Lenny Keeler a congressman and I'll have a friend on the House floor. Somebody to sit around and pass the time with. You're going to tell your state party chairman that if he nominates anybody else, then he can kiss his sweet ass good-bye. You're going to tell every political action committee in town that if they raise one red cent for anybody except Lenny Keeler, then they can kiss their asses good-bye, too. You're going tell everybody in your local organization that as long as Lenny Keeler is their congressman they're going to keep everything they've got and they're going to get more. You're going to work your old district on behalf of Lenny Keeler if you have to, and you're going to play your phone like an accordion to make sure he wins, Ezra. And on the day he wins, you're going to get all the correspondence, all the evidence." He paused to gauge Congressman Wheezle's reactions. "Do you get me?"

Congressman Wheezle looked down at the floor and into his heart. He thought of his first election and of the years he had spent making himself the Caesar of an empire that spread from one congressional district boundary line to the other. He surveyed, with the fleeting velocity of retrospect, the long road to his current position, and then looked up to the mountaintop of the presidency. Was he really going to hand over his empire to a callow youth anointed only because of a senile old man's passing fancy?

You bet he was. "Yes, Senior, I do."

Senior Younger, Jr., reached out and shook Congressman Wheezle's hand. "Fine. I'll speak to the young man and get right back to you." He wheeled himself to the doorway, then turned and winked. "Congratulations, Mr. President."

Chapter Twenty-eight

It was six in the morning when the phone rang in Lenny's new apartment in Walcott Falls.

"Hello?" Lenny said, barely awake.

"Get up! It's Senior Younger," Senior Younger, Jr., announced.

Lenny sat up and struggled to find the clock. "What's wrong? Is something wrong? It's six in the morning."

"Where is the closest newspaper?" Senior Younger, Jr., demanded.

"It's on the front stoop," Lenny answered, rubbing his eyes.

"Get it."

"What the—" He propped himself up. "Wait a minute."

He went to the front door and swept the paper up. He took the paper back to bed, spread it across his lap, and began to read.

LOCAL CONGRESSMAN EZRA WHEEZLE

TO BE ELECTED PRESIDENT

House of Representatives Ballot to Be Held Today

Lenny scanned the front page for some indication that it was a joke, or that he was dreaming, but found none. Instead, there was a file photo of Wheezle and a story that confirmed the headline in gory detail.

Congressional sources confirm that the House of Representatives will meet today to elect Congressman Ezra T. Wheezle (D.-Pa., 4 C.D.), sixty-eight years old, as President of the United States, using their Constitutional authority to select a president following a deadlock in the Electoral College. Spokesmen for Speaker of the House Rollo D. Plank (D.-Oh., 10 C.D.) refused this evening to confirm or deny the rumor, but sources close to The Speaker and the party leadership stated this evening that Congressman Wheezle was selected in a closed-door meeting in the offices of Speaker Plank as a compromise candidate capable of unifying House Democrats. Sources also reveal that Congressman Wheezle has undergone a series of medical tests and has been found fit to serve as president, despite his recent illness, many details of which remain unspecified.

"Jesus Christ!" Lenny blurted into the phone. "Is this true? I mean, how did it happen?"

"Rollo has always wanted to have a president all his own," Senior Younger, Jr., replied, "and this was his chance. All he needed to do was get the caucus to agree on somebody, and Ezra has all the qualifications, the perfect compromise candidate. They've been all over the Hill the past few days drumming up support for him."

"After what he did to you? We've got to expose him before it's too late."

"Expose him?" Senior Younger, Jr., laughed into the phone. "Why would we want to do that? We've got the President of the United States right where we want him."

Lenny was silent as he reflected on this notion. Senior Younger, Jr., was right. They had the president dead to rights. "I—I guess so," Lenny stammered. "But what are you going to do with him?"

"I told Ezra I would shut up about the whole thing if he supported you for his congressional seat."

Lenny gulped audibly. "Me? Why?"

"Plenty of reasons. I'd like to have a friend in Congress, and you're just about the only friend I have left. Besides, you have more intelligence and strength of character than most of the Congress, although that really doesn't say much. But you also have a hook up the president's rear end, and that distinguishes you from most other potential candidates."

"What did Wheezle say?"

"He didn't take to it, at first, but I convinced him." Lenny said nothing, as the situation began to catch up with him. "Well, will you do it?" Senior asked.

"I'm not sure."

"Well, one of Wheezle's people is going to call and offer to fly you down to Washington and put you up as part of the transition operation. Get yourself down here. After that, whatever you decide is fine by me. Now, hop to it," said Senior Younger, Jr., and hung up.

Lenny stared straight ahead, the phone in his lap, and wondered whose fate was the more outlandish—Congressman Wheezle's, or his own.

Lenny really only began to understand the seriousness of his situation when he arrived in Washington late that evening and a chauffeured car took him from the airport to the Four Seasons Hotel. "It's taken care of," was the only thing the driver said, the same thing the hotel clerk said when he checked Lenny into one of the better suites.

Lenny had been there only a few minutes before there was a demanding knock on the door.

"Who is it?"

"It's Ezra Wheezle."

"Come in," Lenny replied, but before his words were spoken the doors flew open and Wheezle entered, accompanied by a sea of men in blue suits with short hair and grim expressions, traveling just as Don Green had traveled not long before. The men quickly scanned the hotel room and found nothing but a hotel room, and then dispersed, one to a position by the window, the others back out into the hall.

Congressman Wheezle sat down slowly and officiously. "Lenny, how are you?" he asked.

"I'm fine, Congressman Wheezle," Lenny said.

"It's President-elect Wheezle," he corrected. "And Congressman Keeler."

"Not yet," said Lenny. "I'm not sure."

Visions of Senior Younger, Jr., before The Speaker with a lapful of incriminating documents flooded Congressman Wheezle's mind. "I'm offering you something very rare," President-elect Wheezle said. "We're not talking about a lousy staff job anymore. We're talking about being a United States representative. Who knows where that might lead? You could serve ten terms and be a senator before you were fifty. Hell, you could wind up president, just like me. Think of it, President of the United States!"

Lenny was unmoved. "I just don't know."

"Be reasonable. What do you want?"

Lenny looked up abruptly. "An explanation. I want an explanation for what you did to Senior."

Congressman Wheezle paused. "Senior didn't want an explanation," he offered, as if that were an explanation in itself.

"Well, I do."

"Don't you get it? Senior didn't need an explanation. He understood. He knows what it's like being a congressman. After ten years, you know what you're going to accomplish. After twenty years, if you haven't accomplished it, you can write it off. Why should I have to spend the rest of my life waiting for Senior to die? Senior's already doing that, so why should both of us have to? Would that have been fair to me? I bided my time the way I was supposed to for thirty-six years. When these New Economic Direction guys came to me and said we could beat Senior in his district, I figured, what the hell. Senior had his day. I wanted mine. What's so wrong about that? It had nothing to do with my respect for Senior. Nobody has warmer feelings for him than I do. It's just business. He and I discussed the situation and there are no hard feelings. All he wanted was for me to get you my seat in Congress. Now, do we have a deal?"

"I'm not sure," Lenny said, trying to sort it all out.

Congressman Wheezle's face reddened with frustration. "You'd better make up your mind pretty damn fast, then. We've got a press conference scheduled tomorrow morning to announce your candidacy."

"I'm sorry," Lenny said, rising from his chair and walking to the window. "I have to think about it. I'll call you first thing tomorrow morning."

Congressman Wheezle saw there was no more he could say or do. "All right, then. But remember, son, I'm going to be the next President of the United States." He gave his lapels a grandiose tug and smiled at Lenny, the soul of paternalism. "You wouldn't want to disappoint the President of the United States, would you?"

Lenny just stared at him and they both knew he wasn't buying it.

"Then would you want to disappoint Senior?" Congressman Wheezle allowed the thought to set.

Lenny sighed and said nothing.

"Very well. Good night." Congressman Wheezle rose. He turned to the Secret Service man who stood by the window. "Let's go," he barked, and with that the Secret Service man raised his cuff to his lips and whispered furtively. In a moment the entire squadron reappeared, pouring through the door with their swiveling heads and ranging eyes. In an instant they swept back out of the room and blew down the hall with Congressman Wheezle, like an entire herd of sheepdogs herding one sheep.

Lenny rubbed his eyes. It was already past midnight. He was going to be a congressman, just as Steve Lowry and Jeff Monge would be White House staffers, and Wheezle a president. He had come to believe that people obtained power because they chose to. That seemed to be the rule—the key to having power was seeking it, for no one who bestowed power bestowed it cheaply or liberally. They were forced to share it only with those who sought it aggressively, and as a result, the ranks of power were peopled with those who wanted it most. But now he saw that there was one other precondition to power—being there when power struck. Dead-ass luck. Its beneficiaries adopted varied demeanors, but they shared this common good fortune, coupled with single-minded relentless drive. But he was the opposite. His fortune hunted him down and captured him. It made no difference that he was apathetic to power. Power, it turned out, wanted him. It made him want to drink.

It was almost three in the morning when Lenny went downstairs to the hotel bar. The place was deathly quiet. The tables had already been cleaned and set up for the next day. The bartender stood at the far end of the bar, talking to the only other customer. His back was turned to Lenny, and he only noticed him when he heard Lenny's chair scrape against the floor. He ambled down the bar.

"What'll it be, friend?"

"I'll have a bourbon neat and a draft chaser," Lenny said. The bartender quickly prepared his drink and served him. Lenny lifted the shot glass and poured it back. "Again," he said, putting the glass down and reaching for the beer.

The bartender put another drink on the bar. "You all set now?"

Lenny nodded, then picked up his beer and sipped. The bartender walked back to the other end of the bar and resumed his conversation, speaking to the other patron with a fawning familiarity. "Well," he said, "lots of us never expected to see you around here again."

The man at the bar grunted into his drink.

"But you're always welcome here," the bartender hastened to correct what he now thought sounded like a slight. "I mean, you're always welcome around this town, you know. Shucks, I think you did the right thing, myself."

The man grunted again. "Thank you," he might have replied.

The bartender turned to stack glasses and Lenny saw the face of the man at the bar. He was handsome, in his mid-sixties perhaps, with a thick graying mane of brown hair, broad shoulders, and a wide chest that kept them apart. Lenny knew him from somewhere. The man saw Lenny looking and turned a bit, not enough to hide himself but enough to show that he didn't want to be studied, but Lenny was already off his stool and walking toward him. Lenny recoiled when he realized who it was. "Wait a minute! You're—"

President Hoak turned toward Lenny and swatted the air in front of him. "Yes, yes," he said, "I'm Wade Hoak. And I'm going to get right the hell out of this seat if you don't shut up! Can't I just drink?"

"Don't be bothering President Hoak," the bartender intervened.

"Sure, sure," Lenny said, modulating his voice. "Here," he said, fumbling in his pocket, pulling out a folded wad of twenties and placing them on the bar, "get the president another round." He turned back to President Hoak, who looked down into his glass. "What are you doing here?"

President Hoak tipped back the rest of his drink and then pushed the empty glass forward, taking a fresh one from the bartender. Without turning, he said, "I'm here to see my lawyer."

"Your lawyer?"

"My wife is leaving me, all right?" He shook his head and sipped his drink.

"But you seemed more interested in her than in being president," Lenny said.

President Hoak chuckled. "Shit, boy, I was more interested in every piece of cooze that came walking down the alley than I was in being president."

Lenny sipped his drink. "But you were the President of the United States! How could you possibly—"

"Because I was the President of the United States, that's why," President Hoak interrupted forcefully. "By the time I realized I had the power to do anything I wanted, all I wanted to do was leave. If I'd had half the sense of a jackass, I'd have never taken that job." He shook his head. "Fuck it."

"But you had the ultimate power of war and peace, the fate of the world in your hands. You had the power that everybody else craves."

"Crap!" President Hoak said. "Who the hell needs it? One night, Euraline says, 'Wade, we don't need this. Get us some money and let's get out of here.' Now she's picked me clean and left."

Lenny was flabbergasted. "So what are you going to do?"

"What the hell can I do?" he asked, the picture of dismay. "Where the hell am I going to go? Here? No way. Back to Texas? You know how damn hot it is down there? California? With all the weirdos? No, I'm a man without a country now, young man. A *president* without a country!" He tipped his drink back again and tapped the bottom with his finger to shake down the last drops. "That's how it is, you know," he muttered as Lenny caught the bartender's eye and nodded toward President Hoak's empty glass. "You never see the country, anyway. You don't drive down the interstate and stop in the roadside joints or in a bar with sawdust on the floor. You get taken from place to place in a helicopter and never see anything in between. What country is that in?" he asked. "Tell me! What country is that? It might as well be . . . wherever," he said, the names of countries escaping him. "The country isn't the point, anyway. It's the power. You live your whole life running after power and after a while it doesn't make a lot of difference what country it is.

"It's the same the whole world over. Capitalist. Communist. Whatever. Sometimes I'd meet some younger guy, some guy who ran a smaller country. Damn good at doing his job. Maybe he'd just overthrown somebody. There'd be fire in his eyes. Did his job, kicked ass. And I'd think to myself, 'Come back in ten years, pal, and let's see your fire then.' In ten years he'll be a man without a country, same as me. Flying over land he doesn't recognize and waving to people he doesn't know. All the time thinking, *I'm doing a great job*, right up until he realizes that the job's being done to him."

Lenny looked at President Hoak. He was the last stop, Park Place, the pot of gold at the end of the rainbow, and he was drunk and alone. He was the ultimate winner: he won the most powerful position on earth and then traded it for enough money to live the way he wanted for the rest of his life. And all he now had to show for it was inebriated heartbreak. President Hoak was curled up in an alcoholic twist because he had been cursed with a simple man's heart and it could not lie to him. President Hoak had lost the people, and as a result lost himself. He had ceased being one of them long ago and had drifted away from them like an untethered balloon. He was forced to resort to leading them with his smile and his platitudes, likes and dislikes, and when he lost the stamina to keep pace with this charade, he fell back on the pleasures of the senses, but his senses had been abandoned along with his sensibilities and this, too, had failed him.

It didn't have to be that way, Lenny thought. He peeled off as many bills as seemed right and walked away silently.

When Laslo appeared at Dickie's office, it took Miriam a minute to realize it was Laslo. He was dressed in a gray business suit, with a white button-down shirt, a blue pattern tie, black wing tips, and a matching alligator belt. A Cuban cigar sat on his lower lip. "Hello, Miriam," he said in a pleasant tone that she found hard to associate with Laslo. "May I come in?"

She stepped aside and he walked to the center of the office. "What do you want?" she asked warily.

"Well, I thought I ought to come back here and clear the air," he said, blowing a puff of cigar smoke into it, "after our last discussion." Laslo paused and turned to Dickie. "You're a United States senator now, Dickie. Do you remember the trouble we had getting Moss to pay attention to us?" he said nostalgically, omitting that, for him, it had been no trouble at all. He looked around for a moment, at what had once been Senator Moss's office, surveying the elegant moldings and the large window with its view of the Capitol. "Remember when we sat on that couch and Moss turned the operation over to us?" he asked with a satisfied expression.

Miriam prodded him impatiently. "Come on, Laslo. What's the point?"

"Point?" he asked. "No point at all," he said, rolling his cigar with his fingertips. "I just wanted to come by to say a few things."

"Say then," she said testily. "The senator's a busy man and he hasn't the time."

Laslo suppressed a sneer and nodded toward Dickie deferentially. "Of course. Well, first, about the other afternoon. I suppose I got a little carried away," he admitted with a small shrug, "but damned if I don't just get a little too intense sometimes. Besides, a man has to have some faults, doesn't he?" he asked with a what-are-you-going-to-do grin. "So let me take this opportunity to apologize, to both of you," he said with a great show of sincerity.

"Accepted," Miriam said tentatively, unprepared for anything remotely resembling an apology out of Laslo, interrupting Dickie before he could say the same. "Two," she snapped.

"Two," Laslo continued, "is that I've gotten calls and letters in the last few weeks the likes of which I've never seen."

"From Daylighteers?" Dickie asked.

"Daylighteers? Hell no! From trade associations! From interest groups! From congressmen and senators just like yourself, Dickie!"

"What do they want?" Miriam asked, her curiosity aroused.

"They want me to be a consultant for their campaigns!" Laslo said with a gleeful look. "Five thousand dollars a day, some of them are talking! Can you imagine? There was this one company—what was it?—Message Concepts, Limited, that was it. Seems they just got rid of their main guy, a guy named Youngblood. Apparently he pissed too many people off. I didn't follow all of it, frankly, but the offer they made was incredible! Gross, net, expenses, equity, points: you name it, they offered it."

"Are you going to do it?" Dickie asked.

"Oh, hell no." He shook his head with a smirk. "Always been my own man. I'm going to open my own office instead. Be my own boss. That's why I came by, really. I want you folks to know that we're all going to be in the same industry, so to speak, and if there's anything I can ever do for you, just speak up and I'll be there, I promise. And that goes double for you, young lady," he said to Miriam with a wink. "Yes, ma'am. You can count on me. And if I've ruffled some of your feathers along the way, I want to tell you that one day I'll make it up to you."

Miriam might as well have been told that she was born on Mars. "Well, I appreciate that, Laslo. I guess there were some times when things got a little tense between us, but I suppose we can work together if we want to, particularly for Dickie's sake," she said tentatively.

"Absolutely!" Laslo extended his hand toward Miriam and shook it with surprising gentleness. "Now, Dickie, my boy. Come out from behind that desk and shake the hand of your old swamp buddy."

Dickie got up as Laslo beamed at him. "Lots of luck to you, Laslo," he said awkwardly, shaking Laslo's outstretched hand.

"Dickie, you're always going to be like a son to me," Laslo said, grasping Dickie's hand in his and swinging him around so that he could put an arm around Dickie's shoulders. Locked in this demi-embrace, Dickie walked with Laslo toward the door. "We've come a long way, Dickie, and you and I will always have a special bond. Right from the first moment I saw you sitting at your desk, I knew we were going to do big things together. Big things." Miriam winced at the recollection.

"And here we are today," Laslo said as they stepped into the doorway and he turned to face Dickie. "Good luck to you, Senator," he said emotionally, and with a sudden lurch, embraced him in a manly hug. "And don't ever forget," he whispered fiercely into Dickie's ear, "if you cross me, even once, you're going to get it just like Moss did. Understand?" And with that he pushed Dickie back from his grasp and held him at arm's length. "Stay in touch," he said with a twinkling smile. "So long!" he called back to Miriam, and with that he was gone, his Florsheims clicking down the marble floor.

Chapter Twenty-nine

Lenny pushed Senior Younger, Jr., into a hearing room on the first floor of the Cannon House Office Building where microphones were awaiting them. He stood behind President-elect Wheezle, his new chief of staff, Steve Lowry, and Speaker Rollo Plank. Reporters stood attentively with their pads poised. President-elect Wheezle gave them a smile and began speaking about the congressional seat he was vacating. He would miss serving the people of the Fourth Congressional District of Pennsylvania, he said, and he wanted to ensure that after his departure for the White House they would receive leadership for a new generation. That was why he had approached an outstanding young man from Walcott Falls, Lenny Keeler, to run for the seat in a special election to be held in February, and that was why he was giving Lenny Keeler his full support, as would Speaker Plank and the entire apparatus of the Democratic party.

Lenny glanced about as he listened. He looked down at Senior Younger, Jr. Senior Younger, Jr., returned his glance and motioned for Lenny to lean over. "Are you sure this is what you want to do?" he asked, just as he had a moment before when Lenny finally conceded to himself what he had to do and informed the old man.

"Yes," Lenny replied.

"Don't worry about what I want or don't want," Senior Younger, Jr., assured him.

Lenny nodded and shook his hand. When he looked up, President-elect Wheezle was introducing him.

Lenny stepped up to the microphones. "Thank you," he said uncomfortably. "I never thought about running for Congress, even when I was working in a congressman's office. It always seemed that being in Congress was for somebody else, for a different kind of person. But now that opportunity is being offered to me."

He drew a deep breath. "I owe it to President-elect Wheezle and Speaker Plank to explain why I'm going to turn them down." He did not need to turn to see the expression of surprise and anger on their faces. "The reason is, I don't want to be a part of the Congress class. I don't want to be part of a governing elite that's distinguished from everybody else mainly by their desire to be a part of that elite, and little more. I don't want to be a part of a system in which all of the voices on one side and all of the voices on the other are made indispensable just because the other side exists.

"The system began before I got here and will go on after I leave, no matter what I do. The system won't be shamed, because it has no shame. It never looks beyond its own agenda so it can point to imminent danger. It simply makes everything go on, just like it always has."

He paused and looked around the room. "I wasn't propelled here by logic or accomplishment, or even desire. I'm here because I'm the product of a deal, just one little deal out of the hundreds of deals and agreements and nods and winks that go on every day.

"I don't think we need leaders whose qualifications are their desire to be qualified, or the imminent danger posed by the other leaders, or their willingness to shake hands behind the scenes. Those who really lead us in life are those who care and serve and sacrifice. And I'm not that either, at least not yet. So I'm not going to run for Congress. I'm going to go home instead."

He turned and gave Senior Younger, Jr., something between a wave and a salute and nodded at President-elect Wheezle, and then walked past the microphones and through the mass of reporters. President-elect Wheezle looked agitated, but Senior Younger, Jr., rapped him with his cane.

"Don't worry, Ezra. You kept your part of the bargain," he said. "Let him go." Senior Younger, Jr., gave President-elect Wheezle a brown envelope, then folded his hands in his lap and watched Lenny proudly as he bulled his way through the doors, out of the government and into America.

Lenny walked out into the street where his nation began, and it went on wherever the street went. On those streets was America, all of it different but all of it the same, going to work and to school, sewing clothes and shopping for food, praying and bowling and reading and worrying, minding its children and mowing the lawn, washing, hoping, running the bases, living, dying, and in love in between, a tribe made up of many tribes, strewn from sea to shining sea. The great nation was like an incorrigible child, bright and ripe with possibilities, prodigious yet undisciplined, capable of great things, great mischief, and great charm, capable of breaking the hearts of those who had put their trust in it and melting the hearts of those who vowed never to let their hearts be broken again.

He was not cut out to lead, not cut out to be apart, not cut out to take the risk that he would end up like President Hoak or President-elect Wheezle, or even Senior Younger, Jr., who beat the system by confessing to himself that it had already won, and then regaining what he truly believed under the cover of going along.

And it was only then that Lenny really understood why Senior Younger, Jr., sang "Home on the Range" back in Pocatello. It was because when he had sat as a young boy under the sky listening to Cicero Younger and John Marshall Bonners, he had heard them talk about preserving the home of the people. That was their plan. With incredible clarity Lenny discerned Cicero Younger and John Marshall Bonners's voices through Senior Younger, Jr.'s, voice, telling him that the jockeying for position and power was irrelevant to Americans' true concerns, that the capital of the nation was not in Washington, D.C.; it was in Pocatello, and it was in San Bernardino and Grand Junction and Gary and New York City and Charleston and Pawtucket, it was in the rolling desolation of the southwest Texas desert and the tract houses back in Walcott Falls, and that each tumbling piece of sagebrush and each worn bus transfer and each hot ingot rolling through a mill was a national icon as much as every document scrawled by our Founding Fathers. The point wasn't the range, but the home, wherever Americans were at home, no matter where it was, so long as they could make their homes in self-respect and peace, be it on the range or in the cities or the subdivisions. There was room under the sky for all of it, and if someday there was no more room, then America would build a bigger sky.

That was what Senior Younger, Jr., meant—the lesson he had learned that night under the Idaho sky, then forgot over 110 years, and then relearned. And that was why when he was twenty points down and sinking, when he had the opportunity and the obligation and no alternative left, he spoke the truth, the only truth he knew:

> *Home, home on the range*
> *Where the deer and the antelope play*
> *Where seldom is heard*
> *A discouraging word*
> *And the skies are not cloudy all day*